Airy Somethings:
The Extraordinary Life of the Aviation Pioneer Horatio Barber

By Terry Grace and Maggie Wilson

Copyright 2019 Terry Grace and Maggie Wilson

ISBN: 9781701503830

Independently published by the authors

All rights reserved

Images: Every effort has been made by the authors to establish copyright of the images in this book.

Front Cover Photo – original painting by Terry Grace

Title Page photo – Horatio Claude Barber from the Royal Aeronautical register of members. Barber was the 30th person to acquire an aeronautical certificate on October 22, 1910.

Back Cover Photo – from *The Goldfields of Larder Lake by* Horatio Barber

Acknowledgements

The authors wish to thank our readers, Reiner Mielke and Debra North, who assisted by reviewing first drafts of the manuscript.

Table of Contents

Introductions..1

Airy Somethings: The Extraordinary Life of the Aviation Pioneer Horatio Barber

Chapter 1	1875 to 1892, Son and Student	5
Chapter 2	1893 to 1897, Gent and Secretary	9
Chapter 3	1898 to 1902, Speculator and Newlywed	15
Chapter 4	1903, Newlywed Again	19
Chapter 5	1903, Orchardman: A Novel Way to Make Money	22
Chapter 6	1904 to 1906, From Rogue to Riches	27
Chapter 7	Additional Cobalt Photographs	53
Chapter 8	1907, at Larder Lake	58
Chapter 9	1908, Barber in Hiding	72
Chapter 10	Barber's Co-Stars in Ontario	79
Chapter 11	1908 to 1919, Barber the Aviator	92
Chapter 12	Barber's Aeroplanes	132
Chapter 13	1910 to 1915 Another Divorce and Another Marriage	150
Chapter 14	Barber as Insurance Broker	156
Chapter 15	Barber the Author	165
Chapter 16	On Jersey and Travel in Retirement	174
Chapter 17	On Nevis, Mr. Barber Causes an Earthquake	178
Chapter 18	The Story Ends	185

Appendices

Appendix 1	H. C. Barber Timeline	189
Appendix 2	Barber's Siblings and Family Tree	191
Appendix 3	The Mystery of Barber's First Aeroplane	198
Appendix 4	Barber's Firsts	208

Appendix 5	Barber's Signatures	209
Appendix 6	Barber's Patents	211
Appendix 7	Dear John	216
Appendix 8	Herbert Campbell Barber	224
Bibliography and Resources		227
Index		232

Introductions

From England, Terry Grace, co-author

I first became aware and then interested in Horatio Barber whilst attending a guided walk around the Lark Hill airfield site led by Mr. Ted Mustard and Tim Brown, author of the excellent book *Flying with the Larks*. Based on their enthusiasm for the man, it was obvious that Horatio Barber was a hero, and this pair's eagerness to share his story, piqued my interest. The tour actually started at what is believed to be the site of Horatio Barber's aeroplane shed, a thirty-foot concrete plinth said to be the base of the shed doors.

An aviation display in the George Hotel, Amesbury, contained more information about Barber that had been collected by Mr. Norman Parker. Some time later, I became a volunteer at the Amesbury History Centre, to where the aviation display had been moved and where Norman is also a volunteer. My interest in Barber now rekindled, I was able to discuss the pioneer aviator with Norman and in greater detail, and I am grateful to him for that.

Although Barber's aviation achievements are fairly well documented in the early aeronautical publications of the era, especially *Flight* magazine, there was little known of his life prior to 1909 when he first appeared at Lark Hill. Norman's account contains a brief sentence suggesting that Barber made a fortune in Canada, possibly in the mining industry, but no more detail than that.

At first, simply to satisfy my own curiosity, I began to research Barber's time before 1909. After discovering that Barber had made his fortune in Canada, my wife Alison and I travelled to Cobalt to discover more. Whilst in Northern Ontario, we were very fortunate to meet up with Maggie Wilson, the chair of the Cobalt Historical Society (CHS). I told her what I had discovered about Barber's time in Cobalt and Larder Lake, and when further snippets of information started to emerge, she became interested in the subject and her enthusiasm was soon to match my own. She started researching documents in the CHS library as well as online newspaper archives. When we returned home, Maggie and I began our correspondence. This co-operation has continued, with literally hundreds of emails crossing the Atlantic on this subject, and I am indeed indebted and most grateful for her encouragement, enthusiasm and assistance.

Terry Grace was born and lives in Wiltshire. England. Since taking early retirement from the Ministry of Defence, Terry has run a small Bed and Breakfast establishment in Amesbury. He has always had an interest in aviation and especially in the history of the pioneering days.

He is a Trustee and volunteer of the Amesbury History Centre which is a charitable Trust. To contact Terry, email him at terry@catkinlodge.com

From Canada - Maggie Wilson, co-author

Winters in Cobalt are long and cold. But I barely noticed last year since I was happily engaged in research into the life of Horatio Claude Barber. What a fascinating project this has been, and I am so pleased that I have been able to help fill in some of the gaps in the man's story.

When Terry first wrote to me, he asked, "Do you know about a man named Horatio Barber and his business The Cobalt Open Call Mining Exchange?" He also wanted to know more about how the aviation pioneer had made his money in mining in Canada. Being new to the area, I was not familiar with Barber, but knew I had seen references to the Open Call Exchange somewhere…

What follows is the product of our combined research. We will answer Terry's questions, and fill in the missing details of how Barber came to Ontario to set up shop as a stockbroker and mine consultant.

Aviation Pioneer Horatio Claude Barber 1875 to 1964

The existing published biographies about Barber are a good start but not comprehensive. Grace's Guide to British Industrial History[1] for example, sheds no light on the first twenty-eight years of his life. Here are the initial four entries in Barber's timeline:

- 1875 - Born in Thornton Heath, son of Charles Worthington Barber and his wife Isabella.
- Educated at Bedford and abroad. Trained at Amesbury and Hendon.
- 1903 - May 27th. Married in Jersey City, USA, to Elsie Mabelle Porter and they lived in the USA, Canada and Greece before settling in London.
- 1909 - He was a civilian experimenter when he obtained permission from the War Office (as it was called then) to use a piece of land on Knighton Down, known as Larkhill.

Horatio Claude Barber Royal Aeronautical Society register of members

Nothing in the brief biography explains how he made his fortune by 1909. Consider the period from 1904 - 1908. The missing years may not seem all that noteworthy to the casual observer but after reading our story, you will see that that the period perfectly coincides with the boom phase of the Cobalt silver mine camp.

How did he come to Cobalt? We supposed his story was no different than thousands of others. After the discovery of silver in 1903, prospectors and promoters and stockbrokers arrived by the

---

[1] gracesguide.co.uk

trainload to the new Cobalt station. News of the bounty travelled across the globe, and many came to Cobalt hoping to get rich.

By 1907, most, if not all of the available land around Cobalt had been claimed, and the prospectors and promoters looked further north, and in our man's case, to the Larder Lake area – eventually a good gold producing region.

Barber referred to himself as a mining man, and offered his services as a consultant. Judging by his status as a wealthy man in 1909, we can assume he was successful as a mine promoter. Grace's Guide calls him a "civilian experimenter" which could be another way of saying "entrepreneur": someone who is comfortable with taking risks.

As research reveals, Mr. Barber was indeed involved in some risky business.

From the 1910s and 20s, the written reports in magazines and journals speak in glowing terms of Barber's achievements, his skill, and his passion. Not one mentions his time in Cobalt.

Take for example the December 1912 *Flight* magazine titled "Aircraft in Warfare, a Chat with Mr. Barber." The author intended to discuss Barber's recent trip to Turkey.

"I went," Mr. Barber explained, "just to see what there was to be seen and learn what there was to be learned."

The interviewer suggests that this attitude perfectly describes the man's character. Looking around the "cozily furnished consulting chambers," he sees evidence of someone who has followed his impulses, apparently all around the globe. A stuffed alligator from Mexico that Barber had clubbed hangs over the doorway. On the walls are photographs of his Australian ranch and of a visit to Hawaii. Under his desk are parcels from the trip to Constantinople.

Perhaps if there were pictures of Northern Ontario landscapes or mine workings, or a sample of silver or gold ore, they were overlooked by the star-struck interviewer. After our research, though, I'm comfortable suggesting that no such evidence was on display.

Together, Terry and I have filled in some of the gaps in Barber's history with some rather remarkable, if unflattering stories of Barber's life after he was educated at "Bedford and abroad."

Follow us as we follow Barber from the UK to Australia, British Columbia, California, and finally to Cobalt and Larder Lake in Northern Ontario. We will fill in the missing bits and then some. According to available documents, Barber was by turn a scholar, gent, speculator, stockbroker and mining consultant, pilot, Captain, insurance broker, and a colonial development officer. It seems that the man never sat still. Was this impulsive behaviour? Was he running after dreams or running from the law? Or all of the above?

Maggie Wilson was born in Kitchener, and lived her working life in several communities in Southern Ontario. She met her husband, a geologist, who introduced her to rocks and minerals and the Town of Cobalt. In 2016 they retired to Cobalt and could not be happier with the decision.

In 2017, with the sudden loss of Vivian Hylands, Maggie accepted the position of President of the Cobalt Historical Society. So began her interest in the fascinating history of the area. Besides mineral collecting, Maggie enjoys research and writing, and she looks forward to sharing new stories about Cobalt and its mining heritage. The work is like a treasure hunt and the discoveries are just as exciting as stumbling upon a nugget of silver.

You can contact Maggie at the Cobalt Historical Society chs@heritagesilvertrail.ca

Chapter 1

Barber the son and student: his childhood and early life, 1875 to 1892

Themes of headline news, broken hearts, and the pursuit of riches occur frequently in Horatio's story. To begin, and to set the scene, we return to Victorian England in 1863, twelve years before his birth. His aunt, Barbara Edith Barber sued her fiancé Robert Fenton for £5,000 in respect of damages for breach of promise of marriage.

In an era when an engagement was often considered as legally binding as a marriage, Aunt Barbara's story was newsworthy. Many lengthy articles were written in the press throughout England. The reports detailed his initial attentive wooings and one paper published his love letters to her. The article[2] goes on to report that "In spring of 1863 he went to Ireland, and whether he there met with somebody who supplanted the plaintiff in his esteem, the learned council was unable to say, but upon his return his love had evidently cooled." Fenton told Barbara he had never loved her and that he would not marry her.

In an eloquent address, the judge contended that the defendant broke off the engagement not because he had formed another attachment, but solely because he found that he did not love the plaintiff sufficiently to warrant that he marry her. The jury returned a verdict for the plaintiff and £3,000 damages were awarded.[3]

Horatio's Parents

In his twenties and before marriage, Charles Worthington Barber was a cotton broker and cigar merchant in Manchester. He reported on the 1861 census that he was also an insurance broker, working alongside his father, William Barber.

Charles was married twice, first to Maria Walker. Her mother, Eleanor Walker was the daughter of a silk manufacturer, Thomas Kenyon Walker. A year and a half after marrying, Maria died in December 1865. She bequeathed equal shares of her estate to her husband and to her mother.

Maria's brothers contested the will saying that she was prone to drinking in excess and not of sound mind and that she allowed her husband to influence how the will was written. This suggests that the siblings thought little of Barber. The case was eventually thrown out. When mother-in-law Eleanor Walker died in 1866, she left her entire fortune to her son-in-law, Charles Worthington Barber. He was, according to the probate calendar, the sole executor of her estate.

---

[2] *London Gazette* October 14, 1873
[3] £3,000 in 1863 would be equivalent in buying power of approximately £370,000 today. In her will, dated 1930, she was listed as Barbara Edith Barber a spinster and her estate was valued at £895 8s 11d.

In 1868, Charles married Isabella Loughborough. He was presumably well off financially, however, by 1869 he was declared bankrupt.

The couple had eight children between 1868 and 1881. Horatio Claude was a middle child, born on September 11, 1875. See Appendix 2 for details of Horatio's siblings.

Horatio's parents were divorced in 1883 when he was eight years old. Judging from the decree, life in the Barber homestead was unpleasant, especially if and when father was home. One might conclude that Horatio's childhood was perhaps a troubled one.

London Gazette *October 14, 1873 Charles Worthington Barber bankrupt*

Isabella declared in the divorce petition that Charles was a violent man who kicked at and threatened to throw knives at her. He withheld financial support. He was accused of debauchery with one of the servants and of serial adultery with a landlady and several other women.

Barber vs Barber divorce petition 1882

The 1881 census indicates that Isabella was supported by her father. She was living on her own, with six children and three servants.

According to the 1891 census, Isabella, possibly to avoid the shame and stigma attached to divorce, declared herself a widow.

Meanwhile, her ex-husband was alive and unencumbered by a wife and family, living in Africa. "After the failure of his second marriage, Charles Barber left for South Africa where he became the proprietor of a boarding house in Kimberly. He died there of throat cancer in February 1893."[4] The obituary recalls Chas Barber was one of the "earliest in pegging out the Premier Mine,"[5] an interesting connection to Horatio's later occupation in mines and stock promotion.

We can reasonably assume that Horatio's father was not close to his son. It could be argued that Horatio's mother also was not very close to him or in fact to some of his other siblings, as is suggested by the following events.

In Brighton, Sussex, 1892, Horatio's mother Isabella married The Rev. William Dewhurst Pearson who was nineteen years her junior. It is believed that Pearson was previously engaged to Isabella's daughter Maude Helen Barber.

After her death in 1915, Isabella's estate was divided between her youngest child Percy Charles Barber and her solicitor, a situation which perhaps suggests a distance between her and the majority of her family. She left nothing to her husband.

Apart from the life lessons young Barber would have acquired at home, Horatio received a formal education at the Bedford Modern School for four terms from 1891 to 1892. He left school at seventeen. Other references place him at Harrow School and Oxford University, but both of these institutions report that he had not attended.

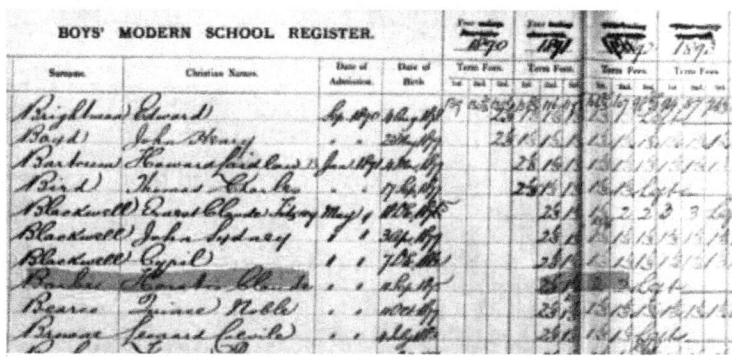

Bedford Modern School Register. Young Barber left school in 1892

We now encounter a wall in our research as we can find no record of Horatio between 1892 and 1895. He left the UK at some point after his last term at Bedford. Exactly when and where he landed, however, is unknown.

One might imagine that he travelled to South Africa, possibly to join up with his father before Charles died in 1893. But that is conjecture.

It is possible that Horatio took the first opportunity to travel when he was about eighteen years old. In the 1930 US census, when he was 55, Barber declared he immigrated to the US in 1893, but we cannot verify this information. Nor can we rely on his declarations. We know that during his time in Canada, because of his work as a mine promoter, he was inclined to overstate or to outright lie. Barber was comfortable bending the truth.

While in Ontario, Barber claimed to have "had experience in most of the mining fields of the world."[6] In his advertisements, he says he was a seasoned "practical mining man." Both

---

[4] Simon Doyle, email correspondence
[5] *Unknown publication* Kimberly – 1893 obituary Charles Worthington Barber
[6] *Cobalt* – a pamphlet written by Barber in 1906

statements are deliberately vague. Unfortunately, this leaves future researchers with the notion that one must take Barber's words with a generous helping of skepticism.

In 1895, we find a Horatio Barber in Honolulu who had been released from Queen's Hospital. Was this our man, on vacation, as reported in the 1912 *Flight* interview "A Chat with Mr. Barber"?

We think not, for later news items announced that after a lengthy stay, the Honolulu Barber died in the Queens hospital in 1899 – he was in his late 40s. We are inclined to connect the 1895 news report to the later one and conclude that the Honolulu Barber is not our Horatio.

For now, we have a three-year gap in his timeline.

Chapter 2

1893 to 1897: Barber in Australia. Travels, Adventures and a Taste for Gold

Brother George Walter Barber

Horatio's older brother George[7] came to Australia after he met Janet "Jessie" Watson Salmond while he was a ship's surgeon with the Peninsular and Oriental Steam Navigation Co. They settled in Kalgoorlie in 1895,[8] and married in 1896.

Perhaps Horatio travelled to Australia to attend his brother's wedding in August. We do know that later that year, the papers announced that Dr. Barber, the new medical officer for the Kalgoorlie hospital had appointed an H. C. Barber as secretary of the same institution.

During this time, Kalgoorlie was at the height of the gold rush. An ad for a Kalgoorlie open call exchange lists Dr. G. Barber as a member.[9] Even if the younger Barber did not dabble in the stock market, he could not have escaped the culture of the mining boom.

An anecdote from Simon Doyle, George Barber's great-grandson, suggests, however, that Horatio had enough money to indulge in luxury.

Doyle writes, "Horatio seemed to be a bit eccentric. Kalgoorlie gets blisteringly hot. He apparently took to filling his baths with ice and sipping champagne. This would have been very expensive since water was so scarce, some entrepreneurs were known to fill their whole baths with champagne instead."

Wildcat Mines

Before we describe the investment scene in Kalgoorlie, we need to go back a few years earlier to 1893 when the global financial markets were in a deep depression. In London, people with money to invest turned to the Australian gold mine stock market. The actual gold producing operations, however, were not as attractive to some investors as were the

Telegraphic News *November 5, 1896, above, announcing Barber's appointment. Below, the Kalgoorlie Hospital, 1896 from the* Outback Family History Blog

---

[7] See Appendix 2 for more on brother George Walter
[8] Simon Doyle correspondence
[9] *Kalgoorlie Western Argus* April 9, 1896

"wildcat" mines – those questionable ventures which offered a quick and highly profitable return.

Basically, two types of wildcat mines were promoted or "floated" by either unscrupulous or impatient promoters.

1. The mine is utterly worthless and the land contains no ore.

2. The mine has potential based on proximity to a working mine or prospectors discover evidence of minerals, but an ore body has not yet been proven.

A further definition of a wildcat mine comes from the 1895 *Thames Star*:[10]

"…prospects that have every chance of becoming valuable but that are entirely undeveloped. In the latter case the original promoters are in too great a haste to turn their find into a marketable commodity; in other words, too anxious to realize at once on what is looked upon as a stroke of luck.

"This is not legitimate mining, but speculation pure and simple. If the property is a promising one it is better in every way to develop it to the fullest extent possible … then, when floated, the investing public will know what they are, and the promoters will stand a chance of reaping a much greater profit on their original outlay."

Yes, wildcats were a risky investment, but taking a chance was part of the appeal and in 1893, London was known as the "casino" of Australian gold mine stocks.[11]

Australia certainly had its share of these mines. Some were spectacular duds, and even then, investors were not discouraged. All that mattered was the opportunity to make a quick profit. Promoters floated companies, puffed up the news to buoy share prices, and hushed bad news to prevent a downturn. Blainey writes that a new Australian company was formed every day for two years. In April of 1896 alone, 81 companies collected more money from the investors than all of the Western Australian mines made in gold in two years.

Londonderry Mine Coolgardie – share certificate right with same vignette of the gold camp inset.

---

[10] Editorial, *Thames Star*, 21 October 1895, p. 2
[11] *The Rush that Never Ended* Geoffrey Blainey

The Londonderry Mine was one of the more infamous Australian wildcat schemes.[12]

> John Mills was an Irishman from Londonderry. He was part of a prospecting party of six who had conducted a fruitless search in early 1894 for gold near Widgiemooltha. Virtually broke, they were prospecting as they made their way back to Coolgardie. Mills sat down under a tree to rest, depressed about his lack of fortune, when he idly pushed a rock aside with the heel of his boot. The underside was covered in gold. As the party explored the site, it was found the stone in the outcrop was hanging together with gold. This incredibly rich tiny deposit yielded 8000 ounces from dollying in a few weeks.
>
> One of the party became ill and returned to Coolgardie. Here he got wildly drunk and with a loose tongue, soon most of the town had heard about the find. The next day virtually the entire town arrived at the site, and leases were pegged in all directions.
>
> The prospecting party sold the lease to speculators, who sealed the hole with a metal plate. A company was formed in London and Paris, raising 750 000 pounds. It was a staggering amount, considering the most promising mines in Western Australia at the time could only raise about 50 000 pounds. In the period after, with the hole still sealed, it developed almost mythical status. [The mine was] promoted as what would become no less than the biggest gold mine in the world.
>
> Eventually after several months, the company was ready to start mining, and the seal was broken with much pomp and ceremony. After a few days, it was revealed only a thin gold shell remained, and all the rock beyond this was barren. Hundreds of leases nearby were immediately abandoned, after thousands of pounds had been spent developing them. Investors lost in some cases their life savings, and went bankrupt. Recriminations flew. It was the first of many scandals on the Western Australian goldfields, because when it comes to greed, people have short memories.

In 1907, during his Larder Lake days, Barber referenced the celebrity of the Londonderry Mine to promote his partners' company, the Larder Lake Proprietary Goldfields Mine. He wrote the following about a gold nugget supposedly found in that area of Northern Ontario:

"… it was extraordinarily rich, and almost on a par with the showing which I saw in the year 1897 on the famous Australian Londonderry Mine, which property sold for £800,000, the entire development consisting of a 12-foot hole."[13]

The above quote reveals several pertinent details. Firstly, if we take him at his word, we have confirmation that Barber was in Australia in 1897. He was savvy in terms of marketing by drawing upon sensational details to pump up the stock. He was also shrewd enough to know that most people would have forgotten the Londonderry fiasco. What he, of course, failed to disclose in his promotion was the true story of the Londonderry Mine.

---

[12] mindat.org
[13] *The Goldfields of Larder Lake* 1907 HC Barber – see Chapters 7 and 8 for the Larder Lake episode of Barber's career.

Open Call Exchanges

An ad[14] for an open call mining exchange described the venue as the opportunity for every man to profit by the sale of stock without the high fees of a middle man. The exchange was conveniently "open" to all, during evenings after working hours, and the commission paid was "infinitesimal."

In 1897, Albert F. Calvert colourfully described a Saturday evening at Hannan's:

"Of all nights in the week at Hannan's, Saturday is *the* night. The main street is thronged with people. Every miner from all the camps for ten miles round the town finds his way there to spend a social hour."

…and "as for the 'open exchange' in the middle of the crowded main street on Saturday night, it is an honoured institution. All hail to the 'exchange,' the disciple of the mining interest, which is the idol of the town! The pavement stock-broker takes the full licence of the place. He sets up a torch on the sidewalk, roars himself hoarse, collects a crowd and chokes the "gangway." The stock-in-trade of one of these roaring hawkers of scrip, consists of a strident voice and a good knowledge of the ruling rates of stock. … a start is made by the operator announcing that he has a buyer for Devonshires at 49/-, a seller at 65/-. Then he demands to know whether there is a better buyer or a lower seller. He asks the question, perhaps, ten or a dozen times – each time more impatiently than before, until, perhaps, the buyer will advance 2/6, and the seller will abate 2/6 of the original offer." Eventually, a deal was made.

Or perhaps not, and lamenting, the broker appealed to the crow that he must make his bread! The next trade was announced, and he found his enthusiasm once again.

The pavement or curb broker selling shares at an open call exchange. Illustration from Calvert's My Fourth Tour in Western Australia. *1901 The Library of UCLA*

---

[14] The *Age* Melbourne November 27, 1889

In his book *The Rush that Never Ended*, Geoffrey Blainey writes that "share auctions were the nerve centre of the [Australian] gold towns," and "share buying was the duty of all, for the mines depended on speculative money."

While Methodist ministers preached against gambling, they turned a blind eye toward share speculation because it was necessary for the well-being of the community. Mining syndicates formed in the vestry after services, and in one mining town, the building that housed the stock market during the week also served as a place of worship on Sunday.

The Kalgoorlie Open Call Exchange 1895 from The Rush that Never Ended, *Geoffrey Blainey. Note the alternate spelling of the town name, Kalcurli.*

Coolgardie Street scene - no shortage of opportunity to buy shares. From The Rush that Never Ended, *Geoffrey Blainey*

Time to move on

In 1896 and 1897, the papers in Australia reported on the exciting news of the gold rush in the Klondike. One article[15] mentioned Archie "Coolgardie" Smith, the president of an open call stock exchange in Coolgardie. He had travelled to Canada to investigate the prospects in Rossland, British Columbia, a gold mine camp under development since 1890. Barber likely knew of him, if not more closely.

---

[15] *Coolgardie Pioneer* September 11, 1897

By invitation or under his own volition, Barber was compelled to follow in Smith's footsteps.

A few short weeks later, the December 3, 1897 edition of *The Kalgoorlie Miner* announced that H. C. Barber resigned his post as secretary and he planned to move to British Columbia.

> Mr H. C. Barber, who has capably filled the position of secretary to the Kalgoorlie Government Hospital, has sent in his resignation, it being his intention to travel to British Columbia. He will leave Kalgoorlie on Tuesday next.

The Kalgoorlie Miner *announcement of Mr. Barber's resignation is noteworthy in that it could be argued to be his first attempt at self-publicity; the phrasing is not dissimilar to future promotional material.*

But before he landed in Canada, Barber returned home to the UK.

Chapter 3

Barber as Speculator and Newlywed 1898 to 1902

After Horatio resigned his position with the Kalgoorlie Hospital in Western Australia, he boarded a Peninsular and Oriental Steamship and returned to England on February 5, 1898.

To Ontario, Canada

Two months later, we encounter our man on April 4th at the altar of Bishop's Palace, York, Ontario.[16] Somewhere along the way from Kalgoorlie to present-day Toronto, Horatio met, fell in love, and married Edle Annita Margarete Pippe.[17]

The marriage document illustrated here is the one and only piece of evidence we've been able to find regarding his first wife. Here's what we know:

In 1898, the bride and groom were both twenty-two. Ms. Pippe was born in Cologne Germany probably of Italian or Austrian stock. Her place of residence at the time of marriage was London, England.

Barber, on the other hand, declared he lived in New Westminster, British Columbia, Canada, which is today a member municipality of Metro Vancouver. His occupation was "speculator."

We can't help but wonder: where did Barber meet the mysterious Margarete? Did they meet in Australia?

Or, on the Atlantic crossing to North America, did they have a whirlwind, shipboard romance? This is a distinct possibility as Horatio was known to be somewhat impulsive as is suggested by the events of his second marriage.

Regarding his west coast address: was it possible that he made the trip from the UK to North America, crossed the continent to set up in British Columbia, and then returned to Toronto all in the eight weeks between his February 5 arrival in England and his April 4 wedding in Toronto?

It leaves one breathless to consider that he may have done!

---

[16] York is a former city within the present-day city of Toronto. Bishop's Palace is also known as St. Michael's Palace or Cathedral
[17] Grace's Guide indicates that Barber was married only once, in 1903. In fact, he was married three times.

15

Or perhaps, for the purposes of the wedding records, he may have been anticipating his future career in New Westminster when he identified his occupation as "speculator." Either way, by April 1898, we can surmise that his mining and/or speculation experience was acquired in Australia and perhaps the western Canadian goldfields.

The witnesses at the marriage ceremony were sisters Mildred and Bertha Murray. They lived in their family home in the high-class neighbourhood adjacent to the church. Perhaps Barber stayed with the family. If that is the case, we have insight into his station in life.

More research along this line of inquiry might be fruitful. In later years, the sisters' brother, W. Parkyn Murray was a member of the Canadian Club (1902), a director of the North American Accident Insurance company (1916), and also in 1916, he was a director of Canadian Aeroplanes Limited. As Alan Sullivan, Lt. RAF, wrote in *Aviation in Canada 1917 to 1918*, this organization "turned out some 2,900 aeroplanes… the undertaking was that of the Imperial Government acting through the Imperial Munitions Board… the primary purpose was that of supplying aeroplanes for the Royal Flying Corps."

In other words, Murray's career somewhat paralleled Barber's. How long had they known one another at the time of Barber's marriage in 1898? Or is their common career path just a tantalizing coincidence?

The Bishop's Palace September 2018 Terry Grace photos

On to British Columbia and the West Coast

If we attribute several later newspaper articles to our couple, we can conclude that they travelled to the west coast. The February 18, 1899 shipping news in the *Times Colonist* reported that a Mrs. H. C. Barber arrived in Victoria by steamer from San Francisco. She returned to California a few weeks later, travelling alone.

Also in Victoria in April of the same year,[18] an H. C. Barber was arrested and jailed for not paying his hotel bill. It is unclear if the author of the news report is indignant on behalf of Mr. Barber or if he is mocking him. Either way, this Mr. Barber who had been living "for some time in Victoria, was subjected to the unpleasant experience of being arrested on *a capeas*[19] at the insistence of the landlady of the Vernon Hotel who was fearful of Barber's taking French leave without going through the formality of discharging a board bill amounting to $215."[20]

Toronto Daily Star *February 25, 1905*

The euphemistic term "French leave" is given in the OED as, *"The custom (in the 18th century prevalent in France and sometimes imitated in England) of going away from a reception, etc. without taking leave of the host or hostess. Hence, jocularly, to take French leave is to go away, or do anything, without permission or notice."*

Two days later, in another paper[21], we learn that the judgement was reserved. We also discover the name of the landlady – a Mrs. Walt of the Vernon Hotel.[22] "Mr. T. M. Miller, who appeared for Barber, held that the affidavits were not sufficient to hold his client and at any rate he had no intention of leaving the city."[23]

With knowledge of events to unfold in 1903 specifically, and knowing his habit of staying in any one place for a very short time in general, if the 1899 Mr. Barber is *our* Mr. Barber, we find the line "he had no intention of leaving the city" somewhat amusing. On several other occasions, Horatio used similar words. For instance, on travel documents, he declared he was taking up permanent residency when he had absolutely no intention of staying.

Other possible reports that might be about our roaming speculator include a passenger list dated August 1899, when an H. C. Barber sailed from Sydney Australia to San Francisco. This chap worked as a waiter to pay for his passage.

If the reader has concerns about our connecting Horatio to the Vernon Hotel and "working as waiter" stories, we understand. Up to this point in the story, Barber appears to have been

---

[18] *The Province* April 7, 1899
[19] a writ or warrant ordering the arrest of a named person
[20] $215 hotel bill from 1899 would be worth approximately $CAD 6500 or £5100 in 2019 currency
[21] *Victoria Daily Columnist* April 9, 1899
[22] Online 1899 directory of Victoria Mrs. M Walt at 66 Douglas, proprietress of "The Vernon," a boarding house.
[23] This is also not the only instance of Barber's activities making the news in more than one paper, as we shall see in the next chapter.

wealthy, as illustrated by the "sipping champagne while bathing in ice water" anecdote, or the fact that he was rubbing shoulders with high society at the time of his wedding in 1898.

To Summarize

We know that Barber left Australia with the intention of working in British Columbia and this is confirmed by him on his wedding certificate. We know that, according to the December 1912 *Flight* interview, "A Chat with Mr. Barber" he claimed to own a ranch in Australia. We know he was a speculator. Perhaps by the time he was ready to "take French leave" of his Victoria boarding house and found himself before the courts, he was broke. Given the story of a Californian scam included later in this book, a scheme which we are certain was carried out by him, we believe that the man who was arrested for non-payment of his lodging bill was, in fact, Horatio. In which case, the H. C. Barber who sailed from Australia to San Francisco while working as a waiter could very well be him.

In 1901, two papers, the *San Francisco Call* and the *San Francisco Examiner* announced that an H. C. Barber arrived at the Palace Hotel in that city, via New York.

As mentioned at the top of this chapter, apart from the marriage registration, we are unable to find any firm evidence of his first before or after the 1898 wedding. However, we do have 1901 news[24] from San Francisco where an H. C. Barber seeks a divorce from his wife Margaret L. Barber, citing desertion, followed by news of the divorce decree, citing infidelity.

The "L" in Barber's wife's name is most likely a transcription error. It has been suggested that Edle went by the name Margaret.

On May 2, 1902, The *San Francisco Call* reported an H. C. Barber arriving in California from Honolulu. If this is our man, perhaps the vacation pictures in his 1912 Pall Mall office are from this time in Hawaii, a place where he "had spent many pleasant months."

We know that he was in New York in 1902, as declared on a border crossing dated October 1903, when he travelled between Canada and the US at Quebec, en route to San Francisco, the setting for the next episode in his story. 1903 was a big year for Horatio.

1903 was also a very big year for many people in Horatio's circle.

---

[24] *San Francisco Chronicle* April 6, 1901

Chapter 4

Newlywed again, in 1903

Let us witness the happy occasion of Horatio's marriage to Elsie Mabelle Porter, in New Jersey, May 27, 1903.

CALIFORNIANS WED IN JERSEY.

Bridegroom Claims Residence in State on One Night's Lodging.

Justice of the Peace John F. Lee of Bayonne, N. J., was called to the Jersey City office of Assemblyman James Hammil yesterday to marry Horatio Clarke Barber, a broker, to Miss Elsie Mabelle Porter.

Both bride and bridegroom said they were from Los Angeles, Cal., but the groom said he lived in the Hotel Washington in Jersey City. He slept there on Tuesday night. He gave his age as 27 years and Miss Porter said she was 18 years old.

The Sun *May 28, 1903, note Clarke instead of Claude – another transcription error. Note also the mention of the ages of the bride and groom.*

Came East to Marry.

New York, May 28.—Justice of the Peace John F. Lee, of Bayonne, N. J., was called to the Jersey City office of Assemblyman James Hammil yesterday to marry Horatio Clarke Barber, a broker, to Miss Elsie Mabelle Porter. Both bride and groom said they were from Los Angeles, Cal.

The Pittsburgh Press *May 28, 1903, Horatio Clarke Barber comes east to marry – an out of state paper reports on the newsworthy nuptials.*

Elsie Mabelle Porter Barber - a rare image of Horatio's second wife ca 1910

According to the marriage certificate, Elsie was 18 and lived in Los Angeles, and he was 27 and claimed he lived in Jersey City. They were married at the courthouse – a routine affair, one would think, and hardly newsworthy – yet it was reported and carried in at least three papers. One headline from the *Sun* read, "Californians Wed – Bridegroom claims residence in State on One Night's Lodging." The address on the marriage return was for the Hotel Washington. The Justice of the Peace was called in to confirm the ages of the two, and he performed the rites.

This is a tantalizing little bit of news and begs the question: why was it reported?

Did Barber make a fuss when he encountered resistance from the officials? Was there a rush to get married? Was the couple trying to beat marriage laws because she was too young? Was this a slow news day and the journalist just happened to be by the chambers and heard people arguing?

Was age of consent an issue? No, for at that time, in both California and New Jersey, the age was sixteen.[25] If we are to believe courthouse documents, Elsie was two years older. Are those records reliable? Rather, can we rely on the respondents to tell the truth?

The answer again is no. Passenger lists and subsequent census declarations[26] indicate that Elsie was born in 1888 or 1890. This means her age in 1903 was fifteen or thirteen. Either age would have been an excellent reason for marriage officials to be concerned. Elsie was approximately half of Barber's age.

---

[25] Incidentally, in 1850, the age of consent in California was ten.
[26] In later years, Elsie married a salesman Rutgers S. Kasson and they relocated to the US. She changed her first name to Barbara.

Barber's occupation on the marriage return is also interesting. He has made the transition from speculator to broker. In later years, more information regarding his dealings in these two professions will emerge, but we know little of his business in the investment field in 1903.

We do know that he was involved in a novel money-making scheme for the rest of 1903.

Chapter 5

Barber as Orchardman – a Novel way to Make Money

We have seen that 1903 was a big year for Horatio, as well as for his new bride, Elsie. The year was noteworthy for others as well. For example, in Northern Ontario, about 100 miles north of North Bay, the Temiskaming and Northern Ontario Railway crews had reached Long Lake. Two tie-cutters, James McKinley and Ernest Darragh were looking for suitable timber. As they walked along the shore, they discovered silver nuggets in the gravel. A few weeks later, Alfred Larose, a blacksmith working for the railroad, found a vein of silver. Within weeks, the McKinley-Darragh Mine and the Larose Mine were in production.

The summer of 1903 at Long Lake, soon to be renamed Cobalt Lake, was momentous not only because these three men were soon wealthy beyond all expectations. The discovery of silver in 1903 was a turning point, an event that would have an impact on the future of Northern Ontario and the lives of countless people, including those like Horatio Barber, who, in two years' time, took advantage of the opportunities that the new frontier had to offer.

In the meantime, in 1903 California, another frontier attracted Barber's attention. According to the Barber family lore, Horatio tried his hand managing an orange grove in California. "He made a somewhat bad job of it," is how the story is told.

We cannot confirm that the newlywed couple returned to the west coast, together. It is just as possible that Barber travelled solo while Elsie remained in New Jersey. Her name, or mention of "Mr. Barber's wife" does not occur in the media reports from early 1904 when the San Francisco newspapers were abuzz with the story of a British tutor who had swindled five of his countrymen. This was sensational news and the press stirred up indignation on behalf of the victims.

Here's what happened, according to the newsmen in attendance at the inquiry. We start with this this eloquent but damning statement submitted by the *Chronicle*.[27] "It appears that Barber leased a ranch in Santa Clara two years ago [in 1902] and set out to make money. Whether suggested to him by former schemes[28] or out of his own wit he decided that the best money-makers were the well-to-do Englishmen."

> THE SAN FRANCIS[CO]
> **TUTOR WORKS BOLD SWINDLE**
> Deserts Five Young Englishmen Who Gave Him $3750 to Instruct Them in Farming
> **VICTIMS ARE STRANGERS**
> H. C. Barber Installs Them on Rented Ranch Near Mountain View and Then Disappears

San Francisco Chronicle, *Feb 14, 1904*

---

[27] *San Francisco Chronicle* July 20, 1904
[28] An ad of one such possible "former scheme" from the *Times* (London, England) October 19, 1899 reads thus: "ORCHARD HOME, MIDDLE CALIFORNIA – A gentleman resident for many years in the Santa Clara Valley near San Jose, one hour by rail from San Francisco, wanting to return to Europe, desires to SELL his beautiful ORCHARD HOME and extensive ORCHARD to a gentleman's son who desires healthy occupation and profitable investment in a beautiful climate. Fine mansion and park, stables, waterworks, wind and steam power, drying plant, all in full running order. Will stay a year to teach the business. First-class references exchanged. No agents."

2 ENGLISHMEN LIVE TO LEARN AND TO LOSE

TWO FARMERS FROM ENGLAND

Young Britishers Duped by an Offer to Teach Them All Branches of Agriculture.

UNITED STATES STEPS IN AND SCHEME FAILS

Complaint Filed Against H. C. Barber, ex-Ranchman and Instructor in Agriculture, of Mountain View Ranch.

IMPORTING FOREIGN LABORERS.

SAN FRANCISCO, July 19.—Five complaints were filed in the United States District Court today against George W. Mosher and H. C. Barber, who are alleged with having imported alien laborers. Mosher is a contractor at Palo Alto and Barber formerly conducted a farming school at Mountain View.

FIVE BRITONS HIS VICTIMS

Lessee of Mountain View Ranch Disappears With Money Obtained for Ranch Schooling.

HEAVY FINES ARE SUED FOR

Palo Alto Contractor May Have to Pay Uncle Sam Three Thousand Dollars

ALIEN LAWS VIOLATED

Mountain View Farmer Absconds After Having Started a Bucolic School

Other headlines from the newspapers reporting on the "Bold Swindle" case. Clockwise from top left: San Francisco Examiner, *July 20, 1904;* San Francisco Chronicle, *July 20, 1904;* San Francisco Call, *July 20, 1904;* San Francisco Chronicle, *February 14, 1904;* Los Angeles Time, *July 20, 1904;* San Francisco Examiner, *July 20, 1904*

Barber then travelled to England and placed ads in the papers "…saying that H. C. Barber, owner of a beautiful ranch in the Santa Clara Valley, California, was willing to teach[29] the various branches of farming to those who desired in return for a small sum."

George Perez and John Inwood were just two of the five or more who did desire it. According to the headline illustrated here, these "students" paid the 2019 equivalent of almost $CAD 22,000.00 or £17,000 in tuition fees.

"All went well at first but the story runs that the eating proved less than expected and the work more. As they became accustomed to the American way of computation, they realised they were paying Barber a large sum for the pleasure of being his hired men, and at the end they were assured only one month's employment."

Late in December, 1903, Barber left the ranch on a business trip to San Francisco, saying he'd be away for two weeks. However, Barber disappeared, leaving local businesses, his creditors, and at least five young men stranded in California, in debt and without work.

He never returned. According to the press, he had sailed on a steamer to Japan or Australia, possibly Hawaii.

We are able to confirm that Horatio Barber travelled to the UK at some point, and then returned to North America with his students aboard the same vessel. The October 1903 *SS Canada* passenger lists shows him traveling first class.

---

[29] By this time, Horatio Barber had owned a ranch in Australia for about seven years and therefore could possibly have those skills. More likely, he considered himself sufficiently experienced in fruit growing to be able to make the claim.

On the same voyage, but listed in steerage (third class or lower deck) were John Inwood and George Neaves Perez, two of the men who were taken in by the swindle.[30]

[Ship manifest image: S.S. Canada sailing from Liverpool, Oct 14th 1903, showing passenger list with Inwood and Perez (Pareg) boxed at entries 12 and 13.]

The victims sought justice through the British Consulate, who in turn approached the office of the United States Attorney General. The Attorney General's office filed two complaints against Barber for violating the Act of Congress March 3rd 1903 entitled "An act to regulate the immigration of aliens into the United States". Barber was sued for $2,000 for bringing in foreign labour, and being in violation of the alien contract law.

The news reports revealed further details of the contract made between the tutor and his students, whereby they were to be employed on Barber's farm at Mountain View, Santa Clara as farmhands at wages of $50 per month each.

The two students paid Barber £100 each and contracted to pay him another £50 each not later than May 2nd 1904. In return Barber agreed to give them board, lodgings and washing at his ranch for a period of not less than one year or more than 18 months. He agreed to instruct them during this period in the various aspects of farming. He also guaranteed employment at $50 a month after the initial 12 or 18 months, at his option.

---

[30] Barber's name is newsworthy enough in those days to be mentioned in the *Gazette* of 23rd October 1903 as a passenger aboard the steamer *Canada*, which, incidentally was associated with the *Titanic*: On June 14th, 1912 at the British investigation, *Canada's* captain R.O. Jones testified that he had been in the same ice field as encountered by *Titanic* on April 14; that he too had received ice warning wireless messages, but he "kept the *Canada* going at full speed as he always had done for 20 years."

It is worth quoting some of the contract details:

> "It is further agreed upon and promised by the party of the second part that he will put his being to such work as shall be required of him by the party of the first part, and in all matters pertaining to the work required of him do as the party of the first part or his representatives directs and orders. Also in the matter of and in such matters of punctuality at meals and the hour of retiring at night the party of the second part promises and agrees to conform to the rules of the party of the first parts establishment."

In plain English, they are to do whatever Barber tells them to do, at all times.

When we first read these reports, we immediately dismissed them and concluded they were referring to another H. C. Barber. At first glance, we could not reconcile the story of Barber the scam artist with that of Barber the aviation pioneer a decade later. The former is completely out of character with the latter.

However, after further research and considering the entire story yet to be revealed, we came to the conclusion that Horatio Barber's moral compass could be redirected. We have little doubt that this swindle was the work of our protagonist, who "made a somewhat bad job" of orchard management.

To date we have not been able to discover how this case was resolved. We found no follow-up reports in the newspaper archives.

How actively did the authorities pursue these sorts of cases in that day? Judging from reports of similar frauds, the frontier was populated by many disreputable sorts: men, who like Barber, may have been described as possessing a character of "base guile and unrighteous shrewdness."[31] The police likely could not deal with each and every scam.[32]

Where did he go after this episode? He would not have been welcome in the UK or the US. Did he quietly pay his fine,[33] or was he hiding in another country? Did he return to his Australian ranch? Recalling that 1912 *Flight* interview[34], perhaps this is when he took that Hawaiian vacation. Or Mexico! He had to capture that alligator at some point in his travels.

Perhaps Canada?

---

[31] *San Francisco Chronicle* Jul 20, 1904
[32] Extradition laws at the time were relatively ineffective, especially regarding new frontier borders and British commonwealth countries. Scam artists took advantage of loopholes and fled to neighbouring countries to avoid arrest.
[33] Perhaps Barber came up with the $2000 at some point since he certainly returned to the US many times in his lifetime.
[34] *Flight* December 1912, "A Chat with Mr. Barber"

Chapter 6
From Rogue to Riches 1904 to 1906

The Barbers' first son Claude Percy was born October 29, 1904, in the County of York, Ontario. From that date, we can calculate that Mr. and Mrs. Barber were together early in 1904 after he had left the Hale Ranch in California. Barber himself registered the birth December 1, 1904, and his occupation was listed as stockbroker. We do not know where the couple lived in York or Toronto when they first arrived.

Meanwhile in Mining News from Cobalt, Ontario

From 1903 to 1904, headlines about the silver discovery in Northern Ontario gained only languid attention even though the Provincial Geologist, Dr. Willet Green Miller spoke enthusiastically about the potential of the area. By the end of 1904, the railroad connected Cobalt to Southern Ontario and the mines began to ship their stockpiles of silver to southern refineries. Now, seeing was believing, and investors began to take note. The mining syndicates, groups of businessmen, lawyers, capitalists, and other opportunists who hoped to profit by investing in the new frontier, began to grow in number.

TORONTO 1905

The arrow points to a listing under "Barber" from the 1905 Toronto Directory

In the 1905 and the 1906 City of Toronto directories is a listing of Barber's new company, Incorporation and Securities Company of Canada, at 72 Queen Street West. He was the manager. We are unable to find any other references or any variation of the company name. We do not know if he was sole proprietor, or if he had a partner, or if he worked for someone else. That Barber made the move from fraudster to business manager in this relatively short space of time is typical for him, when you consider his multiple careers and mailing addresses. He was certainly not one to let the grass grow under his feet.

Annex to Toronto City Hall 1905 the Manning Chambers Building. Toronto Public Library. Judging from the insurance company names on the building, many men who dealt in finance passed through these doors.

We assume that this firm was set up to advise clients on the process of incorporation, which is loosely equivalent to forming a limited company. As well,

Mr. Barber would have helped his clients' companies with financial transactions related to the stock market. Just how qualified he was to be in an advisory position is open to debate.

72 Queen Street West was the address of Toronto's City Hall and at the time, many organizations had their offices here. According to the directories, several architects, barristers, and brokers conducted business in the Manning Chambers building,[35] which was built in 1900 to be an annex to the city hall.

Toronto 1906

The Barbers' second son Conrad Hope Barber was born in the York district of Toronto, January 1906. By this time, the young family lived in a posh Toronto neighbourhood at 76 Admiral Road and Horatio's occupation was listed as stockbroker.

According to the 1904-05 edition of the Tyrell Blue Book,[36] "a reliable directory to over 4,000 of the elite families of Toronto, Hamilton and London…" a Mrs. Mary Moore, widow, lived at 76 Admiral Road.[37] She was also at this address in 1905 according to the telephone book.

Here we have the entry for our family from the 1906 Blue Book.

> Barber, Mr. and Mrs. H. C.
> 76 Admiral road
> Receives 1st and 3d Wednesday
> Mrs., nee Porter

You will note that Mrs. H. C. Barber (nee Porter) received guests on the 1st and 3rd Wednesday of the month. All rather grand, yes?

Note that Conrad's birth registration was not completed until February 1908, some two years after Conrad was born, and by someone other than the parents. Barber was probably too busy with his business dealings at the beginning of 1906 and the matter of documenting his child's birth was forgotten. That someone other than Barber made the return early in 1908, with the permission of the Registrar General suggests that the family was no longer in the country.

---

[35] The architect of the Manning Chambers Annex was E. J. Lennox – he designed Casa Loma, the home of millionaire Henry Pellatt who made his fortune in Cobalt. Pellatt and his partners drained Cobalt Lake to gain access to the riches beneath the water.
This is not the first time we'll hear the Lennox name in this story. Lennox & Lennox were barristers who were associated with several wildcat mine companies in Cobalt and Larder Laker. They were also Barber's solicitors for his brokerage firm, Canada Mines Limited.

[36] *Tyrell Blue Book*, Toronto Public Library.

[37] 76 Admiral Road is located in "The Annex" a neighbourhood that "was popular among the city's elite in the late nineteenth century. The original conception is attributed to E. J. Lennox [there's that name again!], the most prominent architect in late nineteenth century Toronto." en.wikipedia.org/wiki/The Annex

Cobalt 1906

Today, Cobalt is a small, quiet, ghost-like town, sitting on a slope overlooking Cobalt Lake. Evidence of this once booming town can still be seen all around in the form of deserted and decaying headframes and mill foundations. Its population today is 1100 people, but in the early 1900s, it saw a silver mining boom almost equivalent to the 1849 gold rush in the United States. At its height, the area had a population of some 6,000 people with a further ten to fifteen thousand itinerant workers coming and going as work became available.

We've touched on Cobalt's story briefly in earlier chapters and how the origins of the town can be traced to 1903 when the Temiskaming and Northern Ontario Railway (T&NO) extended the railway into the northern regions to encourage settling in the area. Contractors who were cutting logs for the railway ties, or sleepers, discovered nuggets of silver in the gravel at the south end of Long Lake, later renamed Cobalt Lake.

Left is an illustration of Cobalt ca 1905 as it emerged from a tented encampment. By this time, silver fever had taken its grip, and people arrived by the train-load. The town was easily reached by rail from Toronto, today, the largest city in Canada and Ontario's capital. During the silver rush, however, the southern metropolis was demoted to second-place status when people referred to Toronto as "the place where you catch the train to Cobalt."

Cobalt ca 1905 Canadian Mining Journal

As with similar mineral rushes, the people who made the big money were not only the lucky or hard-working prospectors or mine owners, but the men who dealt in shares in these mining operations. It is around this time i.e. late 1905 or early 1906 that we find evidence of a Mr. Barber appearing on the scene.

The Cobalt Open Call Mining Exchange

The *New Liskeard Speaker* carried the announcement that Mr. Barber arrived in Cobalt Saturday, March 24, 1906, ahead of the big opening[38] of the Cobalt Open Call Mining Exchange. A week later, on March 30, 1906, Barber and his associates chartered the company. The provisional directors were Horatio C. Barber along with Capt. Wm. A. Marsh, R. H. C. Browne, and C. H. Moore, all of Cobalt and J. H. Hunter, capitalist of Cincinnati, Ohio. The media release

---

[38] Several advertisements also appeared in international papers, such as the following in the New York *Herald* dated March 25, 1906, announcing the opening on or about April 2. "Information concerning the listing of stocks, private memberships system of operation &c., may be secured by addressing the Secretary of the Exchange at Cobalt, Ontario."

indicated that membership was limited to 50 people and the fact that "it will be their aim to list only legitimate stocks."[39] Investors could buy shares in mines or in the Open Call Exchange itself.[40]

> The Mining exchange recently operated at Cobalt has been incorporated and will work under a provincial charter. Its official name is The Cobalt Open Call Mining Exchange, Limited. It has a capital of $40,000 and its provisional directors are Horatio C. Barber, Wm. A. Marsh and R. H. C. Browne, all of Cobalt. The first 25 seats were sold at $50 and the next 25 fixed at $100. Evening meetings will be held.

From the Canadian Mining Review of May 1906, announcing the incorporation of the Cobalt Open Call Mining Exchange, with Horatio C Barber as one of the directors.

Barber most likely wrote the media releases himself. From these announcements, we can deduce that Horatio had been in the area for several weeks before the opening, if not earlier in 1905. However, building space was limited and time was of the essence when it came to establishing oneself in Cobalt. Residences and offices were erected literally overnight.

> Truly, the great little town of Cobalt, that New Ontario hummer, doth take unto itself a more and more metropolitan character every day. The latest, according to the official gazette, is a company being formed to compile records and distribute information as to stocks and bonds of mining companies, and—above and beyond all this—to "provide and regulate a suitable building or rooms for a Stock Exchange," etc. Horatio Claude Barber is the name of one of the prominent organizers of this up-to-date concern.

Monetary Times *May 1, 1906* The article prints his full name, Horatio Claude Barber. In most media reports, he is referred to as H. C. Barber or simply Mr. Barber. Later in the chapter, we'll confirm that the stock-broker from Cobalt is one and the same as the aviation pioneer from Lark Hill.

It would appear that Barber modelled the Cobalt Open Call Exchange on a similar facility he knew from his time in Australia. Membership was open to all who could afford the $50 fee.[41] Meetings were held on a regular basis in the evenings and members could trade shares amongst themselves without the need of a broker. However, a small transaction charge for each sale was paid to the exchange.

---

[39] *New Liskeard Speaker* March 30, 1906
[40] *Detroit Free Press* June 3, 1906
[41] $CAD 50 from 1906 adjusted for inflation is about $CAD 1,500 or £875 in 2019

An April 28, 1906 news article in the *Province* from British Columbia is revealing for several reasons. We learn about the news from the Cobalt mining scene as well as new prospects further north. These, we've uncovered, are projects involving Barber's associates.

The *Province* also describes the purchase of the site upon which the Exchange was built. "The sale of squatters' rights continues and many fancy figures are given for certain sites. The Imperial Bank purchased squatters' rights from a French-Canadian named Boivin when it located its branch here, and later, the Cobalt Open Call Mining Exchange building is located upon a foundation purchased from another squatter."

At right is the account of the opening night of the exchange. Judging by the author's writing style, and the details discussed, we feel comfortable suggesting that Barber himself may have submitted the piece to the newspaper.

The site of the Open Call Exchange was located in what is still today known as "The Square", the irregularly shaped intersection of Argentite Street, Prospect Avenue, and the former road to Haileybury, now known as Lang Street. The building sat two doors north of the Imperial Bank.

> **Cobalt's Mining Exchange**
>
> People here are confident that the Cobalt Open Call Mining Exchange will be the scene of great activity in speculation during the ensuing summer.
>
> At the opening Saturday, a special train brought two hundred prospective speculators from Liskeard, nearly every man of whom carried stock in his pocket which he was seeking to market. Cobalt swelled the inaugural crowd with several hundred more, and there was rarely a moment throughout the night that there were not five hundred people on the floor of the exchange.
>
> In spite of this, trading was slow. The rules, explained for the first time by Mr. Barber, the secretary of the exchange, were new to all. To the prospectors from a distance who formed part of the crowd, the stocks were strange. Stock lists there were none. In spite of this nearly two thousand dollars changed hands.
>
> Prior to the opening of the exchange, speeches were delivered by Mr. Barber, its secretary; Reeve Finlan, introduced as the "Reeve of the richest township in Canada;" Captain Marsh and Colonel Sol White, ex-Mayor of Windsor, both of whom are shareholders in the corporation.
>
> *From the* Province, *April 28, 1906*

An April 1906 report in the *Canadian Mining Review* said that "a site for the building has been secured for $8,000, and a commodious structure will be at once erected…" The article reiterated previous claims that "wildcats[42] will be carefully excluded."

Barber was a promoter, not only of stocks but also of his businesses and of himself. He was comfortable embellishing the truth. One must approach the media releases with skepticism. The April 28 article in the *Province* illustrates a common practice of the time in that an advertisement or promotional piece for a mining company was submitted to the papers disguised as bona fide journalism.

---

[42] Wildcat definition: a property that has the potential to be a producing mine, but work has not yet been done to prove it.

Consider the $8,000 price tag of the building site. Even though it was located in the most desirable section of town, this seems extraordinarily overpriced considering similar lots were sold for far less, in the hundreds of dollars range. Adjusted for inflation, the syndicate would today (2019) pay $CAD 292,000 or £175,000 for that tiny lot on a rock outcrop. It could be that the $8,000 price was overstated to impress prospective clients. Then again, perhaps Barber's syndicate purchased a double or triple lot with plans to erect a larger, permanent exchange building.

Then we have the crowd size to consider. Would that many people have attended this event? As a matter of fact, yes. It is difficult to appreciate the scale of interest in the silver boom. Author Douglas Baldwin offers insight in *Cobalt: Canada's Forgotten Silver Boom Town*.

"For three consecutive days in 1906 mounted police in New York City cleared Bond Street of expectant investors who were obstructing traffic in their efforts to buy Cobalt shares from the curb brokers. The word Cobalt was on every tongue. Visitors and prospectors came from around the world to inspect the area."

Photos and written memoirs from the period give ample support to the hundreds of people who arrived on a daily basis. Yet, 500 people inside the exchange building? A single lot would have been roughly 10 x 15 metres. Assuming that the building occupied the entire space, it is difficult to imagine that many people being crammed together.

Then, of course, we have the laughable claim that only legitimate stocks would be sold. Laughable, that is, once you know the entire story.

For the moment, we, like the novice investors from 1906, have no choice but to take him at his word.

Left to right - the Open Call Mining Exchange, legal offices, the Imperial Bank. Today only the bank building is standing. Cobalt Mining Museum collection. See Chapter 7 for additional images of Cobalt Square and the Cobalt Open Call Mining Exchange.

Barber as Fiscal Agent for the Hudson Bay Extended Mine

Below is the heading of an expensive half-paged ad that was placed in the *New Liskeard Speaker* May 4, 1906. H. C. Barber's name appears twice in the heading: once among the officers and directors, and again, more prominently in a larger, italicized font, on a separate line, indicating his function as "fiscal agent." In this ad, he promotes himself and the Hudson Bay Extended Mine.

Today, a fiscal agent is usually an institution, such as a bank, for example, that conducts financial business on behalf of a client. We cannot confirm if the same definition applied in 1906, but it would appear that Barber was taking care of the money end of business for the partners involved with this mine.

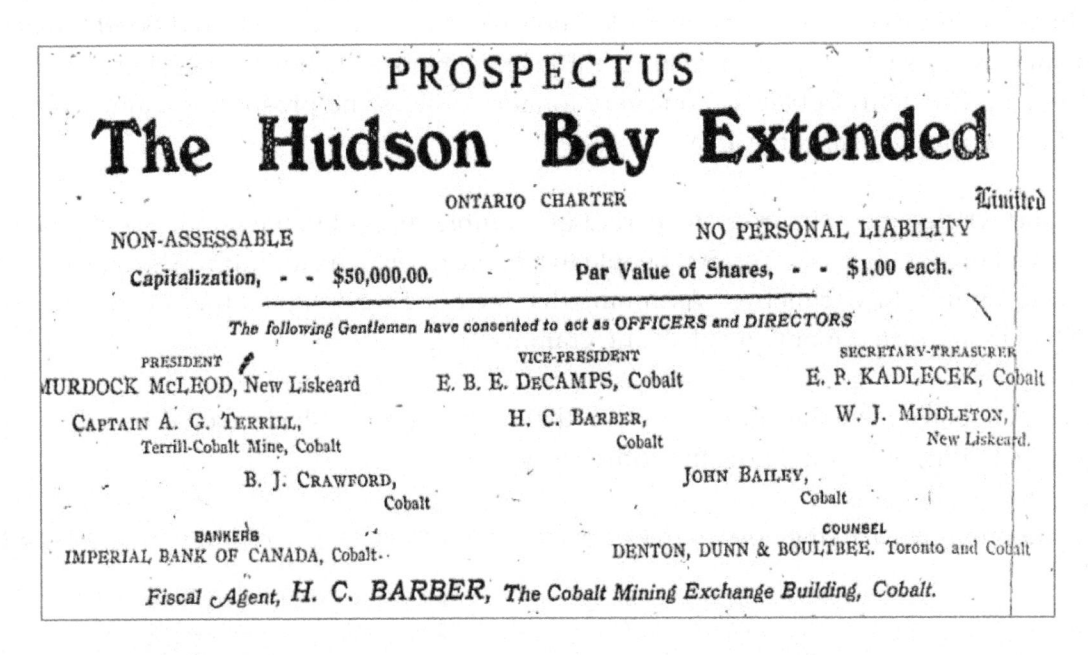

```
                    PROSPECTUS
         The Hudson Bay Extended
                    ONTARIO CHARTER                              Limited
   NON-ASSESSABLE                           NO PERSONAL LIABILITY
   Capitalization, - - $50,000.00.      Par Value of Shares, - - $1.00 each.

         The following Gentlemen have consented to act as OFFICERS and DIRECTORS
        PRESIDENT              VICE-PRESIDENT              SECRETARY-TREASURER
   MURDOCK McLEOD, New Liskeard  E. B. E. DeCAMPS, Cobalt   E. P. KADLECEK, Cobalt
   CAPTAIN A. G. TERRILL,        H. C. BARBER,              W. J. MIDDLETON,
       Terrill-Cobalt Mine, Cobalt      Cobalt                    New Liskeard
              B. J. CRAWFORD,                    JOHN BAILEY,
                      Cobalt                            Cobalt
                 BANKERS                               COUNSEL
   IMPERIAL BANK OF CANADA, Cobalt     DENTON, DUNN & BOULTBEE, Toronto and Cobalt

   Fiscal Agent, H. C. BARBER, The Cobalt Mining Exchange Building, Cobalt.
```

The Hudson Bay Extended was a wildcat mine. That is, an ore body was possible, but not yet discovered. Generally, promotion of such properties was premature, wildly optimistic, and often carried out with the intention to defraud. 1968 mine records[43] compiled since the early days, indicate that the Hudson Bay Extended was never considered to be a producing mine.

Several clues in the ad content (not shown) are dead giveaways as to the legitimacy of this mine and its promoter.

- The writer addresses the reader with a note of urgency: *"A limited amount of this stock… is offered for sale."* A variation of "buy now, don't be disappointed!" Typical advertising hype.

---

[43] *Silver Cobalt Calcite Vein Deposits of Ontario* A. O. Sergiades 1968

- The mine site is adjacent to a producing mine and is therefore likely to have minerals. Or at least, that is what the promoter wants you to believe. The advertisement states, "In naming this Company it has been the object to signify exactly just what the company is, and the name The Hudson Bay Extended, Limited implies exactly the proper thing, vis: that *the most valuable property of this Company is geographical, an extension of the famous Temiskaming & Hudson Bay mines."*

This is a misleading statement. Yes, the "Extension" mine butts up to the first mine which is a "famous" wealthy producer. Yes, veins of ore can and do run beyond the borders of a staked mining property. But if the drilling or other exploration work has not yet been completed to prove that ore is underneath the "extension" property, the promoter is wrong to suggest that his mine bears ore of the same quality as the adjacent producing mine.

- Exploration has revealed *"well-mineralized calcite veins."* When hunting for silver, prospectors looked for "indicator minerals," such as the white calcite or pinkish dolomite veins in the rock. But in the ad, Barber mentions only the mineral cobalt being present, not the more valuable silver. As the provincial geologist Dr. Miller lamented, a carbonate vein of calcite or dolomite is not final proof that precious metals are on the property.
- The ad reports that assays have been conducted, and show *"very promising values in silver."* The description of the geology of the mine site is long on hyperbole, but short on facts. The prospective investor must trust that the promoter is knowledgeable and reliable.
- Typically, a promoter spares no expense when it comes to advertising. The larger, the better. The fact that this ad took up half a page is evidence that the writer wanted the readers' attention. The bona fide producers rarely advertised for investors.

Barber as an organizer of the Long Lake Company.

Barber was also busy with the Long Lake Company Limited along with Hunter, Marsh, and Solomon White. This particular Long Lake was in Charlton, some 70km north of Cobalt. The syndicate had plans to acquire the townsite, "a large sawmill there, timber limits[44], water power rights... and certain mines." Their intention was to also build an electric railway to join Charlton to the TN&O. In all likelihood, Barber

Long Lake

We hear that a company is being organized, to be called the Long Lake Co., Limited. Among the organizers are Col. White, ex. M. P. P., J. H. Hunter, Captain Marsh and H. C. Barber. The Company is taking over the town site of Charlton, a large saw mill there, timber limits, water power rights capable of producing 3,000 horse power and certain Mines. As we are advised, the Company intends to form a subsidiary company for the purpose of building an electric railway between Charlton and the Temiskaming and Northern Ontario Railway and to generally develop that part of the country.

Charlton

The Hon. Sol. White, Capt. March and Mr. Watson, were in town last week, looking after the interests of the Long Lake Co. Ltd. We understand that the company intend taking over the mines and mill plant belonging to Mr. Ryan, on 1st of July.

McColl's Bay looks like a miniature Cobalt just now. Several companies have gangs working the mines there.

C. H. Vint, of Mimico, intends settling in this vicinity.

Russell Draper is back on his farm again. Poor old bachelors!

Mr. Ryan has a gang of men on the lake taking down the drive.

Capt. Marsh thinks that the town site here, is "ideal."

New Liskeard Speaker March 30, left, and June 15, 1906. Note the editorial "we." As a promoter of his associates' business interests, Barber would have sent these media updates to the paper. Note also Mr. Ryan's name, right.

---

[44] "Timber limits" are the rights to harvest trees for lumber, or timber, within a designated area.

would have assisted with the incorporation of this company, either as their agent or consultant, drawing on his experience from his days as manager of Incorporation and Securities Company of Canada.

Important Evidence

What follows is a letter written in regards to the Long Lake project. It is perhaps the single most important piece of documentary evidence we found about Barber's activities before his aviation career. The letterhead is followed by the two-page document. We transcribe it on the next page.

The correspondence links the Horatio Claude Barber who referred to himself as a stockbroker who lived with his family in Toronto at 76 Admiral Road to the Cobalt Open Call Mining Exchange[45] and therefore to the man who went on to aviation fame in the early 1910s in the UK.

The letter[46], presently in the collection of the Cobalt Historical Society, is dated May 6, 1906, and was written from H. C. Barber to lawyer Albert Norton Morgan of New Liskeard. The full letter is transcribed, right.

> 76 Admiral Road,
> Toronto,
> May 6, 1906
>
> Dear Mr. Morgan,
>
> I am hard at work on the Long Lake proposition and have already excellent prospects as far as raising the requisite amount of capital is concerned. The people I have interested will probably want to visit Charlton and investigate within a week from now and everything depends upon getting an option from the Ryans without a day's delay. I hope you are losing no time. If it will facilitate matters and save any time at all telegraph the Ryan's to come to you at New Liskeard at once and if necessary I will put up their expenses -- though if you offer them that, it will have to be done in such a way as not to put them "up in the air" too much. Please use every means possible to get the Ryans together and to secure the option at once. You can imagine what would probably happen if my moneyed connections should get "next" them before I have the option! I expect to be in Cobalt next Wednesday.
>
> Yours Faithfully
> H. C. Barber

---

[45] Note also the tag line to Barber's business heading: "Mining Properties Bought and Sold. Capital Furnished to Develop Properties." These are the very words used on the notice board on the left side of the exchange building.
See Appendix 5 for a collection of Barber's signatures from an assortment of documents during his lifetime.

[46] Note from author Terry Grace: It is true to say that much hard work and travel has been necessary to accomplish the story of this particular part of Barber's life, but that serendipity too has played its part. The letter referred to above, surfaced at the most opportune moment. Whilst we were in Cobalt researching Barber's time there, we went into the most fantastic second hand book shop and spent a long time talking to its owner Deborah. She promised to let me know if she came across any references to him in the local history publications. During our time in Cobalt we met up with Maggie Wilson of the Cobalt Historical Society. I had previously been in contact with Maggie, and in helping me with my enquiries into Barber's time in Cobalt, she too had become interested in the man. A few weeks after our return to the UK, Maggie received a call from Deborah who knowing that she was interested in that period, let her know that she had just received two boxes of letters written to A.N. Morgan, a lawyer who practiced in the nearby town of New Liskeard. The boxes had been donated by the Cramahe Ontario Heritage Board, who explained that "...they were recovered from a garage clean out on a property owned by one Sally Marshall, who was a daughter of a long-time resident doctor of the town of Colborne. She incidentally was an executive assistant of Pierre Trudeau (probably pre-government days)." It is quite miraculous that this 112-year old letter which had been sitting in a garage for decades, fell into our hands at this time.

Barber was obviously very keen to close the Long Lake deal and this is made even more obvious by the telegram sent the very next day which reinforces the urgency.

Telegram dated May 7, 1906 to Mr. Morgan [lawyer] "I have the capital assured. Everything depends upon getting option. Use haste and every means possible. Wire me if you know anything yet. R. C. Barber." Note that the "R" in signature is a transcription error.

The *Canadian Mining Journal* included the Long Lake Company among the Cobalt companies that were incorporated at the close of 1906. The list came with the following caveat:

> "Some of the companies originally incorporated on a modest basis have altered their figures from hundreds of thousands to millions, and the tendency always is towards inflated figures. People who have studied Cobalt at all carefully admit that the potentialities of the camp are great. It has been pronounced by disinterested expert mining men as the greatest silver camp on the globe. It is the great value of the silver deposits there that constitutes the greatest danger for the unthinking public. The exploiting of "wild-cat" companies is a consequence. In the matter of investment, the Canadian public must be its own judge. Some mining companies operating in Ontario under state incorporation have not complied with the Provincial requirements in taking out a licence to do business here. Some of these companies assert that they are not legally required to do so, and the provincial Secretary's Department is now giving the question of the standing of these alien combinations consideration that foreshadow the adoption of some course of action at an early date."
>
> *Canadian Mining Journal* Vol.28 1907

Perhaps the Long Lake company fell afoul of the legislation at an early date, as there seem to be no more references to the venture after the June 15 media release in the *Speaker*. Perhaps Morgan and/or Barber were unable to make a deal with the Ryans. Col. Solomon White, who was mentioned in both clippings as an interested party in the Long Lake Company, did have a property in that town called Lake Farm. Perhaps he bought out the rest of the partners.

Regarding the outcome of the Long Lake project in Charlton, as usual, we are left to speculate until more information comes to light.

Barber as Mine Operator

In his pamphlet about Cobalt, Barber referred to himself as a mine operator.[47]

We have not found his name associated with any bona fide mine operation in the region - neither as a board member, director, employee, or contractor. He was not involved with the development of a mine and the actual work of building a facility or extracting and processing ore. We assume that he identified himself as a "mine operator" to enhance his credentials. In reality, he was an operator in the disparaging sense of the word.

Barber also promoted himself as a mining consultant and later writers such as Dufresne and Thompson[48] described him as such. Barber was in Cobalt to set up shop and gave the impression of being the man at the front, the man in the know, the man to talk to if you wanted the latest news and insider information.

Barber as Promoter

While in Cobalt, Barber referred to himself as a stockbroker, director and secretary, fiscal agent, an organizer, and mine operator. The one title he didn't use, but best describes his activities was promoter.

By 1908 the Cobalt area proved to be the biggest global producer of silver and of cobalt. However, in the early days of the evolution of the mining camp, any notion of worldwide status was based more on speculation than substance.

Initially, huge nuggets of nearly pure silver were found on or near the surface of the ground. This created the international interest and the prospectors' subsequent rush. Before long, geologists and other professional mining men determined that the extent of the silver ore body was limited to the area around the growing town and that it would be necessary to mine much deeper in order to produce significant quantities. This did not stop the speculation and the rush to buy shares in the silver mining ventures.

At its height in 1906, investment in mines in Cobalt and the surrounding areas, either operating or proposed, was estimated to be $75 million. This was fuelled by brokers and promoters who vastly exaggerated the silver content of the ore being extracted. Indeed, most of the ads and articles in the press regarding Cobalt investment opportunities were either overly optimistic on one hand or total fabrications on the other. The provincial geologists, and editors of the *Canadian Mining Journal,* for example, issued notices to the public, urging caution when it came to the speculative claims made by rogue dealers. But these occasional warnings were drowned out by the constant stream of ads and promotions.

---

[47] *Cobalt - The Mining District Containing the richest deposits in the world of Silver and Cobalt* by H. C. Barber
[48] *Canada's Forgotten Gold Rush: The Goldfields of Larder Lake* 1999 Vernon Dufresne and Clark Thompson

COBALT

Immense profits are being made, and for some time will continue to be made in Cobalt stocks, but it is absolutely necessary to have the right kind of information.

I Am a Practical Mining Man

—was one of the first in the Cobalt field, and am personally acquainted with every mine of any importance.

MY NEW BOOK, "Cobalt," furnishes the latest authentic information—includes map and Government report.

MY WEEKLY NEWS-LETTER gives reliable and up-to-date particulars concerning the Cobalt stocks—market conditions—and the latest news direct from the field.

THE ABOVE MAILED FREE TO ANY ADDRESS.

Write, wire or 'phone me when buying or selling Cobalt stocks. Prompt and efficient service.

H. C. BARBER

43 Adelaide Street East, Toronto.

Ottawa Citizen *November 10, 1906. This ad appeared in several papers. Referring to oneself as a "practical mining man" was a strategy employed by many similarly-minded "entrepreneurs" from this time.*

Barber advertised his services in the major papers throughout North America first as "The Cobalt Open Call Mining Exchange" then under his own name. Later, he opened a business called Canada Mines Limited, a name that implies that the operation was national in scope. The title was nothing more than a fancy name for his promotional schemes. A selection of his earlier ads is shown on the next page.

COBALT.

COBALT STOCKS—the right kind—offer immense opportunities for large and immediate profits. For the past few months high-grade ore has been piling up at the mines, shipments being withheld pending the completion of the new smelter. This has resulted in many stocks being quoted by those not understanding conditions at a price far below their real value. Shipments are now commencing, and great returns, not to speak of advances in stock market prices, are assured. Many ground-floor opportunities exist now, but the market is daily becoming more active and NOW IS THE TIME TO ACT.

My booklet (including Govt. report) and weekly news letter furnish full and up-to-date information. They are free.

H. C. BARBER,

Mines   Stocks   Syndicates

45 Adelaide St. E., Toronto, and Cobalt.

Birtle Eye Witness 28th August 1906

COBALT—BY FAR THE RICHEST SILVER field in the world, offers the most wonderful opportunities for large and immediate profits. The ore runs as high as $100,000 to the car, and more than one company has paid back several times its entire subscribed capital in its first dividend. New and rich discoveries are being made weekly, and investors are reaping enormous profits. These are facts—cold facts—and the field yet in its infancy. Now is the time to pick up those stocks which, from the valuable properties behind them, are bound to pay immense dividends and to advance to many times their present price. The time to get in is now, before the inevitable boom and inflated prices. There are large profits to be made, but don't rush too quickly, act warily, and first of all secure really authentic information. The Canada Mines, Ltd., chartered by the Ontario government, directed by well known Canadians known to everyone, and managed by H. C. Barber, well known as a successful and practical mining man, affords you a safe and responsible medium through which you can secure the right kind of information concerning the immense opportunities for large and immediate profits certain Cobalt stocks offer. Booklet, government report, map and weekly news letter free. Write to-day. Opportunity waits for no man. Canada Mines, Ltd., 45 Adelaide street east, Toronto.

Manitoba Free Press Winnipeg 22nd Sept. 1906

COBALT.

THE OPPORTUNITY OF THE AGE.

100% TO 15,000% PROFITS.

A 1,500 PER CENT. DIVIDEND PAID LAST WEEK.

COBALT, the new silver field, by far the richest the world has ever seen, has already brought investors from 100 to 30,000 per cent. profits. One company last week paid a 1,500 per cent. dividend; one stock has jumped from 40 cents to $119; another from $5.00 to $30.00; another from $1.00 to $5.25; another from 80 cents to $3, etc., etc.

The field is yet in its infancy, new and extraordinarily rich discoveries are being made daily and there are immense profits to be made by those getting in now. Canadian laws are so strict the investor is protected as never before, and Cobalt presents the opportunity of the age for large profits combined with safety.

The CANADA MINES, LIMITED, chartered by the Ontario Government and directed by conservative statesmen and business men known to everyone in Canada, affords a really safe and responsible medium through which you may take advantage of the immense opportunities for large and immediate profits contained in the Cobalt silver field.

Authentic information, Government report, maps and full particulars concerning Cobalt stocks free on request. Write today and get the facts.

CANADA MINES, LIMITED,

45 Adelaide street, Toronto, Can.

The Sun Baltimore 11th November 1906

BUSINESS OPPORTUNITIES

COBALT

THE OPPORTUNITY OF THE AGE

100% TO 30,000% PROFITS

A 4500% Dividend Paid Last Week

BY THE T. AND H. B. COMPANY.

COBALT, the new silver field, by far the richest the world has ever seen, has already brought investors from 100 to 30,000 per cent. profits. The T. and H. B. Company last week paid a 4500 per cent. dividend; one stock has jumped from 40 cents to $135; another from $5.00 to $30.00, another from $1.00 to $5.25, another from 80 cents to $4.00, etc., etc.

The field is yet in its infancy, new and extraordinarily rich discoveries are being made daily, and there are immense profits to be made by those getting in now. Canadian laws are so strict the investor is protected as never before, and Cobalt presents the opportunity of the age for large profits combined with safety.

The CANADA MINES, LIMITED, chartered by the Ontario Government and directed by conservative statesmen and business men known to everyone in Canada, affords a really safe and responsible medium through which you may take advantage of the immense opportunities for large and immediate profits contained in the Cobalt silver field.

Authentic information, government report, maps and full particulars concerning Cobalt stocks free on request. Write today and get the facts.

CANADA MINES, LIMITED,

45 Adelaide st., Toronto, Canada.

The Philadelphia Enquirer 25th November 1906

> A million dollar deal took place at Cobalt last week when Mr. Hunter of Cincinnati and Captain W. A. Marsh of Toronto secured a tract of land in the Abbitibi district near the southeastern watershed and within five miles of the T. & N. O. railway. The land is leased and the title perfect. On the tract is a mineral vein ninety-five feet wide containing gold, silver and copper. The new owners will put in a diamond drill at once and proceed to take out ore for shipment. Experts pronounce the property one of the most valuable in Northern Ontario.

To promote his businesses, Barber submitted regular mining news updates to the newspapers. In these articles, he usually focused on his partners' projects.

For example, consider the snippet on the left. It is a paragraph from an article[49] that went to press just a few days ahead of the opening of his exchange. Barber described a million-dollar[50] deal involving two of his cohorts Hunter and Marsh, and a 95-foot wide vein, with gold and silver and copper.

The average reader would reasonably conclude that a 95-foot vein was an impressive size to merit a million-dollar deal. However, 95-foot veins of gold do not occur in Northern Ontario geology. The discovery of an equally imaginary 9.5-*inch* vein would have been cause for jubilation. Perhaps the vein in question was exposed on the surface for a good length, perhaps it had particles of precious minerals, maybe even a nugget or two of visible gold. But to lead on the impressionable reader without backing up the claims with assay results and omitting the names and qualifications of the "experts" is dubious at best.

Barber didn't go quite as a far as another brokerage, Willis Abbott & Co. This firm played on the prevailing sentiment against foreign ownership of the Canadian silver mines. An eye-popping headline in a large, nearly half-page ad that promoted The Southern Belle Mine, shamed the reader to "Be a good Canadian. If you can't, then be a Yank and grasp the "silver" opportunities as they are offered."[51]

Canada Mines Limited

In September 1906, Barber incorporated Canada Mines Limited and opened an office in Toronto. This was a strategic and important move. A posh location in the heart of the financial district and a lavish suite of offices would help him to impress prospective clients or business partners.

Canada Mines Limited, Barber's offices at 45 Adelaide St. East, Toronto in 1906 above, from the pamphlet, and in 2018 Terry Grace photograph.

---

[49] *Vancouver Daily World* March 26, 1906
[50] A million 1903 dollars adjusted for inflation is about of $CAD 38.1 million or £17 million, in 2019 values. In those days, the currency in arrangements like this often involved shares or options of an equivalent value, not cash on the barrel head.
[51] *New Liskeard Speaker* January 11, 1907

COBALT

The Mining District

Containing the richest deposits in the world of

SILVER AND COBALT

ALSO COPPER GOLD NICKEL ARSENIC

Canada Mines Limited
Canadian Mines and Mining Stocks

45 Adelaide Street East, Toronto and Cobalt, New Ontario

To promote this venture, he wrote a pamphlet about Cobalt.[52] By way of introduction, he assured his readers that his company owned no mines and was therefore unbiased. He subtly offered his guidance to potential investors. His tone was serene, almost modest.

We've parsed his text, below, and point out his strategic comments, exaggerations, and blatant falsehoods, with our comments in bold.

"I, the writer may say that I am a practical mining man, having had experience in most of the mining fields of the world." *(We know he was in Western Australia and also in British Columbia and may have been in Mexico. However, to say "most" is stretching the truth.)*

"I was one of the first in the Cobalt field," *(He may have arrived as a tourist in 1905 once the T&NO established passenger service, but he was hardly the first.)* "…and the first man in Cobalt to do active business in mining properties and stocks." *(This is likely true as his business The Cobalt Open Call Mining Exchange appears to have had no competition initially.)*

"This spring my business had increased to such an extent that I found it necessary to open Toronto offices in addition to those I had already established in Cobalt." *(He opened the Canada Mines Limited offices at 45 Adelaide St. Toronto around August 1906 but was trading there under the name H. C. Barber at least a month before that.)*

Barber continued, "Soon after that my business had gained so much in magnitude that, following what seemed to me to be the next step to take under the circumstances and at the earnest wish of some of my friends who desired to be associated with me, *(Barber promoted himself as an important man, with a large, successful business. So important, people were clamouring to align themselves with him.)* I obtained a Government charter for my business to be conducted under the name of CANADA MINES, LTD." *(Barber wanted his readers to be assured that his was a legitimate business, chartered under the auspices of a government body.)*

"I wish my clients to understand, however, that the policy of the business is in no way changed and that the CANADA MINES, LTD., will under my management, continue to follow those same lines on which I have built up my valuable and esteemed connection. *(More self-promotion: He is valued. He is esteemed.)*

"The CANADA MINES, LTD., does not bias its judgement by owning or operating mines or trading in stocks on its own account. The business of the company is to render faithful and efficient service to its clients in buying or selling, undertaking the management of and reporting

---

[52] *Cobalt - The Mining District Containing the richest deposits in the world of Silver and Cobalt* by H. C. Barber. See Bibliography and Resources for a link to an online copy of the pamphlet

upon mining properties in Canada- and in executing commissions for the sale and purchase of mining stocks." *(It is unclear what he meant by "management of ... mining properties." After all, this is in conflict with the previous statement about remaining unbiased. Perhaps he was referring to the management and dissemination of information about mining properties.)*

"It is hardly necessary for me to say very much concerning my associates- the names of this Company's directors on the opposite page speak for themselves. *(The people aligned with Barber were men of rank, status, or title. This was a typical strategy used by wildcat mine promoters who wished to give their business legitimacy, similar to celebrity endorsement of a product. If the name of the company director was not someone the reader knew, then the reader clearly did not travel in the right sort of crowd; after all, it was "hardly necessary" for Barber to say much more on the subject of the men's qualifications.)* "The services of the foremost mining engineers in Canada have been retained by the Company and in short, no stone has been left unturned to afford the public a really safe *(Unmitigated temerity!)* and responsible medium through which they make take profitable advantage of the mineral wealth now being opened up in Canada."

The content of the pamphlet is a blend of fact and fiction. Barber included descriptions of the mines which he collected from other publications and from mine owners, in what we would today describe as a "cut and paste" fashion. This data contained the provincial geologists' reports. However, he also reprinted newspaper articles that raved about the riches to be encountered and the wonderful opportunities not to be missed.

Throughout the text, by using a bold font, Barber strategically highlighted key phrases to catch the eye of the reader. "Expert Opinion of Prof Miller" – **Barber was name dropping here – Dr. Miller was much admired and respected in mining circles.** "Second only to Klondike" **was meant to stir the sentiment of those who recalled the excitement of the Yukon gold rush.**

One particular caption at the top of a page caught our eye, and with the benefit of hindsight, the words strike us as more than a little cynical, if not downright mendacious: "Cobalt Ores Richest in the World, Mining Laws so Strict <u>no 'Wild Cat' Schemes Can Flourish</u>." [additional emphasis by the authors]

In closing, Barber added a postscript. "Since the foregoing appeared much has happened - so much that it would be impossible within the limits of this booklet to treat the subject fully. "There are some thirty shipping mines, scores of others developed far beyond the experimental stage, and numerous rich discoveries have been made, and are constantly coming to light, showing the mineral field to be of immensely larger area than was before thought. *(Barber was correct. The number of financial transactions in those days, as well as the frequency in which a mine was bought and sold and then sold again, was breath-taking.)* "Smelters are in course of erection and many thousands of experienced prospectors are at work exploring the country. *(While many men were experienced prospectors, many were greenhorns trying their luck. This is another example of Barber overstating the facts.)*

There is now no doubt that the mineral deposits will prove of permanent value and that New Ontario will rank among the greatest mining fields in the world. *(If Barber believed that the mining camp was permanent, he was alone in this line of thinking. The Town of Cobalt did not invest in waterworks, hospitals and other social services because the prevailing sentiment was that the silver would run out in short order. Barber was either naïve, or misleading the potential investor, yet again.)*

There is little doubt that the basic organization of Barber's business was legitimate. But he was not averse to selling shares in wildcat properties, specifically those of the Abitibi and Cobalt Mining Company.

Barber's Wildcat

In his *Cobalt* pamphlet, among the list of the successful mines such as the Larose, Buffalo, and Nipissing is an entry for Abitibi and Cobalt Mining Company. The yearly provincial Bureau of Mines report indicates that the company was incorporated March 10, 1906.[53] Barber probably handled the paperwork. The provisional directors were all merchants and businessmen from Sault Ste. Marie, Michigan. The solicitor representing the group was from Ontario.[54] The company name does not appear in other mine reports, nor in the Davis Handbook or Sergiades[55] – two authorities on the Cobalt mines.

While reading the pamphlet, a prospective investor might reasonably conclude that since the Abitibi and Cobalt Mine is listed alongside the other bona fide producers and big money generators, it must be equally rich. This was exactly Barber's gambit.

Recall that Barber was the fiscal agent for the Hudson Bay Extended Mine. That organization pinned its hopes on the possibility that silver veins from the producing mine immediately next door reached their property. In the case of the Abitibi and Cobalt Mine, the several sites staked by the company were very far outside the range of the silver-bearing rock. The main camp at Gillies Depot, for example, was five kilometres from the nearest shipping mine. This company, (and its promoter, Mr. Barber) pinned its hopes on the likelihood that the investor wasn't paying close attention to geology maps.

In his pamphlet, Barber makes it clear that the mine is not yet a producer, but the property is "very good looking" with "good values" and the camp is "one of the best in the district." He

---

[53] Dept of Mines annual report 1907
[54] *Cobalt and its Silver Mines* by William Starr Bullock 1906
[55] *The Davis Handbook* of *The Cobalt Silver District*, by HP Davis, 1910 Silver Cobalt Calcite Vein Deposits of Ontario A. O. Sergiades 1968

says, "I am informed by the officials of the Company that they anticipate shipping... at an early date. From all appearances, this Company should prove a big shipper and very successful." While positive-sounding, these vague words do not convey meaningful information about the mine. The statement that his mine was "one of the best in the district" is nonsense.

Generally, the shares of the larger producing mines were very closely held by the company directors and select investors. If a customer wrote to Barber asking to purchase shares in the Nipissing Mine, for example, Barber would have explained that he had none to sell, and besides, the price was perhaps more than the client could afford. He'd then direct the investor to the Abitibi and Cobalt Mine that had plenty of affordable shares for sale. Classic bait and switch.

During our research, it became apparent that whoever chose Abitibi and Cobalt as the name of the company, did so with marketing in mind. In most alphabetical listings, the A&C ranked first. Including the word "Cobalt" in the name was also a strategic move. Investors who were hungry for any news about the silver mine town would eagerly scan the financial pages, looking for updates from Cobalt.

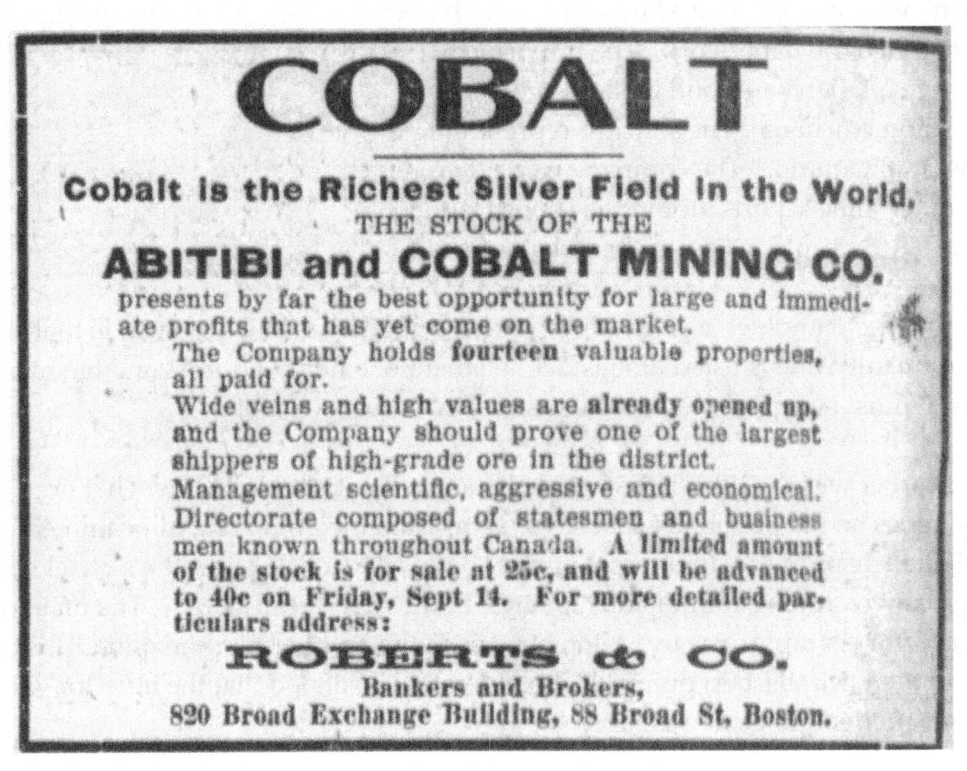

COBALT

Cobalt is the Richest Silver Field in the World.
THE STOCK OF THE
ABITIBI and COBALT MINING CO.
presents by far the best opportunity for large and immediate profits that has yet come on the market.
The Company holds **fourteen** valuable properties, all paid for.
Wide veins and high values are already opened up, and the Company should prove one of the largest shippers of high-grade ore in the district.
Management scientific, aggressive and economical. Directorate composed of statesmen and business men known throughout Canada. A limited amount of the stock is for sale at 25c, and will be advanced to 40c on Friday, Sept 14. For more detailed particulars address:

ROBERTS & CO.
Bankers and Brokers,
820 Broad Exchange Building, 88 Broad St, Boston.

The Boston Globe, *September 9, 1906*

Barber purchased advertisements to promote the sale of Abitibi and Cobalt Mines starting around September 1906. It appears that he sold blocks of A&C shares to other brokers for resale.

For example, the firm of Roberts and Co. in Boston[56] urged interested parties to "buy now" before the price increased from twenty-five to forty cents.

Barber's self-promoting newspaper advertisements and articles were ubiquitous during 1906, but a quarter-page ad in the *Chicago Tribune* to promote "Cobalt – Land of Fortune" was most striking in style and tone, one with a certain Edwardian ring to it.

Chicago Tribune *September 23, 1906*

The ad was seemingly written to address concerns about the wisdom of investing in the Cobalt silver mines. Barber used this platform to address any reluctance investors had and to set their minds at ease. Buried at the end of the piece, we discover the real reason for buying this expensive advertisement: he urged his readers to buy shares in Abitibi and Cobalt Mine.

The date of the advertisement, September 23rd is worth noting, as it was near the end of Barber's days in that particular area of Northern Ontario. This is perhaps why we detect a note of urgency in his words, "seize the present opportunities… and [act] quickly."

In the ad, he promoted himself and repeated the assertion, "I claim to know mines and mining, having been actively engaged in that business for years, in the different camps of the world." He makes the grand assertion that "I have never advised my clients to purchase any Cobalt stock that has not afterwards materially advanced in value. I believe I may say that I stand alone in this record, which I think is due to the fact that I am a *practical mining man* [Barber's emphasis] rather than a broker…"

Several paragraphs in the essay/advertisement talk about the safeguards that the authorities have arranged to protect the investor and the mining industry. Judging by his apparent familiarity with the Torrens Law Title Act [57] and the watchdogs in the provincial government who must approve a mine, we wonder if he was speaking from experience. One imagines that he would have been irritated by the legal hurdles he encountered.

---

[56] The *Boston Globe*, Sep 9, 1906
[57] Torrens Law refers to the legalities related to land registration and title.

He reiterated that there is no such thing as a wildcat mining operation in the Cobalt mine camp. After all, how could there be, with "safeguards" in place? He wrote, "A hole in the ground is not a mine in the estimation of the authorities and hence an investor may be sure when he finds out that the mine has a charter [and has been incorporated under provincial laws], that his stock represents real value." This is a bald-faced lie.

The final sentence is remarkably shrewd in that Barber lays the blame for any stock performance failure at the feet of the investor. "Nothing but bad management can prevent his stock from being a good investment." [58]

Abitibi and Cobalt Mine, lower left. The distance to Cobalt Lake in the upper right is about 5 km, as the crow flies.

At the end of his essay, Barber included a plug for Abitibi and Cobalt shares. "The stock I am pushing and that I firmly believe will be a money maker is the Abitibi & Cobalt Mining Co. – whose mines are right in the heart of the producers – in Coleman Township."

So that our readers are able to appreciate Barber's falsehood, the map illustrates the location of the mine. In the lower left, the large arrow points to a marker which is the symbol for a single mine site. This is the location of the Abitibi and Cobalt Mine. The circles with numbers in them indicate multiple mines sites located side-by-side.

---

[58] Barber employs an excuse that has been around for some time. "It is complained that some sellers and buyers of the shares in mines are fraudulent. I concede it. But can they deceive anyone except a stupid, careless man, unskilled in mining matters?" Georg Agricola, De re Metallica 1556

Rather than being located "right in the heart of the producers," the Abitibi and Cobalt Mine was located *far* outside of the mineral-bearing property of the Town of Cobalt and Coleman Township. The distance to Cobalt Lake in the upper right is about 5 km, as the crow flies.

Goodbye, Cobalt

October 1906 was a watershed moment in Barber's Cobalt career. During October, we find no ads from him related to the Abitibi and Cobalt Mine.

As a matter of fact, Barber seems to have left Cobalt altogether since he abandoned the substantial sum of $733.62[59] in his company's bank account after October 18, 1906 – the last date on record. Upon close examination of the photos of the open call exchange, we can see that the building (and thus by inference his business) was for sale in 1906.

Another view of Cobalt Square and the "For Sale" sign on the Cobalt Open Call Mining Exchange building. In 1907, the building was a boarding house, the American Palace. Cobalt Mining Museum photo.

Why did Barber leave Cobalt? If we indulge in armchair analysis of his personality, we propose that the following character traits contributed to his decision to move on.

Firstly, Barber had a tendency either through preference or necessity to change direction at the drop of a hat. He was a man who until his retirement did not stay long in any one place. He enjoyed travelling and new challenges. He possessed a self-assurance that compensated for

---

[59] From March 15, 1932 *Maclean's* magazine entitled "Have you forgotten your Bank Balance" in which the authors investigate large sums of money left in Canadian bank accounts. $CAD 733.62 in 1906 adjusted for inflation = $CAD 20,900.00 or £12,700 in 2019 values. We assume that the funds were never claimed.

whatever he lacked in skills or education. In some instances, this confidence propelled him into trouble. In the case of his later aviation career, of course, his self-belief was warranted.

Secondly, after he had achieved success in Cobalt, perhaps he was pulled away by the allure of greater accomplishments and of greater wealth, as we shall see in the Larder Lake chapter. Thirdly, he was possibly forced to remove himself due to professional and legal reasons. An assortment of news articles from late 1906 reveals an unpleasant situation in which Barber was entangled.

We expand on these factors by discussing…
- The timing of a wildcat scheme
- A new broker on the scene
- Gold discovered at Larder Lake
- The Guggenheim effect on the New York Stock Exchange

Stock Market Timing

When trading in wildcat mines, the best time to make a decent return is at the very beginning, just after the company has been introduced to the stock market. At this point, the successful promoter will have spared no expense in advertising the venture. Barber's work promoting the mine was completed that October. He would have been ready to sell any outstanding shares he owned, if he hadn't done so, already.

With high demand comes high prices. In order to profit, the shrewd investor will sell quickly and get out of the market while other investors are willing to buy. But before long, only those with stock to sell will come to the exchange, and that's when stock prices fall, usually never to rally again.

Once he was back in the UK, Barber was known to be wealthy. We must assume that he made a significant amount of money in Cobalt and through his offices in Toronto. Why, at the height of the boom, did he abandon Cobalt at the end of 1906?

It's time we introduce a new character to the story.

Meet Homer L. Gibson

In early October 1906[60], a new player to the brokerage scene announced his Detroit business specializing in the Cobalt mines. Interestingly, Homer L. Gibson also promoted himself as a "practical mining man," and he had just returned from a six-month visit to Cobalt where

Injunction Against Broker.

An ex-parte injunction was obtained at noon on Saturday from Mr. Justice MacMahon by Homer L. Gibson against H. C. Barber, mining broker, of this city and the Canada Mines Company, Limited, and the Abitibi Mining Company, Limited, restraining Mr. Barber and the Canada Mines Co. from disposing of any shares now held by him on his contract for the sale of stock of his co-defendant the Abitibi Company, and restraining the latter company from transferring any shares of capital stock of Mr. Barber until November 15.

The Globe *November 12, 1906*

---

[60] *Detroit Free Press, October 9, 1906*

he encountered Barber and associates. The two struck some sort of deal, but one that appears to have ended badly.

In early November[61], a judge issued an *ex parte* order to restrain Barber, Canada Mines, and co-defendants Abitibi Mining Company from selling shares of the A&C for two weeks.

What happened? Like many of the other Barber storylines, we have the first part of the account, but little or no follow-up, nor any indication as to why these events occurred in the first place, or how they were resolved.

Perhaps Barber had revealed his plans to close up shop in Cobalt and focus on his next project up in Larder Lake. He may have declared his intention to sell off his remaining holdings in Abitibi and Cobalt, thereby flooding the market with shares and lowering the value of the stock.

Perhaps Gibson had purchased a block of shares from Barber and needed time to finalize a sale. When he couldn't reason with Barber, he went to the courts and requested the restraining order.

Whatever the details of their contract, it came to an end on December 7, 1906, when Barber placed a notice in the *Speaker* announcing the termination of "the partnership lately existing between myself and Rosser I. [sic] Gibson of Cobalt, Ont." The spelling of Gibson's name is a transcription error.

> **Notice of Dissolution of Partnership.**
>
> I hereby give notice that the partnership lately existing between myself and Rosser I. Gibson of Cobalt, Ont., Has been dissolved and that the said Rosser I. Gibson has assumed all liabilities in connection with the business heretofore carried on in Cobalt under my name
>
> H. C. BARBER.

We believe this was the last time Barber and Gibson crossed paths. (See Chapter 10 Cobalt Co-Stars for more on Gibson.)

Meanwhile, in Larder Lake

Through the spring and summer of 1906, prospectors explored for mineral riches further north. Rumours began to trickle down to Cobalt about gold discoveries in Larder Lake. In October, Dr. Reddick, an early prospector and investor in the region, gave an interview in the *Globe*.[62] He verified the existence of gold, and the new rush was on.

Barber, no doubt, paid attention to the news from Larder Lake and recognized an opportunity. Since we know this was his next stop in the story, we assume that he pounced at the chance to "be first" in the camp, and capitalize on the opportunity.

---

[61] *Toronto Star* November 10, 1906 – judge issues *ex parte* order - usually as an emergency measure when the complainant stands to be harmed by actions of the defendant, for example in domestic abuse cases. The defendant (Barber, in this case) is not necessarily present before the courts when the order is made

[62] *Canada's Forgotten Gold Rush: The Goldfields of Larder Lake*, 1999, Dufresne and Thompson

The Guggenheim Effect

Local Cobalt historian Charlie Angus writes about Daniel and Murray Guggenheim and the impact of their interest in the Nipissing Mine in Cobalt. Toward the end of 1906, the price of shares of the Nipissing Mine skyrocketed when the Guggenheims invested. However, they did not exercise an option to buy additional shares. The New York market crashed December 1, 1906 "when the Guggenheims suddenly announced they were pulling out of the deal. The consortium never explained the abrupt turnaround."[63]

What Angus writes next perfectly describes the situation of the Abitibi and Cobalt Mine: "Many small brokers went bankrupt being caught out with shares in Cobalt companies that didn't have ground anywhere close to a producing mine. Thousands of other investors lost their savings having purchased stock based on the myths being perpetrated by a profusion of wildcat stock promotions."

Mr. Barber was in a no-win situation. It appears that he cut his losses and moved on to a new venture.

Epilogue Abitibi and Cobalt

As for the Abitibi and Cobalt Mine, investors expressed renewed interest in the stock in December 1906 when the papers[64] announced that "Insiders are said to be quietly buying up the stock owing to the report that English capitalists, represented by Senator Ulrey of the United States, have lately taken under option a controlling interest…" (We'll meet Mr. Ulrey later up in Larder Lake.) The uptick in interest was short-lived and in early February 1907, the company's secretary issued a "calming letter" to shareholders, urging them to disregard recent, damaging rumours.[65]

After this point, the press went silent and we have no further news about the mine.

Public sentiment toward the mine had most certainly soured if we consider a revealing human-interest story[66] published six weeks later.

The *New Liskeard Speaker* described a burlesque mounted by the "old boys" at the Cobalt Hotel. Bored with the lingering winter, the gents staged a "mock" exchange. The men had a grand old time creating fictitious names for the mining companies, named after the real mines of the day. For example, the "Maiden on the Hill Mine" represented the Nancy Helen Mine at the crest of Galena Street. The "Close Connection Mine" was used in place of the Cobalt Contact Mine in Bucke Township.

---

[63] *Silver City, An Alternate history of a Frontier Town,* Charlie Angus, unpublished
[64] *Ottawa Citizen* December 8, 1906
[65] *Boston Globe* February 3, 1907
[66] The *New Liskeard Speaker* March 29, 1907

What was the name they chose for the Abitibi and Cobalt Mine?

The Dead Horse.

*** *** ***

Observer, *August 22, 1896*

Rivals as the Prince of Liars

Lost Soul: Please may I come in?

Mephistopheles: And who are you, pray?

Lost Soul: A late mining expert.

Mephistopheles: (emphatically): Get you gone. I want no rivals here!

Chapter 7: Additional Cobalt Photographs

We include here photos[67] of historic Cobalt to supplement those found in Chapter 6. These pictures were taken around the time that Horatio Barber was in the silver mine camp and they illustrate the setting for when and where he conducted business in Northern Ontario.

Cobalt ca 1906

Horatio Barber's Cobalt Open Call Mining Exchange (COCME) was located in the former "Cobalt Square", the commercial centre of the frontier town. The building was located not far from the Imperial Bank.

By examining the evolution of the Bank building, it is possible to piece together a timeline for the existence of the COCME business. Figure 1 shows a very early iteration of the Imperial bank, dated August 20, 1905. The building to the right and behind is Clifton Moore's drug store, under construction.

Figure 1 August 20, 1905

Figure 2 is a later view with the bank exterior completed. Moore's Hotel is across the road on the right and to the far left are the law offices of Boultbee and Boultbee, Barber's legal counsel.

The photographer is facing northeast, looking toward the Haileybury Road, the narrow passage to the right of the bank. This road was rebuilt and widened after the 1909 fire and renamed Lang Street.

Figure 2 1906

---

[67] Unless otherwise noted, the photos are from the Cobalt Mining Museum digital collection.

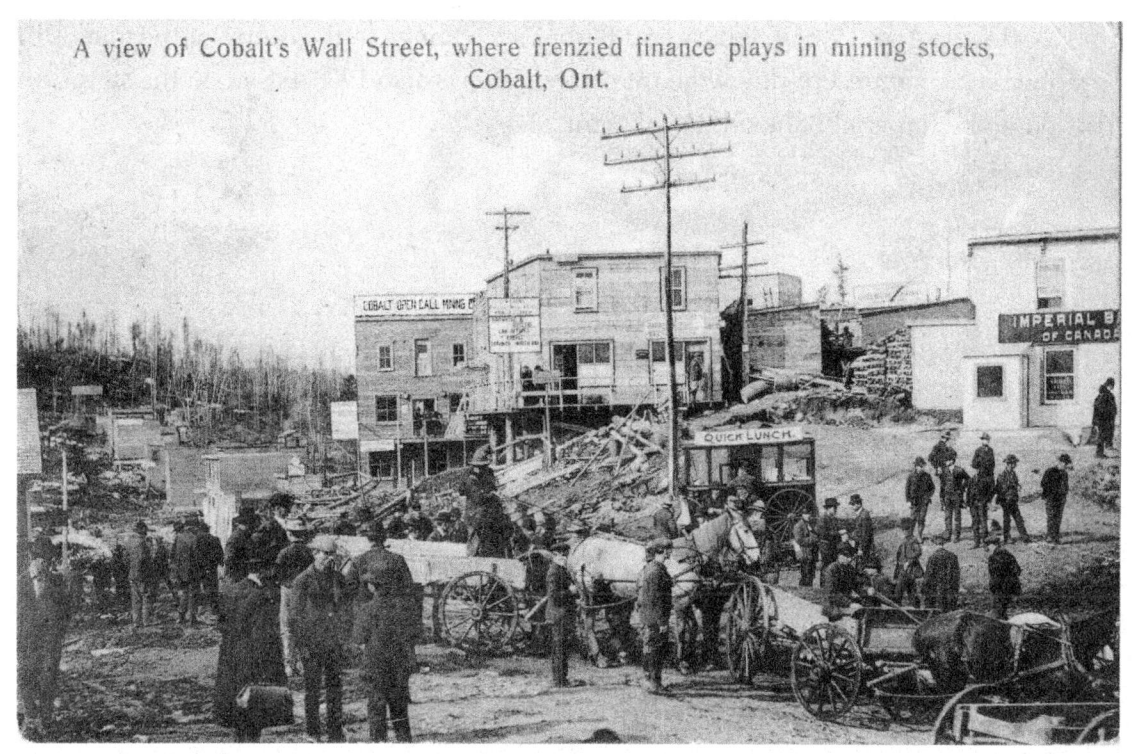

Figure 3 After the opening of the exchange April 1906

The date of Figure 3 is about the same as Figure 2 based on the construction of the Imperial Bank at the far right, but here you can see Barber's Cobalt Open Call Mining Exchange. We know that he opened the exchange in early April 1906, so we can place the date to sometime after that period. Figure 4 below shows an extension being added to the Imperial Bank building which was completed in 1906.[68]

Figure 4 Later in 1906 after the extension to the Imperial Bank

---

[68] *Historical Photo Analysis of the Landscape of Early Cobalt, Methods of Interpretation of Cobalt's Early Landscape Images* Robert Larocque, 2019

In Figure 5 below, we see Cobalt Square and Barber's Exchange in the centre of the image. The photographer is facing present-day Argentite Street. This is also 1906, based on the status of the construction of the Imperial Bank on the far right.

Figure 5 Cobalt Square after the opening of the exchange April 1906 and before the extension on the bank.

Figure 6 is an enlarged portion from the image above in which you can read the name H. Barber on one of the notice boards attached to it.

The sign reads, "MINING PROPERTIES BOUGHT AND SOLD. CAPITAL FURNISHED TO DEVELOP PROPERTIES."

This wording becomes important in establishing Horatio Barber as the author of the two promotional publications which have been attributed to another man of the same initials, namely Herbert Campbell Barber of Toronto. (See Appendix 8) Horatio uses the exact phrasing in those publications.

Figure 6 H. Barber Mining Properties Bought and Sold Capital Furnished to Develop Properties

55

Figure 7 Argentite Street 1907 or 1908 – new occupants in the exchange building

In Figure 7 the photographer stood facing north toward Argentite Street with the Imperial Bank out of sight on the right. The office of the Cobalt Nugget on the left was where R. H. C. Browne would have conducted his editorial duties. By this date, roughly 1907 or 1908, the exchange building has new occupants, including an employment office, a tailor shop, and a stationery store. The bulk of the building was occupied by the American Palace, a boarding house. Below, in Figure 8, is the former bank building from 2019. The trees obscure the empty lots that run north along Argentite, the former sites of the law offices and the COCME.

Figure 8 Argentite Street at Lang Street 2019 Maggie Wilson photo

56

Cobalt today with some of the original mines and headframes around the lake

Terry Grace photos 2018 – an assortment of headframes still standing around Cobalt Lake. Lower left is an open cut, the remains of a mined-out vein of silver.

Chapter 8

1907 Barber at Larder Lake

"Old Larder Lake was just a fake…" [69]

Branch Office at Larder of Canada Mines, Limited, who were the first mining firm to establish offices there.

Mr. Dobbins
C. H. Battersby   H. F. Young   John Martin   H. C. Barber   Howard Wicksteed   Major Cooper
Charles W. Johnson   Chief's Wife
                                                                            Chief,
                                                                            Grassy Lake Indians

Note the wording on the Canada Mines sign. It is virtually identical to that of the Cobalt Open Call Mining Exchange and that of Barber's letterhead, thus linking the two and confirming the identity of Horatio Claude Barber. Horatio is the man standing behind the sitting woman "Chief's wife." Note as well, the name on the far left, C. H. Battersby. His brother, Charles Worsley Battersby was a founding member of the Aeronautical Syndicate with Barber in 1909. Christopher Hayes came to Canada in 1906. This photo and similar images in this chapter were provided by Barber, taken while on his trip to the area early in 1907.

The story of Cobalt is an important one in other ways besides the incredible silver deposits discovered in 1903. After prospectors exhausted the mineral potential in the area, they moved on and searched for whatever precious metals they could find. The silver discoveries at Elk

---

[69] *The Cobalt Song*; Words by L.F. Steenman, Music by R.L. MacAdam, February 1910.

Lake, Gowganda, and Silver Centre attracted the promoters' attention next, thanks to an insatiable appetite for resources and profit from mining and mining investment.

Next came the gold discoveries near Kirkland Lake and Timmins. Today, some of those mines that were developed from the original discoveries are still active and profitable.

The story of the Town of Larder Lake is slightly different. Prospectors searched for gold, and as we noted earlier, Dr. Reddick was credited with making the first discovery in 1906, the same time that Horatio was in Cobalt. In 1907, the new camp was overrun with men who meant to capitalize on the gold rush - prospectors and businessmen and mine promoters – men such as Barber and his Canada Mines brokerage.

Yes, the Larder Lake area was an active gold mining region for several decades. However, not in 1907 or for several years afterward. Development was delayed for many years.

Immediately after 1907, the boom ended as a colossal bust.

Barber aligned himself with a new set of business associates after his time in Cobalt - men who were equally dishonest in the stock market game.

This fact will become more than obvious as the story takes us now to the establishment of the gold camp which was located, as Barber's promotional pamphlet announced, "60 miles north of Cobalt."

The Gold Rush is On!

After Dr. Reddick's interview in late October 1906, when he confirmed the rumour of gold in Larder Lake, prospectors turned their attention to the region. Between October 17 and December 21, 1906, seven mining companies had incorporated. During the winter of 1906 and 1907, about four thousand claims were staked. However, by the end of 1911, of the "hundreds of companies operating in the Larder Lake Mining Division, only eight-five were legally incorporated."[70]

Barber's clients hired a man to acquire property in early January 1907. They called the mine The Larder Lake Proprietary Gold Fields Limited (LLPGF) and incorporated the company in February. The site was strategically well-placed near the Reddick claims. That is, they rode on

---

[70] *Canada's Forgotten Gold Rush: The Goldfields of Larder Lake* Dufresne and Thompson, 1999. In writing this chapter on Larder Lake we relied heavily on this most excellent volume and we recommend this book to readers who wish to get a better idea of the complete story of the area and its mining history.

59

the coattails of the already famous Dr. Reddick and hoped that the presence of gold was continuous across claim boundaries.

Dufresne and Thompson have this to say about the key players on the board of LLPGF: "By the first week of February, two men controlled the company, John F. Marskey from Saginaw Michigan, and Senator G.B. [sic] Ulrey of Fort Wayne, Indiana. "Being mining men of a different school, it was not their idea to go tramping in the bush to find gold. Instead, they preferred to do their wheeling and dealing from the King Edward Hotel in Toronto, and when absolutely necessary, directed the company from Cobalt."

Directors of a mining company, especially a wildcat[71], were usually people of title or rank. Like a supermodel or sports legend endorsing a product, a recognizable name attached to a mining company will give the business a sense of legitimacy.

The directors of LLPGF were politicians, medical military officers, manufacturers, and real estate men. Only two had mining backgrounds, and of those, one was a manager of a gold mine and the other was a stock promoter.

In front of the Larder Lake Proprietary Goldfields office. Barber's company Canada Mines promoted this mine. Barber is second from the left, front row, and Lew Ulrey is fourth from the left.

---

[71] Definition of wildcat: a property that has the potential to be a producing mine, but work has not yet been done to prove it.

- Col. G. Sterling Ryerson –President - physician, politician, Toronto, Ontario
- Senator Ulrey– Vice President – politician - Fort Wayne, Indiana
- John F. Marskey – Secretary-Treasurer – insurance, real estate – Saginaw, Michigan
- Col. A.N. Worthington – politician and mayor of Sherbrooke, Quebec
- Francis P. Buck - mine promoter[72] - Sherbrooke, Quebec
- Chas H. Waterous Jr. – manufacturer, mayor of Brantford, Ontario
- Herbert Lennox – Member of the Legislative Assembly, Toronto, Ontario
- Dr. David H. Piper – physician, London, ON
- Peter Kirkegaard, M. E. – manager of gold mines in Deloro, Ontario

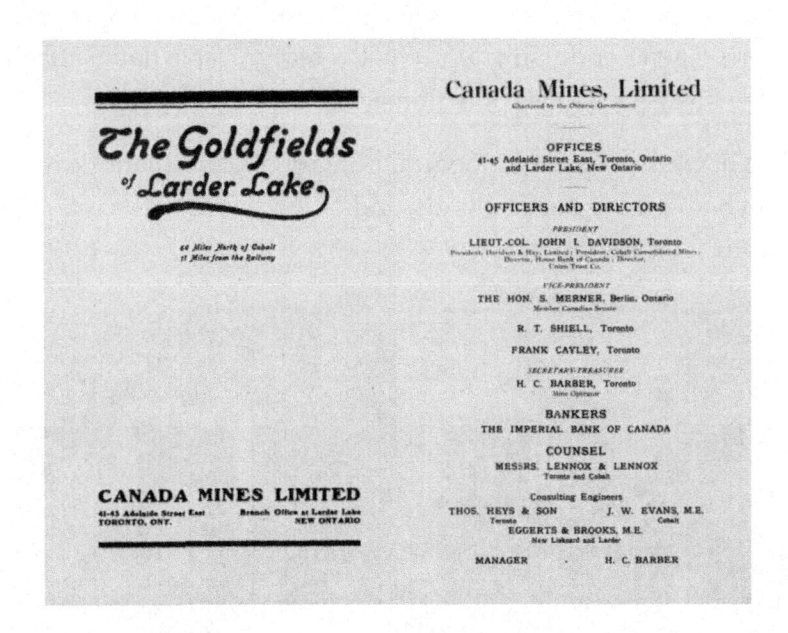

Marketing: More Fact and Fiction

Barber published another pamphlet similar to the *Cobalt* document. Indeed, the preface of *The Goldfields of Larder Lake 60 miles north of Cobalt* [73] is a slightly revised version of the *Cobalt* introduction. This booklet was illustrated with photos from the trip he made in late March 1907. He was there to oversee the building and opening of his northern branch of Canada Mines. His claims that he was the first broker in the camp are true.

Barber used the brochure in exactly the same manner as he did with the Abitibi and Cobalt Mine gambit. He took the opportunity to promote himself, his company Canada Mines, and the wildcat mine that his cohorts were floating in the gold camp, the Larder Lake Proprietary Gold Fields, Limited.

---

[72] Buck was a mine promoter in Rossland BC around the time that Horatio was in the region – an interesting connection.
[73] Barber's booklet *The Goldfields of Larder Lake 60 miles north of Cobalt* is a fascinating read, and is available for download online. See Bibliography and Resources.

Again, the content of the brochure is a blend of fact and fiction. His description of the discovery of Larder Lake sounds more like a travelogue with colourful detail regarding the indigenous people involved in the story.

Before it became known as Larder Lake, the body of water after which the township is named was known as "Tegusiewabi to the First Nation inhabitants and was well known as a place where supply cupboards, or "larders" could be replenished with fish and animals. The name was accepted by the Geological Survey for Canada in 1902.

A slightly later picture of Barber's offices, with a lean-to addition to the side.

Barber offered first-hand accounts of the camp and he assured his readers that for those properties he had not personally visited, he obtained information from only the most "trustworthy" albeit unnamed sources.

He then described the plans to develop the camp. This was meant to be encouraging information; it proved that optimism was high and that the site was worth developing. Barber described access to the region and plans to provide rail services. At the time of discovery, the trail to the camp was arduous and involved several days travel by train, steamship or canoe, and many challenging portages over rugged terrain, in winter. Yet, he described the site as being "within exceptionally easy reach…"

He wrote, "The Temiskaming Telephone Company are beginning work immediately on a line to connect Cobalt, Haileybury, New Liskeard and Tomstown with Larder Lake so that very shortly now it will be possible by using the telegraph wire to New Liskeard and the telephone wire to Larder to transmit quick-time messages to the new camp from anywhere." The first telephone exchange was actually in part of Barber's Canada Mines Ltd offices in Larder Lake.

Barber in front of the telephone exchange

From the brochure: "As in the case of all Ontario mining camps, there is an absence of the disorderly element, gambling, etc., particularly refreshing to comers from other fields." Ontario mining camps may have been a degree more orderly than others. Certainly, the Ontario government prohibited the sale of alcohol within a five-mile radius of a mining camp and the police raided "blind pigs" or illegal drinking establishments from time to time. However, Barber glossed over the fact that alcohol, either smuggled or homebrewed, was freely available in all the camps.

"In short, the conditions are such that there is nothing to deter the economical and peaceful exploitation of this field, which for early promise compares very favourably with the most famous and wealth producing goldfields in the world.

"In conversing with the numerous prospectors entering the field I find that even now, with the rush only just beginning and several feet of snow on the ground, many of them are from fields as far away as the Pacific Coast, Australia, and Africa, and they all speak of having sent word home for their friends to follow on. With the advent of spring, there is little doubt the rush will be immense and from every part of the world, and that a booming city and tens of thousands of prospectors will be making the shores of Larder Lake ring."

These words, as much as those by any other writer, must have fueled the boom which of course was his intention. Although in later paragraphs he warns against "snow claims" he seems here to be promoting the practice.

As Barber detailed the geology of the area, he used glowing terms such as "stupendous bodies of ore" and "immense quartz veins." Again, short on detail, but long on hyperbole.

Since a stream ran through the LLPGF property, in his opinion, "just as soon as the spring break-up is over, valuable placer grounds will be discovered… and will cause a rush even greater than the Klondike." This is nonsense: both the comment about the placer deposit and likening Larder Lake to the Klondike are fanciful fabrications.

Regarding the scope of the ore body, Barber protected himself from liability at the same time as he played to the reader's ego and intelligence. He allowed that it was unknown if the gold continued with depth. That is, yes, gold was found near the surface of the earth, but no one had determined if gold was found deeper in the ground. He agreed that the reason for sensational assays was possibly due to the nuggety habit of the gold in Larder Lake. In these details, he was truthful.

The geology at Larder Lake is such that the gold does not form long stringers or run in continuous masses along the veins. When Barber described the "nuggety" habit of gold, he was referring to how the mineral is found in the earth. Like raisins in a cake, small lumps of the mineral are separated by some distance within the rock. Some of the gold pieces might be significant in size, with correspondingly high ounces-per-ton assay values. However, simply because the lab reported attractive results from one showing of gold in one corner of the mining claim, nobody can state with absolute confidence that the same will be found elsewhere on the property, let alone on the neighbouring mine.

Barber doesn't leave it at that. He goes on to say that he was prepared to vouch for the fact that those assays were a "very big thing indeed, and more than enough to satisfy any sane man in search of wealth by mining." In other words, if you aren't satisfied with the assay results, you are insane, or at the very least, unintelligent and certainly not serious about making wealth by investing in the stock market.

On 28th March 1907 Barber took two photographs of the rush to Larder Lake. These photographs reproduced from the brochure, ably illustrate the snow conditions at that time and indeed the extent of the rush toward the camp.

He made special mention about the 4000 claims that were located during the winter. Most of the properties were staked over deep snow cover and therefore questionable in terms of what lay beneath. Mining law at that time stated that prospectors must provide proof that minerals were on any claimed land, and that the discovery location was marked with a post. Also, it stated that owners of the newly staked claim should, within three months, have completed thirty days on development work such as clearing the land, trenching, or digging a shaft. Of course, this was not possible at Larder Lake because of the snow, but apparently, that did not prevent unscrupulous owners and brokers from selling shares in these ventures. Barber warned the prospective investor to avoid those particular companies, "the stock of which will take the form of prolific "wildcat." Implying, of course, that he would not expose his customers to that sort of risk.

He closed his pamphlet with a series of newspaper clippings from the Toronto press, all speaking in raving and exaggerated terms about the new gold discovery. In these advertisements-disguised-as-journalism, are several references to US Senator Ulrey, the man who represented those British capitalists involved in insider trading in the Abitibi and Cobalt Mine scheme from Chapter 6.

Lewis Valentine Ulrey

In 1906, Ulrey explored new money-making ventures, primarily in oil in his home state, Indiana. In August, he struck oil in Kent County, Ontario[74] and in December, he left Indiana for a month to pursue his energy and lumber interests in Canada, with plans to return February 1, 1907. During this time, if not earlier, he met Barber and associates.

After he became the vice president of the LLPGF company, Ulrey travelled to Larder Lake with Barber, and together with secretary-treasurer John F. Marskey, announced the order of a stamp mill for the new mine. The news was meant to create confidence in the mine. The expense of transporting and installing this large piece of equipment was considered a worthwhile strategy in order to convince investors that gold was in the ground. When people saw that money was being spent to build a mill, they reasonably assumed that the directors had found gold and had determined that there was an ore body. This was not the case.

Indianapolis Star *June 7, 1906 Lewis Ulrey on the right at a political rally in Indianapolis the summer before he got involved in Cobalt and Larder Lake.*

Early Warning Signs

Barber's claims of untold wealth and investment potential in the Larder Lake goldfields were outrageous in their exaggeration. He was not alone in forwarding this type of advertising, but he was certainly one of the most prolific. Many a false claim was made to the public about Cobalt's silver mines, but that region actually had great mineral wealth. Larder Lake did not, at least not with the technology and resources available at the time. This didn't matter to the speculators. Larder Lake soon became a synonym for fraud, and as with Cobalt, the mining journals issued warnings to the public about investing in the area.

The following article titled "Larder Lake" appeared in the *Canadian Mining Journal,* in April 1907.

"At date of writing more than 3,000 claims have been registered around and about Larder Lake. Company after company is being floated with capitalizations which make one dizzy.

"At risk of falling into that obnoxious category of human beings designated "knockers" we wish to express our views. Pick up a prospectus of a Larder Lake company, read it with care. In almost every case you will see the claim made that fabulously rich assay values have been found close to the property being exploited.

---

[74] *The Indianapolis Star* 1906-08-19

"In some rare cases these values, it is stated, have actually been found on the areas of the company whose prospectus you are reading. But it is very generally true that the majority of Larder Lake properties are valuated [sic] on an entirely assumptive basis. The district is hardly yet in the initial stages of development. Not until late in April can systematic prospecting be undertaken. And yet thousands of dollars are being invested in possibilities! Improbabilities even are being capitalized at astounding figures.

"We have not a word to say against Larder Lake as a legitimate and likely field for prospecting. Of its geological probabilities and limitations, we are not now competent to speak. But no camp can survive the reckless and insanely un-business-like "boom" to which this place is now being subjected.

"We wish to add one word in closing and it is this. When statements of assay values are quoted in any prospectus, it is safer and saner to ignore them altogether unless signed affidavits describing the exact places, conditions and method of sampling, the name of the assayer, the size of the sample and the circumstances under which it was shipped can be obtained. This is one very necessary and very much neglected preliminary step. You have at this point, sufficient information to justify you in making further enquiry. Your next step is to engage a competent mining engineer (easier said than done) to go over the property in question and report upon the feasibility of beginning mining operations. In brief, there is no reason under the sun why mining should not be approached in the same business-like attitude which is characteristic of the successful merchant."

Obviously, the mining journals were ignored by the masses who continued to pile their cash into Larder Lake. Indeed, just after the above damning report, the press in Ontario and Indiana reported several sensational stories that "Lew Ulrey is a Rich Man."[75] Ulrey was secretive about how he made his money, neither confirming nor denying "the stories … that the development of the veins owned by the company of which he [was] a leading spirit had made him wealthy." The news article described the gold mine camp. The text was more or less a carbon copy of the Larder Lake pamphlet penned by Barber.

More Marketing

Meanwhile, Barber continued to promote the sale of shares in the gold mine through the month of May. He purchased large, and therefore expensive ads in the newspaper.

The wording was earnest, emphatic, and insistent in tone, but not without doubletalk. "I am not urging anyone to take on Larder Lake Proprietary. The stock is fast selling itself and in a short time will all be placed in Canada and the United States." He was anxious, he declared, to see that his Canadian clients bought into the market at the lower price.

---

[75] *Fort Wayne Daily News* April 11, 1907

To add to the urgency, Barber told his readers that LLPGF would soon be listed on the stock exchange,[76] meaning that more people would have access to what few shares might be available.

He also sent regular updates from the mining camp to the press. As Dufresne and Thompson point out, his correspondence gives us a snapshot of what life was like for the men who lived and worked there. Here are samples of some of those dispatches.

> **Letter from Larder Lake**
>
> "THE GOLD FIELDS OF LARDER LAKE" is the title of a book which has been written by Mr. H. C. Barber, Managing Director of Canada Mines Ltd. Written in particularly agreeable style and containing numerous reproductions of photographs taken by Mr. Barber at Larder. The book is apart from its educational value, well worth reading.
>
> 9th April 1907, *Mail and Empire*

Ironically, we agree: the book is a fascinating education.

The next submission is rather more subdued than most of Barber's writing. We assume the mining company was one of his clients.

> Mr. Barber yesterday received information that free gold has been discovered in one of the properties of the Cobalt and Larder Lake Mining Company. This property is situated scarcely ¼ mile from Dublin's Point on Larder Lake on the south shore of Wilson Bay.
>
> 26th April 1907, *Mail and Empire*

It is astonishing that the following submission passed the scrutiny of the editors. How could this be considered journalism? It is easy to understand the contempt that the *Canadian Mining Journal* held for not only stock promoters, but the press as well.

---

[76] The *Ottawa Journal* Sat, May 4, 1907

> The Larder Lake gold district presents wonderful opportunities for rich profits---also losses. Everyone should thoroughly investigate and get properly posted before getting in. It seldom pays to take a "flyer"- that's usually another name for a "blind chance."
>
> My offices, my engineers and my personal and experienced employees are on the ground. By their aid, and my own personal work, I keep my following reliably advised from week to week and they make money. Thousands will testify to that.
>
> Write to me for my weekly letter, my book "The Gold Fields of Larder Lake" and my map they are free.
>
> H. C. Barber, Managing Director
>
> May 8th 1907, *Mail and Empire*

The *Toronto World* was also happy to run his weekly letters including the following lengthy update. This particular article places Barber somewhere other than Larder Lake since the report was submitted by "his representatives in the camp." Note that special mention is made of the Proprietary Gold Fields Mine, Barber's client.

> LARDER LAKE NEWS - RECENT INCIDENTS AT THE NEW GOLD CAMP
>
> "The sensation of the week has been the discovery of free gold ¼ mile from our office. Beyond this, just over the hill, a find of free gold* has also has also shown up. Free gold has also been discovered on the north side of the lake, just east of the narrows. J. E. Croft of Lima, Ontario, a man who has had large and various experience in all the great mining camps in the world, is now at Larder Lake, acting in the interest of a large firm of New York Financiers. He tells us that his impression of the camp as gold producer is equal to anything he has ever seen.
>
> Captain McGee, of Utica, New York, has arrived in order to inspect the claims and he is enthusiastic as Mr. Croft, as regards the future of the camp. [continued]

*Free gold is the geological term used for native gold. That is, elemental gold that is not bound up in other minerals such as pyrite. Also, in these early days, the gold particles were large enough to be visible to the naked eye. Although we have no way of knowing if free gold was found a quarter-mile from Barber's office, this claim was very common in the advertisements appearing in the press at that time. Good news for one mine was considered good news for another. The *Toronto World* article continued:

> Fred Forrest is in charge of the Proprietary Gold Fields Limited and reports of discovery of free gold on Claims No. 1885, 2024, and 2928. The splendid showing of free gold is also being discovered on the claim adjoining Claim No 2132 of the Proprietary Company. Great discoveries are being reported somewhere north of the Lake (near the Martin group of claims). The New Liskeard Syndicate is commencing operations there.
>
> Prospecting, owing to present conditions, is still carried on with some difficulty, but very shortly, with the final departure of the snow, an even greater number of rich discoveries may certainly be looked for. The influx of new arrivals continues to increase and our energies are somewhat taxed in taking care of the gentlemen arriving with introductions from you [Mr. Barber.]
>
> Your gasoline boat has arrived, and the big boat [the *Geisha*] will be ready to launch when navigation opens shortly. The fleet on the lake numbers nearly a dozen. A tremendous amount of new building is going on, new hotels and restaurants are opening, and the telephone line is fast nearing the camp. Another assay office [Mr. Cameron's] has been started and is working night and day.
>
> May 9th 1907, *Toronto World*

Regarding the "gasoline" and "big" boats: Dufresne and Thompson wrote that Barber's company was the first to use an outboard gasoline-powered motorboat on the lake to travel between Larder city and their properties on Reddick Bay in spring of 1907 before the ice was off the water. The boat travelled in the small open space between the edge of the ice and the lakeshore.

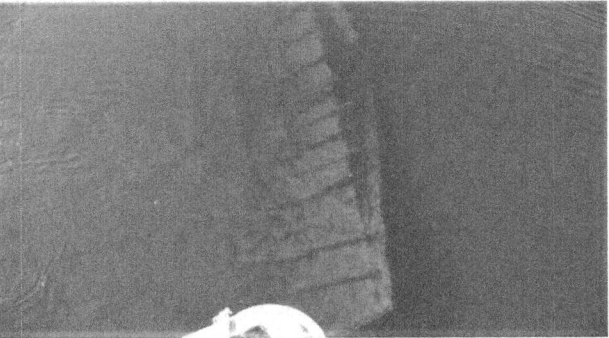

Left, the "big boat" Geisha on its way to Larder Lake in early 1907 and as seen by Barber, courtesy Bruce Taylor; Right, her watery grave on Dublin Bay, thanks to Paul Kelly.

Due to the disappointing gold deposits, and better roads, the Geisha was not long in use. By the spring of 1909, the Upper Ontario Steamboat Company lost faith in the potential of Larder Lake, and sold her to Messrs. McLaughlin and Guilfoyle, a pair of merchants at Larder City. They ran her for at least one more season, but by 1913 she was listed as "not in commission" and shortly afterwards she was gutted by fire, whether by accident or deliberately is not known.

Barber encountered the *Geisha* on his trip to Larder Lake. "On my return from the lake last week, I passed a steamboat belonging to the Northern Ontario Navigation Co. which has been taken to pieces and was being hauled to the lake over the snow. It will be ready to launch as soon as the ice breaks up which will be very shortly now." The *Geisha* was put to great use on the lake. Today, the remains of the vessel can still be seen under water near to Dublin Bay.

In a May publication of "Larder Lake Matters"[77] Barber commented on the "considerable excitement" regarding not one, but two 25-lb. nuggets which were supposedly two-thirds gold, found just southwest of the LLPGF mine. He suggested, "This, I think, was a slight exaggeration… and inaccurate." Had he taken the *Canadian Mining Journal's* cautionary words about overstated assay results to heart? No, he had not.

Instead, he used the story to his advantage. First of all, he diminished the report related to a competitor's mine and took this chance to appear knowledgeable, as only a practical mining man could. Ever the opportunist, he repeated the sensational account, because good news for one mine, was good news for them all. Barber allowed that the nuggets were extraordinarily rich, if not as rich as first reported. He then crossed the line between fact and fiction. He said that the nuggets were "almost on par" with the famous 1897 Londonderry Mine in Australia, a property that "sold for $4,000,000 and the development consisting of a 12-foot hole." Of course, the notorious Londonderry Mine was a wildcat play of spectacular proportions. (See Chapter 2.)

Moving On

We can find no more promotional activity related to LLPGF after May and the last news we hear from Barber as Canada Mines manager is an update about a new silver mine in Cobalt on June 8, 1907.[78]

Being shrewd characters, Barber and his business partners would have made their money when the stock prices were high and then cashed out and moved on to their next venture. In a piece from the *Indianapolis Star*,[79] news from Fort Wayne Indiana suggested that "Mr. Ulrey in a few days will leave for old Mexico to look over Sonora mining fields." Perhaps Horatio tagged along? We know that Ulrey had left North America at some point because he was aboard a steamship returning from England at the end of July.

Mrs. Barber and her sons left Canada on July 19th, bound for Liverpool. G.B. Strathy, Barber's lawyer was on board the same ship. But where was Horatio?

---

[77] The *Ottawa Journal* May 10, 1907
[78] The *Ottawa Journal* June 8, 1907
[79] The *Indianapolis Star* April 26, 1907

The beginnings of Larder City, left, by Horatio Barber and right, a similar view 2018 by Terry Grace

A Postscript from Thomas Alva Edison

Horatio may have fled the country, but his agents or colleagues were still working on behalf of Canada Mines, Limited. The famous inventor Thomas Edison owned a cobalt mine near Latchford, just south of Cobalt. After exploration of the site proved that minerals were scarce, he decided to sell the property. Canada Mines had approached him about representing him. In October 1907, Edison wrote to his manager, "These men [in Barber's group] in my opinion are fakers. We want cash and no use of my name in promoting."[80]

---

[80] *The Darby Mine, Thomas Edison's Latchford Venture*; George Lefebvre in *Selected Chapters of Temiskaming Heritage – proceeds of the 2017 Speaker's Symposium*

Chapter 9

1907 to 1908 Barber in Hiding

Legal Trouble

Apart from the fact that the *Canadian Mining Journal* was keeping a close watch, we suspect that the primary reason that Barber and his Larder Lake business associates had removed themselves from the scene was to escape legal troubles.

At the end of July 1907, Larder Lake Proprietary Gold Fields company was in the news as the shareholders went to court.[81] Dufresne and Thompson wrote, "Court action in Toronto required the LLPGF management give a public accounting of their affairs. An explanation of why family members and others received so much free stock was requested by a group of shareholders." 1,424,306 shares were being held by the Trusts and Guarantee Co. and were supposed to be delivered to the purchasers on July 23, but the LLPGF company ordered the trust company to hold them back. When some of the shareholders demanded their rightful certificates, the trust company turned the shares over to the court under provisions of the Trustees Relief Act.

In a follow-up report[82] a week later, we hear testimony that "Mr. Barber, of the Canada Mines Company, had an option on 800,000 shares at 25 cents, which he was trying to sell in England at 4s 2d. Mr. Bain, lawyer for the Larder Lake Company, admitted that an option at 25 cents had been given on 800,000 shares which were not pooled, [i.e. *not* part of the 1.4 million shares that were now in the safekeeping of the courts]." Chief Justice Falconbridge reserved judgement.

In other words, the people who bought shares in the Larder Lake Proprietary Gold Fields Mine were not allowed access to their share certificates and could not trade them. They were waiting for the courts to rule on the case. Meanwhile, Mr. Barber owned nearly a million shares that he was free to sell as he wished.

Piper v. Ulrey

In the autumn of 1907, lawyers were in court defending one set of the Larder Lake Proprietary Gold Fields company partners against the others.

The October 24, 1907 issue of the Ontario Weekly Reporter provides insight into Piper v. Ulrey, a case that is either related to the July court case discussed above or an additional litigation. Dr. David Piper, one of the company directors, sued the Vice President and the Secretary-Treasurer of the company, Ulrey and Marskey.[83] Ryerson, the mine company president was named a co-defendant, as was Horatio Barber through his connection with Canada Mines, and the LLPGF company lawyers, Lennox and Lennox.

---

[81] The *Gazette* Montreal July 25, 1907
[82] The *Gazette* Montreal August 2, 1907
[83] The *Ontario weekly reporter*, Vol. X. No. 22 Oct 24 1907

In an effort to stall or to alter the case against them, Ulrey, Marskey, and Barber presented a statement of claim in which they tried to have certain paragraphs struck from the suit as being "embarrassing" and "multifarious" or too complex. The defendants lost the gambit. By way of explaining his reasons for dismissing the statement of claim, the judge provided an overview of Piper v. Ulrey – a summary that reveals the questionable details of their business dealings.

"Ulrey and Marskey agreed to join together as a syndicate for the purchase or acquisition of options or mining claims in the Larder Lake district." Next, they formed the company LLPGF. Their company paid $126,000 cash and 1,100,000 fully paid shares for the properties.[84] The plaintiffs, director David Piper and all the other directors were entitled to a share in these transactions.

Then Ulrey and Marskey allegedly issued shares to Lennox, Ryerson, and Barber, all without consideration for the other directors.

"As Managing Director of Canada Mines Limited, [Ulrey and Marskey gave Barber] an option for eight months (from 11 February, 1907) on 800,000 at 25 cents a share, and Barber was given 194,319 shares on condition of his sharing any profit he might make on the 800,000 shares with Ulrey and Marskey, in which profits plaintiffs [Piper, and the others] claim to share.

"The claim is based on partnership, and the defendants Ulrey and Marskey are charged with violating the known rights of the plaintiffs, and the other defendants are alleged to be colluding with them and aiding them in what the plaintiffs [claim] is a fraudulent scheme to deprive the plaintiffs of their rights."

The article ends with the notice that "defendants should plead within a week..."

To date, we have been unable to find any further information about this case. The defendants either won, or settled out of court, or simply wiped their hands of the matter and escaped the consequences. With the benefit of hindsight, we now understand why Lew Ulrey hesitated to confirm or deny how he made his fortune at Larder Lake.

As for Larder Lake Proprietary Gold Fields

Even though *The Speaker* announced "mountains of gold"[85] at Larder Lake on March 1907 and in May, managers were 'hopeful' to ship bricks of gold soon,[86] when the stamp-mill was finally operational, the results were disappointing: only about $314 worth of gold was produced. Eventually, the company was unable to pay its employees. An ad published in the *Canadian*

---

[84] Adjusted for inflation to 2019 values $CAD 5,160,000 or £3,150,000
[85] *New Liskeard Speaker* March 13, 1908
[86] *New Liskeard Speaker* May 29, 1908

Mining Journal dated January 23, 1909, announced the liquidation sale of property and chattels of the Larder Lake Proprietary Gold Fields Mine.

Larder Lake was just a Fake – at the Time

In 1907, every mine in Larder Lake, whether it was legally or illegally incorporated, was a wildcat. In the case of the Larder Lake Proprietary Gold Fields mine, then, it is ironic, if not tragic to note that if the men had had the resources and technology required to dig deeper, they would have encountered rich ore bodies from which the Kerr Addison Mine later extracted over ten million ounces of gold.[87]

Canadian Mining Journal Steps In

This section of the story does not provide anything new related specifically to Horatio Barber or his brokerage Canada Mines, or the LLPGF company, per se. We include it here, however, because the tenacious efforts of the *Canadian Mining Journal* (*CMJ*) may have convinced Barber to leave Ontario, if not North America during the first half of 1907. We have seen already that in April, the magazine warned its readers to be wary of the scams proliferating in Larder Lake.

The editors of the *Journal* rightfully took exception to what they considered outrageous and questionable practice on the part of the mine promoters and the newspapers that published ads and so-called "reporting" from the mining district. The editors cited one particularly offensive piece of "journalism" that detailed the riches to be made in Larder Lake in general, and the investment activity of companies such as Law & Co. in particular, Frank Law owner and broker."[88]

Law was a man with a similar background as the others we've encountered. He had no education in mining, engineering, or finance. The *Journal* wrote in October, "For the benefit of the public, we give the following facts: Frank Law, the head of the firm of Law & Co., was, about four years ago a barber in Montreal. Graduating from life insurance, he started his present business in Toronto, not more than a year ago."

When writing the column for the *Toronto World* titled "Larder Lake Investors Making Money," Law borrowed heavily from Barber's pamphlet, *The Gold Fields of Larder Lake* and he referred to his cohort as a "prominent engineer." Law ended the piece, (and unwittingly foreshadowed the outcome) by saying, "The large display of advertisements by Law & Co. …will be remembered by the Canadian public."

---

[87] *Canada's Forgotten Gold Rush: The Goldfields of Larder Lake* Dufresne and Thompson, 1999.
[88] The full text of the offending *Toronto World* article submitted by Frank Law and the subsequent rebuttals by the *Canadian Mining Journal* are reprinted in their entirety in *Canada's Forgotten Gold Rush: The Goldfields of Larder Lake* Dufresne and Thompson, 1999.

The *CMJ* felt compelled to speak out even more loudly, to not only protect the interests of the investors but those of the mining industry in as well. In October 1907, the *Journal* harshly criticized the *World* for allowing Law's ad to be published as bona fide newspaper reporting.

Law & Co. may well have survived this attack, as they were not the only brokers who dealt in such language when they promoted the potential of mines in Larder Lake. Law's ill-conceived response, however, was his undoing.

Just two days after the *Journal's* rebuke, the following statement appeared in the *Toronto World*:

"Law & Co. Enters Action - Will Sue Mining Journal for $50,000 for Alleged Libel."

This action brought attention to his business practices. Dufresne and Thompson wrote, "In the civil court case to follow, the presiding judge hears enough of the evidence to stop the civil action and orders Law & Co to be prosecuted in criminal court for conspiring to cheat and defraud the public."

In November 1907, the editors of the *Journal* continued to admonish promoters, brokers, directors, and the press for falsely advertising and influencing public perception of Larder Lake. "It has been announced that the district is an enormously rich one. This is false."

A month later the front-page article of the *CMJ* is titled "The Beginning of the End. A History and a Moral." In this piece, the editors described the prompt and effective response from Ontario Government authorities. The lawmakers realized that while the wildcat companies were not breaking the letter of the law, the spirit of the Ontario Companies Act was not observed nor respected.

It's difficult to imagine that the authorities were not aware of the flagrant stretching of the rules prior to the *CMJ* articles. Perhaps lawmakers had turned a blind eye to the matter since some of those authorities and their cronies sat as directors on mine company boards: they obviously benefited from the wildcat promotions. Perhaps investigations were already underway and the *Journal* article accelerated the effort. Whatever the reason, if simply by coincidence, or triggered by the efforts of the *CMJ*, the government responded almost instantly.

Frank Law and company was the first target and he was arrested November 18. The principals of the company were charged with fraud.

According to testimony,[89] when Law's brokerage received orders for shares in the Highland Mary Mine, the Larder Lake gold mine company at the centre of the case, the customers were issued stock certificates, but not from the company treasury. Under normal – that is, legal – circumstances, a customer would buy shares that had been issued to the treasury. The proceeds of the sale would be kept in the company's bank account, under the name Highland Mary Mine,

---

[89] *National Post* November 23, 1907

in this case. The funds would then be used to develop the mine, for example, and for payroll and other expenses. The company had one million shares in the treasury. None were ever sold.

In this scam, Frank Law had been issued two million shares, and it was these certificates that were sold to the unsuspecting investors. The clients' money was deposited into Frank Law's own personal "trust" account. Highland Mary never received a dime from the sale of stock certificates.

W.A. Abendroth was the bookkeeper for Frank Law's brokerage. When he testified, he recalled that about twenty-five thousand ads promoting the Highland Mary Mine were mailed out in a three-week period.[90]

Law was found guilty and he was sentenced to five years in Kingston Penitentiary. The January 18, 1909 edition of the *Toronto World* printed the following headline:

FRANK LAW IS GUILTY JURY OUT IN 8 MINUTES.

In the February 1909 issue of the *Journal,* the writers reflected about how Frank Law was made an example, and that "the whole sordid story will act as a deterrent upon others who may look upon the flotation of bogus mining companies as a legitimate source of wealth."

Then, because neither the legal firms nor the press had been on trial, the *CMJ* took the opportunity to judge these organizations guilty as well. The editors pointed out the connection between Frank Law's brokerage and his legal team of Lennox and Lennox. These men were counsel for several of the wildcat mines promoted by Law and Co. The Lennox team also held several executive director positions on the mining company boards, clearly a conflict of interest. A quick look through the 1910 *Davis Handbook*, a catalogue of incorporated silver mines in the Cobalt region, reveals a half dozen wildcat mines with the Lennox name attached, either as solicitor, director, or both.[91]

Lennox & Lennox Barristers at Larder Lake – Not only were these men Barber's legal team representing Canada Mines Limited, Herbert Lennox was a director of the Larder Lake Proprietary Gold Fields Mine.

The newspapers received similar condemnation. Reiterating their concerns about the number of ads-as-journalism, and to prove their point, the *CMJ* singled out the *Toronto World*. The editors noted that the early 1907 editions of the newspaper ran thirty large ads promoting wildcat schemes. "Five of the promoters of these

---

[90] *Ottawa Citizen* December 18, 1907
[91] The *Davis Handbook* was published by the *Canadian Mining Journal* in 1910, and the content is presented with minimal editorial comment. That makes the following notation attached to the listing for the Silver Bird Mine, Frank Law promoter, Lennox and Lennox solicitors, all the more noteworthy: "The Silver Bird is one of the most notorious of the Cobalt wild cats. There is no rock exposure on the property, and while the diamond drilling may possibly locate ore the result is very doubtful."

concerns are now fugitives from justice. The shares of not one of the thirty companies are worth purchasing today. This is indeed a startling indictment."

Dodging Bullets

No doubt, Barber and his brokerage company, Canada Mines Limited, was one of these five "fugitives." His advertisements used the same template and his legal team, Lennox and Lennox were implicated in the Law story.

The Larder Lake Proprietary Gold Fields company was above board in that they did develop the mine to a certain extent, and money from treasury stock was used to pay for plant and wages etc. But recall those additional 800,000 shares that were issued to Barber. These were apart from the 1.4 million shares that were sold to customers.

Besides the ads and weekly updates in the newspapers, Barber probably bombarded everyone on his mailing lists with circulars extolling the opportunities with the Larder Lake Proprietary Gold Mine. We turn again to the *Canadian Mining Journal* and another warning to investors, this time about the proliferation of ads for Larder Lake gold mine shares.

> Here we may pause to observe that several Toronto mining brokers and promoters are advertising lavishly in the press of the Western and Maritime Provinces.
>
> We wish to warn those who are desirous of risking their money in mining ventures to refrain absolutely from purchasing stock in Larder Lake or Cobalt concerns, until they have consulted either the Ontario Bureau of Mines or some competent and reputable mining engineer.
>
> This is a reiteration of what has been said before. But so glaring, so patently unsound are the statements made in the "display" advertisements, that they provoke renewed attention.
>
> A contemporary mining periodical cites an instance which may well be taken to heart. The LM Sullivan Company, of Nevada, a lavish advertiser, received as much as $140,000 in a single day from the sale of mining stocks which it was promoting, yet so tremendous were its expenses that the company failed and had to be reorganized.

If Barber was reading the news and paying attention – and if he was still in Canada – the 1907 reports by the *CMJ* would have been reason enough to "skip town."

He appears to have gone into hiding as far as travel documents and newspaper accounts are concerned. His name was not on the passenger list that included the other members of his family who sailed to the UK in July of 1907. In early August, it is known that he was trying to sell some of his 800,000 shares of LLPGF in England, but that may have been handled by an agent. His lawyer, G.B. Strathy represented him in the Piper v. Ulrey case, later in the year.

Once again, the trail goes dark.

The urge to solve the mystery of where Barber went after June 1907 has led us to consider several fanciful possibilities. On August 7, 1907, a Mr. H. C. Barber sailed from Liverpool to Forcados, Nigeria on *SS Karina*. Nigeria would have been a good place to maintain a low profile.

Did he sail home with his family in July, perhaps disguised as G.B. Strathy, his lawyer?

Interestingly, Horatio Barber's family told the story[92] that when he left Canada, and presumably before appearing in France, he stopped off in New York. According to the family legend, he hit the jackpot at a casino there and stayed up all night guarding the winnings before he could get it to the bank.

This also sounds fanciful, since at that time in New York, due to the reform movement, gambling was very much frowned upon. He may have concocted the gambling story to explain his newfound fortune. After all, he had defrauded people all over the world by this point and would want to present a believable and less damning explanation for his considerable newfound wealth to his family and possibly the taxman.[93]

In 1913, Elsie declared in her divorce statement that the couple lived in many different locations during their marriage, including Greece. In his book *Airy Nothings*, Barber speaks longingly about the Grecian island of Corfu. Perhaps this was his sanctuary until he felt safe enough to move to France,[94] where he surfaced once again on December 24, 1908.

This was at the automobile exhibition where, for the first time, aeroplanes were on display in the Paris Aeronautical Salon in the Grand Palais des Champs-Élysées. There, he fell in love with the aeroplane and began the next chapter of his life.

---

[92] As related to Norman Parker
[93] Regarding the casino story, we have no evidence one way or another, and recognize that we may do the man an injustice with our speculation.
[94] Various references suggest that he returned to England following "an extended stay in Paris." He could therefore have been in Paris for a year or more.

Chapter 10: Barber's Co-Stars in Ontario

In this Chapter, we feature people who played a supporting role in Horatio Barber's Canadian career. The characters' names are in order as they appear in preceding chapters, the period when Barber lived in Toronto and worked as a stockbroker for companies in Cobalt and Larder Lake, Ontario.

Further research into these men's lives may add to Horatio's story and would be a good project for another day. For now, we offer a brief sketch of these men.

The Cobalt Open Call Mining Exchange

The *Canadian Mining Review* of May 1906 announced the incorporation of the Cobalt Open Call Mining Exchange. Horatio C. Barber was one of the three directors and R. H. C. Browne of Cobalt was another. Other news reports announced C. H. Moore of Cobalt and J. H. Hunter of Cincinnati as charter members of the exchange.

Robert H.C. Browne held several positions while he lived and worked in Cobalt. He was the first editor and owner of the town's newspaper, the *Cobalt Nugget*, a life insurance agent, and the police magistrate.[95]

Browne was an active mining man with interests in several properties. In 1906, he and his partners were among the first in the area to use a diamond drill rig, a relatively new and expensive technique just introduced to the mining camp.[96]

In 1919, he was hospitalized for a self-inflicted axe wound when he was out prospecting in the bush near Matachewan, Ontario. He was fifty-five at the time.[97] We have been unable to trace him prior to his time in Cobalt, or after 1919.

R. H. C. Browne, left, police magistrate and F. Hedley Marsh banker, ca1907; Cobalt Mining Museum

---

[95] *Cobalt: Canada's Forgotten Silver Boom Town,* Douglas Baldwin, 2016
[96] *Bureau of Mines Report for 1906,* pg. 31
[97] *Brandon Daily Sun,* October 14, 1919

Clifton Henry Moore (1879 to 1934) "Cliff" Moore was a businessman and druggist. He arrived in Cobalt in 1906 and owned several enterprises in town including a drug store and restaurant. He also owned the Cobalt Mess at 77 Cobalt Street. This building served the dual purpose of being his home base when he was in town, as well as a meeting place for his visiting colleagues and dignitaries. Later in 1906, when J. H. Hunter built his commercial building in The Square, Moore moved his drug store to this site.

Moore also made money by investing in mine exploration. He "grubstaked" numerous prospectors in Northern Ontario, including the goldfields in Porcupine. He was there in 1911 when the devastating fire tore through the region. He ran the King George Hotel at the time of the fire,[98] and in 1912, he had a real estate office in the newly rebuilt hotel.

He was 55 at the time of his death, in his home in Cobalt.

Cliff Moore back row on right with bowler hat. Unknown date. Cobalt Mining Museum

On the left is Moore's first drug store on the Haileybury Road, ca 1906. One of these two men wearing a bowler looks like Moore, most likely the man with the overcoat. Cobalt Public Library

The image on the right is captioned "Men on Porch Nipissing Mine." Is the man in the bowler Cliff Moore? And who is the chap striking the casual pose with his hands in his pockets? Could that be Horatio?! We believe so! Cobalt Mining Museum

---

[98] *Maclean's "The Fire that Wiped out Porcupine"*, February 1, 1954

J.H. Hunter (1857 to 1916?)

None of the Cobalt records or media reports spell out Hunter's full name. He is identified as a capitalist from Cincinnati who owned considerable property in Cobalt's residential and commercial neighbourhoods.

We believe, however, that Joseph Hendricks Hunter, a man who was arrested for using the mail to defraud in 1893 was the same Cincinnati entrepreneur.

His brother Harry also of Cincinnati posted the $2000 bail bond, but it was forfeited when J.H. fled town - supposedly to St. Louis from where he wrote to his wife. The press speculated that Hunter was following the lead of another character involved with the scam. That man had escaped custody and was known to be in Canada.

Apparently, the newspapers had guessed correctly. According to the 1901 census, J.H. and his family were in Toronto - his occupation was advertising agent and he declared that he arrived in Canada in 1890, but on the 1911 enumeration, he changed that date to 1893.

After his involvement with Barber's exchange, J.H. Hunter was busy with several projects related to townsite development and mining. His most significant contribution to Cobalt was the completion of the Hunter Block in 1907.[99]

By the standards of the mining town, The Hunter Block was impressive looking on the outside. Inside was another matter. It was a cheaply built, three-storey structure without toilets. Note "Moore's Drug Store" sign over the entrance. This building was located across from the Cobalt Open Call Mining Exchange.

---

[99] In 1909 during the typhoid crisis, a new name appeared in the press: C.O. Hunter. This was Joseph's brother Cromwell Orrick who appears to have been acting as agent for the landlord of the Hunter Block or he had purchased the building from his brother. He was fined for non-compliance after he ignored the health authorities' order to install toilets in that building and other rooming facilities in town.

In 1908, J.H. Hunter purchased lots of the Cochrane townsite at the end of the TN&O rail line. The press speculated that he might build another "Hunter" Block, but this did not happen.

By 1911, he was a rich man and lived in a posh Toronto neighbourhood. However, unlike Barber, his name didn't merit an entry in the Blue Book, the directory of high society for Toronto and Hamilton. It seems that by 1916 he had died because his wife declared herself a widow when she lived in Detroit. We have not found a death notice, obituary, or grave marker.

Long Lake Company and the Charlton Townsite Development Project

Long Lake	Charlton
We hear that a company is being organized, to be called the Long Lake Co., Limited. Among the organizers are Col. White, ex. M. P. P., J. H. Hunter, Captain Marsh and H. C. Barber. The Company is taking over the town site of Charlton, a large saw mill there, timber limits, water power rights capable of producing 3,000 horse power and certain Mines. As we are advised, the Company intends to form a subsidiary company for the purpose of building an electric railway between Charlton and the Temiskaming and Northern Ontario Railway and to generally develop that part of the country.	The Hon. Sol. White, Capt. March and Mr. Watson, were in town last week, looking after the interests of the Long Lake Co. Ltd. We understand that the company intend taking over the mines and mill plant belonging to Mr. Ryan, on 1st of July. McColl's Bay looks like a miniature Cobalt just now. Several companies have gangs working the mines there. C. H. Vint, of Mimico, intends settling in this vicinity. Russell Draper is back on his farm again. Poor old bachelors! Mr. Ryan has a gang of men on the lake taking down the drive. Capt. Marsh thinks that the town site here, is "ideal."

The two reports, above, from the *New Liskeard Speaker* March 30, and June 15, 1906, describe the Charlton townsite project organized by Horatio Barber, J.H. Hunter, Captain Marsh, and Solomon White. The plan was to build whatever infrastructure was required in anticipation of another boomtown. It never happened. Barber's syndicate either abandoned their project or were out-maneuvered by New Liskeard entrepreneur, Pete Farrah who eventually built a hydro generating facility in Charlton.

Solomon White KC (1836 to 1911)

Solomon White was born in 1836 near Amherstburg, Ontario, the son of Joseph White, a Chief of the Wyandot First Nations. He became a lawyer in 1865 in Windsor and in 1878 he represented the riding of Essex North in the Legislative Assembly of Ontario. In 1890, he was Mayor of Windsor.

White moved to Cobalt in 1905 and set up a law practice. He ran for mayor in 1911, lost the race, but won on a recount. He died six months later in November.[100]

Solomon White ca 1893 By William Cochrane and John Castell Hopkins - The Canadian Album: Men of Canada.

---

[100] en.wikipedia.org/wiki/Solomon_White

Solomon and his wife spent their time between Windsor and Cobalt and he had offices in a building on Argentite Street – the same building earlier occupied by Barber's lawyers, Boultbee & Boultbee. He owned several investment properties in Cobalt and a farm in Charlton, the latter possibly acquired during the Long Lake Company project.

S. White Law Office located to the left of the Imperial Bank. The dark wooden building to the left is the former Open Call Mining Exchange. ca 1910 Cobalt Mining Museum

As would be expected for a man with legal and political occupations, the media regularly reported on White's activities. Since he was involved with several mining projects as well and was associated with Horatio Barber, some of those news pieces were more sensational than most.

In September 1905, on a return trip to the south, the press reported that he was suitably impressed with the opportunities in Cobalt and that he had aligned himself with capitalists who had set out "to secure the services of an expert mining engineer." It would appear that the expert was Horatio. It would certainly not be surprising to learn that the news report was submitted by Barber himself.

White said, "I expect to return north the first of next month to attend to the business interests I have acquired in the mining territory, and by that time, I will be in a position to know just how valuable my claims are."[101]

In 1907, the lawyer invested in the Larder Lake goldfields. One news report,[102] more of a "puff piece", sings the glories of his King Jumbo copper mine. We can find no such name in the official mine literature. More to the point, Larder Lake had no copper ore to speak of. This wildcat mine was really more fake than the fake gold plays of the day!

Whether or not White did well with his copper mine is not known. He reportedly made and lost fortunes several times over. In 1909, however, he and his three partners who co-owned the Gem Claim were back in the news[103] with the discovery of an enormous 2800-pound silver nugget. Shortly after the discovery, the piece was taken on a promotional tour and the investment pages were filled with ads that encouraged people to put their money in the Gem Claim.

Solomon White died a wealthy man.

Largest Silver Nugget ever discovered was found on the Cobalt Gem Property May 22, 1909. The man with the bowler hat to the right of the newsboy is possibly Sol White. The man seated on the nugget, to the left of the newsboy is Zach Jackson, White's "valet." He is seen in several images of the silver piece as it was taken on a promotional tour. Jackson was a drayman from Windsor, and he drove the team that hauled the giant nugget.

---

[101] *Windsor Star* September 6, 1905
[102] *Detroit Free Press* September 11, 1907
[103] *Windsor Star* June 3, 1909

The Competition - Homer L.[104] Gibson (1882 to 1948)

Homer Gibson was born in Good Hope, Ohio. After he graduated high school in 1902, he moved to Cincinnati and worked as an expressman for the railroad.[105]

He came to Cobalt in May 1906 where he met Horatio Barber. The two men struck a deal regarding the sale of shares in the Abitibi and Cobalt Mine Company. During a dispute, Gibson felt obliged to involve the courts to resolve the issue and by the end of the year, the two had parted company and did not cross paths again.

Gibson stayed in the North working as a stockbroker out of Haileybury and Porcupine. In 1917, he established a brokerage, Homer L. Gibson & Company with branches in northern mining towns, including Cobalt. He applied for Canadian citizenship in 1917.

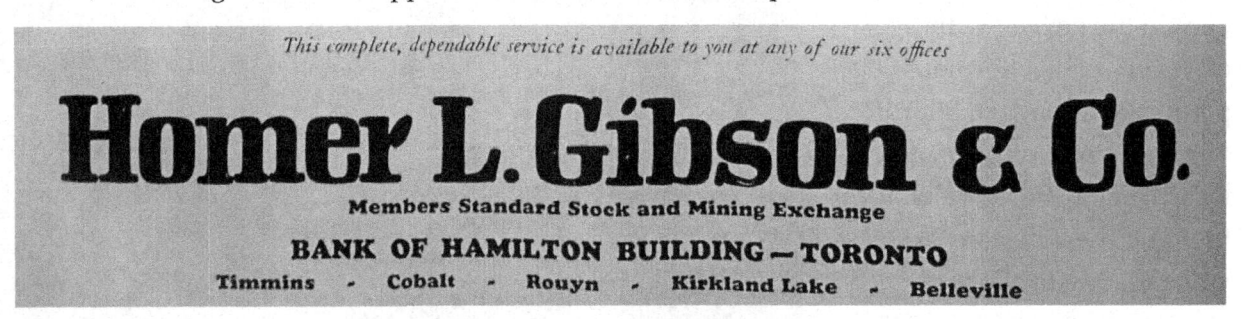

Homer L. Gibson & Co. Brokerage ad 1927 - branches in Timmins, Cobalt, Kirkland Lake, Belleville, Ontario and Rouyn, Quebec

By 1920, Gibson was a wealthy man and he lived in one of Toronto's Blue Book neighbourhoods.

Gibson went on to attain considerable stature in both the mining and financial communities. The image used at top is from the 1929 newspaper account of his re-election as an officer of the Standard Stock Exchange in Toronto. Editors of the mining journals praised his regular reports as concise, informative, and without hyperbole. He hosted a weekly radio show and reported the latest news from the mines.

At the beginning of his career, however, Gibson had no more understanding of geology and mines than Horatio did. Neither man had any formal education in mining or investment.

Where the two men differed was in their personalities. While Barber was impulsive and given to exaggeration, Gibson was restrained and matter-of-fact. In the Abitibi and Cobalt Mine

---

[104] Curiously, we have been unable to determine Gibson's middle name—on military records, and his application for Canadian Citizenship, it is written as "L". On the Ohio Births and Christenings, 1821-1962 record, he is listed simply as Homer Gibson. He was born a Gipson, but the family changed the name to Gibson.
[105] ancestry.com/ReferenceMaterial/Files/A_Genealogy_of_the_Shobe_Kirkpatrick_and_Dilling_Families.pdf

dispute with Barber, it would appear that Barber was possibly outmaneuvered by the more coldblooded Gibson.

Why coldblooded?

In 1930, Gibson allowed Maurice Young, his nephew and employee, to take the fall for him in a notorious stock fraud scandal. During the trial, the defence attorney declared that Young was simply following his boss's orders. The lawyer also alluded to the strong bond between the uncle and the nephew, and that Gibson had suggested that he would one day make Young his heir.[106] The presiding judge in the case instructed the jury to disregard those intriguing details and to remember that only the man before them was on trial, not Homer Gibson.

After the Hunter block burned down in 1926, a new building was erected and one of the occupants was Homer L. Gibson. His nephew Maurice E. Young worked and lived in this building. Ca 1930 Cobalt Mining Museum.

Whatever the relationship between the uncle and nephew, Young, along with two other stockbrokers from the firm went to jail in March 1931.

During the trial, Gibson was in Europe. Two months later on his return voyage, he listed Young as his contact, and the address of his Toronto brokerage as the address. It would seem that he was not aware of his nephew's incarceration.

In the 1930s, Gibson was living and working in the United States. He spent some time in Pasadena, California, and later, he moved to Carson City, Nevada where he worked as the managing director of Dayton Consolidated Mines. He worked for the company until his sudden death in 1948.

---

[106] *The Winnipeg Tribune* October 21, 1930

Larder Lake Proprietary Gold Fields Mine

Frenzy is a word that aptly describes the Larder Lake Gold Rush. Men were clamouring over each other to be first to stake a claim, to open a hotel, or as in Horatio's case, to open a brokerage company. This he was able to accomplish, and he boasted about the fact in his marketing material.

Some people, like Barber and Ulrey, made money from the gold rush, as did the businessmen who contracted their services and charged exorbitant prices to supply the mining camp. Certainly, some prospectors and development miners had employment for a short while.

But in the end, many people were bitterly disappointed by losing their investments. Many employees worked without pay. In the last dying days of Larder Lake Proprietary Gold Fields Mine, men gave up waiting for their payroll and finally walked away from their jobs. When they came out of camp, they didn't have enough money to buy a meal.

Of course, through it all, the legal community profited, whether the lawyers represented the winners or the losers.

Some lawyers, such as those from the legal firm of Lennox and Lennox turned a blind eye to any conflict of interest. T. Herbert Lennox sat as a director of the Larder Lake Proprietary Gold Mine company, representing the shareholders. His brother, John Francis Lennox was the President of the board of directors of Barbers' brokerage Canada Mines, the company that handled the selling of shares in that gold mine.

In the case of the Southern Belle Cobalt Silver Mine, for example, the Lennox brothers' firm represented the company in legal matters at the same time as J. F. Lennox was the president of the board of directors. The Southern Belle, it hardly needs stating, was a wildcat mine.

In Chapter 9 we introduced Frank Law, the stock promoter who made the mistake of suing the *Canadian Mining Journal* and ended up in jail. T. H. Lennox represented him during the trial. The Highland Mary Mine at the centre of the case was a notorious wildcat.

Making Connections

Near the end of 1905, Sir James A. Grant wrote to lawyer Albert Morgan.[107] In his letter, Grant offered to connect him to his "influential friends" who were interested in investing in the Cobalt silver mines. Judging from the fact that we haven't found Morgan's name aligned with any of the wildcat mines, it appears he either took Grant's advice to heart or was already disinclined to take what work may have been offered to him.

---

[107] Barber wrote to Morgan about the Long Lake and the Ryan brothers in Charlton. See Chapter 6.

> December 27, 1905
>
> My Dear Morgan
>
> I called on your father yesterday and was glad to learn you had established a legal office in Cobalt. If you have any good silver claims I might be able to give you a helping hand in placing these with influential friends at a distance and to whom I have been sending papers & geological reports on the subject.
>
> It is a great matter that you are directly on the spot where the recent discoveries have been made. At present the snow places claims out of sight, but I could be at work and make ready for the spring opening.
>
> In all such matters great care and prudence are necessary, and particularly the avoidance of "Wild Cat" undertakings in which I am confident you would take no part.
>
> I will be glad to have a line from you on this subject. Wishing you the compliments of the season, and every possible degree of success.
>
> Very sincerely yours
>
> JA Grant

It stands to reason that lawyers in offices around the province received similar requests, especially those in Cobalt and Toronto.

If a solicitor was associated with one wildcat scheme, chances were excellent his name was associated with several more. In the case of Lennox and Lennox, we find their name attached to at least nine wildcat mining ventures, including Canada Mines, Barber's brokerage.

Someone like Horatio Barber, new to the community and to the laws of the land, would have aligned himself with these men who had the contacts, legal expertise, and access to capital. Perhaps through his relationship with Lennox and Lennox, Barber met people like J. H. Hunter, Moore, and the others.

Lewis Valentine Ulrey (1868 to 1959)

The former senator is a key player in the Larder Lake episode. Of the men who associated with Horatio Barber, Ulrey's name was the one most commonly mentioned in newspaper articles. He was perhaps the most notorious of all when you consider his association with right-wing extremists during the 1930s and 40s.

In 1900, Ulrey was 32 and worked as an insurance agent. He was the Indiana state organizer for The Pathfinders, a fraternal association related to the insurance industry and that was likely his stepping stone to the Indiana State Senate in 1902. [108]

> LEGISLATIVE MANUAL. 213
>
> LEW V. ULREY.
>
> Senator Lew V. Ulrey, of Ft. Wayne, Indiana, was born on a farm in Clark County, Illinois, April 11, 1868. His father, Eli Ulrey, was born in Morrow County, Ohio, and now owns and operates a farm near Coleman, Michigan. When six years of age Senator Ulrey moved with his parents to the birthplace of his mother in Allen County, Indiana. The maiden name of his mother was Angeline Ulrey, his father and mother being cousins. In the public schools of Allen County young Ulrey got the foundation of a good education. His work in the public schools was supplemented by two years' work at Franklin College, and by several years of hard study in the Northern Indiana Normal School at Valparaiso. Senator Ulrey prepared for the law but never practiced. He is State Organizer for the Pathfinders, and is also largely interested in the production of crude petroleum. He was married in 1896 to Miss Ada Denner. He is a Democrat in politics and represents the county of Allen in the Indiana Senate. This is the only office he has ever held.

Lewis Valentine Ulrey's bio from the Indiana state senate legislative manual, 1903.

---

[108] *Fort Wayne Sentinel* March 15, 1902

While he was a senator, he was president of Reliance Oil out of Redkey, Indiana. He then explored further afield, and he found oil in Ontario. From there, he took a brief detour into gold mining and accompanied Horatio to Larder Lake in 1907.

Ulrey in Mexico

Finished with the goldfields of Larder Lake, Ulrey moved on to search for minerals in Mexico during the time of growing social unrest that led to the 1911 revolution. Reports of his lecture tours in 1914 reveal that he lost "a fortune of over $60,000 which he used in promoting… a mineral proposition which promised to develop into the greatest of its kind on earth."[109] Ulrey blamed the "political problems" with President Diaz [who] forced the syndicate to abandon their plans and their investment."[110]

Pilgrim Oil

Pilgrim Oil was incorporated in Boston, Massachusetts, March 1918.[111] Later that year the company was permitted to conduct business in Texas, with offices in Fort Worth.[112] In 1920, Ulrey was president of the Boston branch. The oilman dedicated the next three years of his life drilling for a gusher in the oil fields of Shreveport, Louisiana. By the end of January 1923, after digging wells to record depths, he had not yet discovered oil.

Meanwhile, the United States authorities investigated fraudulent investment practice among oil stock promoters. While Pilgrim Oil in Fort Worth was not the only company engaged in the schemes, the Texas branch was marked as one of the worst offenders. Ulrey claimed he was not involved in the fraud, and his name was not mentioned in reports of the investigation. However, his Louisiana company was no doubt affected by the negative press. The last news of Pilgrim Oil from Shreveport is an advertisement[113] offering used drilling equipment for sale.

In Bryan Burrough's, *The Big Rich: The Rise and Fall of the Greatest Texas Oil Fortunes,* Ulrey is described as "an oil field character… a self-taught geologist who had wandered Louisiana, Texas, and Mexico for two decades before, by his own telling, suffered a nervous breakdown and washed up penniless on a Galveston beach."

Political Leaning

After twenty years of personal and business failures, Ulrey's political leaning had moved to the extreme far right of the spectrum and he crusaded for an America that was free of whatever he felt caused his downfall and interfered with his ability to be a wealthy man.

---

[109] *Daily Deadwood Pioneer-Times* March 15, 1914
[110] *Argus-Leader* May 26, 1914
[111] *Boston Globe* March 18, 1918
[112] *Houston Post* November 20, 1918
[113] *The Times*, Shreveport Louisiana February 9, 1924

He associated with extremely rich and ultraconservative men such as Maco Stewart and Vance Muse. Ulrey coordinated Stewart's anti-Communist campaign and according to Ulrey, "Russian communism was part of an international Jewish conspiracy that had infiltrated the highest levels of American churches, universities and the Roosevelt administration.[114]"

In the mid-1930s, Muse appointed Ulrey as the chairman of the "Christian American Association Inc.," the original "Right-To-Work" lobby front. Their propaganda was racist, anti-Semitic, anti-communism, and anti-unionism. In the late 1930s, Ulrey wrote pro-Hitler columns for a magazine run by Gerald Winrod, a notorious anti-Semite who was arrested during World War Two for pro-Nazi sedition.[115]

Walter Davenport interviewed Ulrey and Vance Muse for *Colliers Weekly* in August 1945. The picture he paints of the former Indiana senator is not flattering:

> "In his thin old voice that frequently rose to a shrill, quavering falsetto, Mr. Ulrey had held forth, his mouth bitter with acrimony, against social liberals, political radicals, labour unions … All of them, he said, were nothing but proponents of Red Russian Communism."
>
> Walter Davenport for *Colliers Weekly* August 1945.

At the end of 1945, when Ulrey advised the Texas state school board to reject a book called *Good Neighbour Russia* from the curriculum, his name was back in the spotlight. He refused to explain why he rejected the text.[116] Into 1946, protestors petitioned for Ulrey's removal from his post as secretary to Maco Stewart Jr., the head of the Texas board of education. It is unknown if Ulrey remained employed with the board.

He lived out his days in Galveston and died on June 14, 1959. He was 91.

---

[114] *The Big Rich: The Rise and Fall of the Greatest Texas Oil Fortunes* Bryan Burrough, 2009
[115] pando.com/2015/03/13/as-right-to-work-becomes-law-in-wisconsin-a-reminder-of-its-inventors-racist-past/
[116] *Austin American Statesman* November 16, 1945

Chapter 11
Barber the Aviator: From underground to above the ground 1908-1919

On returning from the New World, Barber spent some time in Paris during 1908 and it was here that we see the first sign of his interest in aviation, although it is quite possible that he kept up with the emerging science previous to that. He was in Canada and the USA in 1903, so most likely he would have heard of the Wright brothers' success before news of that event crossed the Atlantic.

Paris, 1908
In late December 1908 he visited the Paris Salon de L'automobile, which for the first time exhibited a small collection of aeroplanes or aerodromes as they were sometimes called at that time. Of the handful of machines exhibited, it is said that only the Brazilian Santos-Dumont had actually flown. In actual fact this is probably not correct, and some of the other exhibits may have been aloft, although Santos-Dumont's was possibly the most famous.

Santos-Dumont's Aeroplane 1906 – alamy.com

Barber was inspired by this show and wasted no time in returning to England with the intention of getting involved in the new science of aviation. As we have seen in previous chapters, Barber was able to change career direction very quickly. This particular change was probably his most rapid because within a matter of months he had both an aeroplane shed and his first aeroplane on Salisbury Plain at Lark Hill.[117]

---

[117] The downland in that area was originally known as the Hill of the Larks. The location was called Lark Hill and then Larkhill. During Barber's time here, both names were in use, though Lark Hill more commonly so. The reader will note that both names are used in the text, depending on the timeframe.

Battersea and Lark Hill, 1909
Once back in England, Barber gravitated to Battersea and set up a workshop under some railway arches in this most unlikely place, one of the most important centres of British aviation at that time.

The reason for locating in Battersea is described in *Flights of Fancy* subtitled *Early Aviation in Battersea and Wandsworth* by Patrick Loobey. This area of London became a popular site for gas-filled balloon experiments due to its proximity to the fuel. By the 1880s, Wandsworth gasworks which was situated on the river Wandle had become the site of choice for many balloonists due to the cheaper rate and plentiful supply of gas sold by the Wandsworth Gas Company. Also, there were fewer buildings than in other parts of London.

The Short brothers, C.S. Rolls and J.C. Moore-Brabazon were all early gas ballooning pioneers. A.V. Roe also lived in the area and conducted experiments nearby. The Short brothers and the brothers Howard and Warwick Wright rented railway arches in what is now Sopwith Way, Battersea, so when their attention was drawn from lighter-than-air to heavier-than-air machines, this is where they stayed.

'The Mammoth' launch, at Wandsworth Gasworks, 25th May 1907

Another aviation pioneer who very early on rented a workshop here was Horatio Phillips, whose peculiar "Venetian Blind" aeroplane is reported to have flown in 1907, but this is disputed by many. Philips was also a helicopter pioneer.

Horatio Phillips 1907 "Venetian Blind" flying machine

Barber hired Howard Wright to build his first aeroplane. Wright had been at his Battersea workshop since about 1901. In 1907 he advertised that he could build any kind of machine to the inventor's specification. In that year, he constructed a helicopter for Federico Capone at his brother Warwick's workshop. This machine apparently flew at Croydon. It was tethered and raised to a height of two feet, but owing to its construction of tubular steel, was too heavy to lift a pilot.

Barber's first plane was basically a Howard Wright design and like his helicopter, Wright's plane was also made of tubular steel and was too heavy and therefore not successful. As with some of Wright's planes, this machine had contra-rotating propellers which had recently been patented by F.W. Lanchester of motorcar fame. The propellers were driven via a gearbox in front of the engine.

The design of the plane was very similar to a machine made for Avis, which actually flew, and a machine ordered by W.E. Cooke of the Burnley Motor Omnibus Company in Lancashire, both of which were made by Howard Wright. We do not know how much input Barber had in the design of this machine, but Barber's invention[118], a method of stability by adjusting the wing dihedral is thought to have been incorporated into this aeroplane.

Here we seem to have a contradiction, in that Barber is said to have been inspired by the 1908 Paris exhibition to come back to England and start a career in aviation. Since the 1908 Paris salon exhibition was held from December 24th to the 30th, it seems unlikely that Barber would have been in a position to apply for a patent by January 1909. This suggests that he was interested or involved in aviation prior to the Paris show.

Barber spent a considerable amount of his fortune on aviation projects, and Loobey suggests that he either invested in the Howard Wright's works at Battersea or he worked alongside them in the railway arches for a time. Loobey also suggests that Barber's projects may have been financed by a Mr. Patrick Alexander who awarded cash payments for aviation advancements. However, as we know from previous chapters in his story, Barber was a very wealthy man at this time, so this may just be conjecture.

As early as February 1909, the War Office had notified the Aero Club of the United Kingdom that it was prepared to grant the club facilities on War Department land on Salisbury Plain for flight trials, provided there was no interference with military training. Barber repeatedly requested permission to build an aeroplane shed on this allotted land at Lark Hill but he received no satisfactory answers.[119] He then went to the War Office with a supply of food and drink and stated that he was not leaving until he got a reply. Eventually, he leased a plot of land at Lark Hill and was given permission to construct a 40' by 45' shed on this land. By the end of May 1909 and possibly slightly earlier, Barber's shed had been completed. *The Northern Daily Telegraph* of June 2, 1909, reported that "Away by the Lark Hill Camp the first aeroplane shed

---

[118] Patent number 1999 of January 1909, granted December 1909
[119] See Appendix 7: Dear John. A Letter from Horatio to his son

has been erected for a member of the Aero Club, and a site has been marked out for others." Barber's shed was 60' distance from the Packway, an ancient road running through the Lark Hill Camp.

This concrete plinth at Lark Hill is believed to be the remains of Barber's shed. It is 30 feet long and thought to be the base for the sliding doors to the shed. There is no absolute proof of its provenance, but it is exactly in the correct place to be those remains. The plinth is 60 feet from The Packway, which is where Barber's shed was situated according to contemporary photographs. Terry Grace photo.

Barber's first aeroplane[120] arrived at Lark Hill on June 1909 and his experiments started immediately. We can be fairly sure about the date, since an editorial in *Aero* dated June 8, 1909, reported that when they recently visited the works of Howard T. Wright, they found the new monoplane almost complete. Howard Wright told the reporters that the machine was going away for trials in a day or two, but that the purchaser had asked that the aeroplane not be described in the publication until it had proved a success. The report then goes on to say that the machine embodied some very clever ideas which were absolute novelties in principle, but which should work out in practice. The workmanship was found to be of the highest quality, and the tubular framework was capitally designed. In general, it resembled an Antoinette or maybe the REP, a monoplane built by Frenchman Robert Esnault-Pelterie.

---

[120] For additional technical information and images of all of Barber's aircraft, see Chapter 12.

Horatio Barber in his first plane built by Howard Wright, at Lark Hill 1909. This is probably a staged publicity photograph, with Barber posing in the cockpit. He had not yet flown at that time. From Barber's scrapbook at Hendon RAF Museum.

Obviously, the craft described by *Aero* was Barber's monoplane with its novel features of automatic stability and co-axial contra-rotating propellers. We can assume that the aeroplane arrived at Lark Hill in the first half of June 1909. The fact that its description did not follow in later editions of the magazine suggests that it was deemed a failure, although we can be fairly certain that it did, in fact, get off the ground. The *Aero* article suggests that Barber was working in some secrecy in the early days at Lark Hill, and this fact together with the relative isolation of the site accounts for the lack of information on this aeroplane in any of the journals or newspapers of the time.

Originally the plane was to have had "rotating wing tips" for control, but this was replaced by a wing warping system before production. (Unless the term

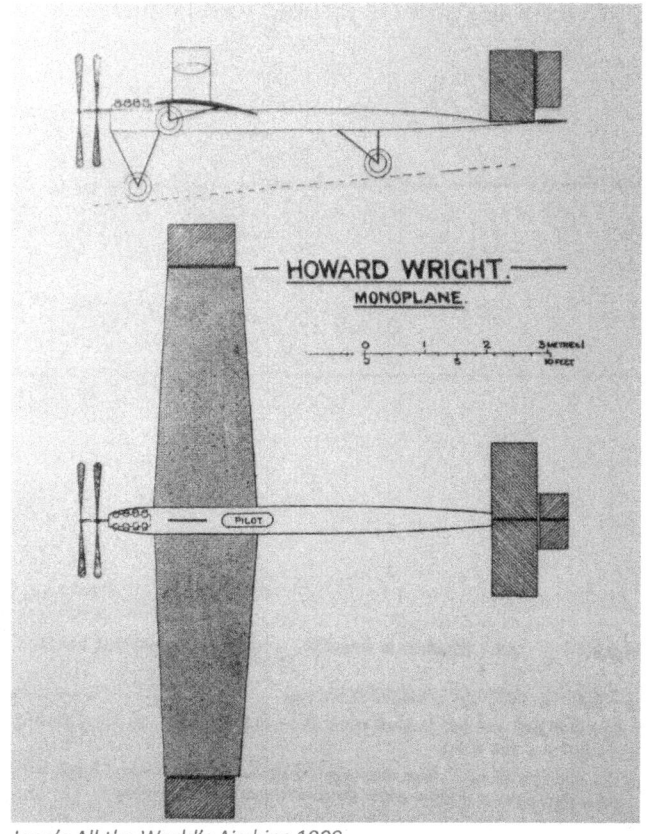

Jane's All the World's Airships 1909

96

"rotating wing tips" is synonymous with "wing warping".) But note that Jane's drawing of Barber's monoplane quite clearly shows separate and therefore controllable wing tips.

In the two images on the previous page, the contra-rotating propellers are plainly visible and this was a feature that Howard Wright incorporated into some of his other planes. The aeroplane was powered by a 50-horsepower, water-cooled, Antoinette V8 engine. Two long radiators ran along each side of the fuselage as can be clearly seen in the photograph. The long rod seen under the fuselage is thought to be Barber's patented wing stabilizing system.

A later photo of the aeroplane reveals that Barber or possibly Howard Wright and W.O. Manning altered the craft by adding an additional lifting surface to the rear, and a larger tail fin and rudder. Also shown is the rod lying under the fuselage and apparently connected to the wings, which could be Barber's patented invention for stability control using dihedral adjustment. The shorter of the two downward projections between the front and rear wheels appears to be a pulley wheel. This is more obvious in the modified aeroplane. (See Chapter 12.)

In the same photograph, the man in the pilot's seat looks much like Howard Wright, or more possibly W.O. Manning who was Wright's designer, so perhaps one of the two were called to Lark Hill to oversee the modifications. It is known that Wright travelled frequently, and certainly travelled to Naples for the trials of Capone's second helicopter. Manning also supervised the testing of Wright machines and supplied many photographs for the aeronautical journals of the time, so it could well be him.

Howard Wright monoplane for W E Cooke

Howard Wright Avis monoplane in flight

It has been suggested that the Cooke monoplane seen on the previous page was, in fact, Barber's first machine, which Wright had retrieved and modified with smaller, less weighty radiators on the fuselage sides. Whilst this is a possibility, it seems at first unlikely because we know that Barber's aeroplane was heavily modified at Lark Hill with much-increased tail and rudder area and also an additional horizontal plane in the position near the tail end of the radiators. In the picture, the aeroplane is seen with the very characteristic Howard Wright tailplane arrangement and no sign of the additional horizontal plane. It is quite clear that the front landing gear arrangement is different from that of the Barber machine. Again, this could have been evolutionary improvements, with the removal of the cart spring undercarriage of Barber's machine to reduce the weight and thereby increasing the ability of the aeroplane to lift from the ground. However, P.D. Stemp in his book *Kites, Birds and Stuff* shows the same photograph above and states that it *was* the aeroplane built for H. Barber and that it was originally "co-axial" i.e. contra-rotating propellers which were later modified to a single propeller. Since it appears that in the picture above only one propeller is present, this story has some credibility. (See more about the Mystery of Barber's First Aeroplane in Appendix 3.)

Worth noting is that Howard Wright was instrumental in speeding up the manufacture of aeroplanes by the standardization of parts. At a later stage, he advertised that aeroplanes could be built in two weeks at his premises in Battersea. While Barber's machine weighed over 1000lbs without a driver, Howard Wright was making monoplanes weighing only 350lbs (without engine) by December 1909 and he had returned to using wood frames instead of steel tubing.

Bertie Woodrow[121]

At this stage in our account, it is fitting to discuss Barber's chauffeur, Mr. Bertie Woodrow who was to become the first official test pilot of powered aeroplanes in Britain and most likely the world.

The story came first-hand to local historian Norman Parker when he first became interested in Barber's adventures at Lark Hill. It goes thus:

Barber, who may have been somewhat reluctant to attempt to take to the air in one of his own contraptions, said to Bertie one day that since he (Bertie) drove Barber's car, then perhaps he should also attempt to fly his aeroplane. To which Bertie replied, "Very good sir."

Bertie Woodrow after his first successful flight on March 5th 1910. Terry Grace collection.

---

[121] Bertie was born February 24, 1888. He married Florence Elizabeth Gibbs in October 1907. In 1932 the couple lived at 25 Ashley Court, Kensington and in 1935 at 3 Dawson Place, Kensington. In 1939 they were living at 62 Waklin Rd. Willesden Middlesex where he was listed as being a Motor Mechanic. He died February 1969 Hillingdon London at 81.

Whilst at Lark Hill, Barber stayed in the comfortable Ivydene Hotel in Amesbury and Bertie Woodrow lodged with the Bannister family in a property behind the Stonehenge Inn, Durrington. Incidentally, H. Bannister[122] worked for Barber at jobs such as repairing the wheels of his planes. He also worked for Captain Fulton on his plane at a later date.

Whilst all this was going on, Barber had formed the Aeronautical Syndicate Limited (ASL) together with a stockbroker, Charles Worsley Battersby[123] and Herman Schmettua. Battersby was the major shareholder. Barber was the manager and never became a shareholder. The company was officially incorporated in June 1909. Barber's patents, his lease and shed at Lark Hill, and the first aeroplane were transferred to ASL. Barber's future aero-experiments were then funded by this company which had an initial capital of £2500.

NEW COMPANIES REGISTERED.
Aeronautical Syndicate, Ltd., 30, Moorgate Street, E.C.—Capital £2,500, in £1 shares.
Handley Page, Ltd., 36, William Street, Woolwich, Kent.—Capital £10,000, in £20 shares. Manufacturers of and dealers in aeroplanes, hydroplanes, &c. First directors, H. Page and F. N. Dalton.

From Flight *magazine July 3rd 1909*

Barber's second aeroplane to appear at Lark Hill was the ASL monoplane, sometimes referred to as ASL monoplane No.2. Typical of Barber, this machine was of a completely different design and was of the "Canard[124]" layout in that it was designed to fly tail first, the tail-like structure at the front being an elevator. This aeroplane was again from the Howard Wright stable, Presumably, Barber would have had a much greater input into the design, although it was officially designed by William Oke Manning, an aeronautical engineer working with Howard Wright. The aeroplane was powered by a 60-horsepower Green engine, driving a propeller of 8' 2" diameter which was to the rear of the pilot and passenger's position. On March 5, 1910, this machine took to the air with Bertie Woodrow at the controls. The flight was commemorated by the presentation of the framed photograph of Woodrow. The inscription on the frame is shown below:

PRESENTED BY THE AERONAUTICAL SYNDICATE, L.TD TO MR. B. WOODROW, UPON THE OCCASION OF HIS FIRST FLIGHT WITH AN A.S.L. MONOPLANE, MARCH 5th 1910.

Inscribed on the portrait of Bertie Woodrow: Presented by the Aeronautical Syndicate Ltd to Mr. B. Woodrow upon the occasion of his first flight with an ASL monoplane March 5th, 1910 Terry Grace photo

Another fascinating story tells of how this aeroplane became free of the ground. Bertie Woodrow was conducting taxiing trials in the new aeroplane when the machine hit a small mound which propelled the aeroplane into the air to a height of about thirty feet. Woodrow had the presence of mind to immediately switch off the engine and glide in a straight line to the

---

[122] H. Bannister's grandson Trevor Bannister was an actor who starred in the sit-com *Are you Being Served?*
[123] Christopher Hayes Battersby, brother to Charles, came to Canada in 1906. He was photographed alongside Horatio in the Larder Lake pamphlet from 1907.
[124] Canard is the French term for "duck."

ground. He had an uncomfortably hard landing that damaged the aeroplane somewhat, but he remained relatively unscathed.

This flight was the first at Lark Hill. That same week, *Flight* magazine of March 12th devoted one and a half pages to this machine and its conquest of the air, including two photographs.[125] Both show Barber in the pilot's position, although Bertie Woodrow sits in the passenger seat of one of the photos. The article points out the similarity of this aeroplane with that of Santos-Dumont's machine, and also the technical differences between this ASL aeroplane and Barber's first machine, which strangely they refer to as the Antoinette Flyer.

This image shows Barber's second aeroplane (usually referred to as the A.S.L. monoplane) being built in the workshop of Howard Wright in Battersea. The fuselage being constructed in the middle of the picture is the ASL, whilst a Bleriot type is in front of it, (towards the window) and the crates to the right hold the wings of the ASL plane.

The reader will note that although Bertie Woodrow's flight was acknowledged by ASL in the presentation of the photograph of him and the subsequent contract awarded to him as "Test Pilot", Barber was in the pilot's seat of these pictures staged for *Flight* magazine. There is nothing in the article about Woodrow being the pilot of this significant achievement, and although towards the latter part of his life Barber reminisces about himself being the pilot, we know it was, in fact, Bertie Woodrow.[126] *Aero* magazine credits B. Woodrow as the driver of the aeroplane and does not mention Barber in its article regarding the first flight in this machine.

Two months later, on May 18, 1910, Woodrow signed a contract to be "Test Pilot" for ASL.[127] Woodrow's contract, which can be seen in the Amesbury History Centre is a very interesting historical document in the aviation world, setting out as it does the conditions of employment for the first-ever test pilot of powered aeroplanes. The wording of the first paragraph is

---

[125] See Chapter 12 for the photos of Barber and Woodrow on the occasion of the first flight.
[126] At the time of his reminiscences to his son John, Barber had been diagnosed with pre-senility, which might explain the discrepancy.
[127] When later asked about his flying experience which led to the contract, Woodrow is quoted as saying, "I just wanted to get the bloody thing back on the ground."

(probably) necessarily demanding. While the phrasing is somewhat reminiscent of the contract Barber drew up for the unfortunate men who subscribed to his 1903 Hale Ranch swindle in California earlier in his career, we have no reason to suspect that Woodrow was treated in a similar manner. £2 per week was a good wage at that time when the average salary was £70 a year.

The first paragraph of the contract states:

>1. The said Bertie Woodrow shall during the term of five years from the date hereof if he shall so long live to serve the Syndicate as mechanic and fitter and shall give his whole time and attention to his employment and shall in all respects diligently and faithfully obey and observe all lawful orders and instructions of the Board of Directors or Manager of the Syndicate in relation to the conduct of the said employment and shall not without the consent of the said Board or Manager divulge any secrets or dealings relating thereto. The said Bertie Woodrow shall in particular test any monoplane of the Syndicate in flight and shall fly in the Monoplanes of the Syndicate at any Competition Meeting or Exhibition when required by the Syndicate so to do.

And in the second paragraph:

>2. The said Bertie Woodrow shall at all times during the period of his employment use his best endeavours for the success of the business of the Syndicate and shall not undertake any other business or fly in any Monoplane or Flying Machines belonging to any other person persons or Corporation than the Syndicate without the consent in writing of the Syndicate.

It seems that there is little further evidence of Woodrow's flying, and we can only conclude that once he had taught Barber the rudimentary skills, he no longer took to the air. Certainly, there is no account of Woodrow flying at Hendon when the Syndicate relocated there a few months later, and all reported flying of Barber's planes there was carried out by Barber himself or by his students. It is quite likely that Woodrow continued to test this machine during its development at Lark Hill and possibly also went on to fly Barber's next machine, the Valkyrie, but there appears to be no evidence for this.

On March 23rd ,1910 Barber applied for and was later awarded Patent No.7289 titled, "Improvements in Monoplane Flying Machines," and it is this patent which led to the Valkyrie.

Flight magazine published two photographs of "A NEW BRITISH FLYER". The aeroplane was called "Valkyrie 1" and the pictures show the aeroplane in flight. This was the first incarnation of Barber's most successful flying machines from which evolved a series of variations. However, as revolutionary as the Valkyrie design appears, a short mention of another such aeroplane is pertinent at this stage.

A NEW BRITISH FLYER.—The above photographs show "Valkyrie I" in flight on Tuesday, September 13th, prior to dismantlement for removal to the new works and school that the Aeronautical Syndicate, Ltd., have established at Hendon. This machine is the fifth of a series of experimental models with which trials have been carried out on Salisbury Plain during the past 17 months. It is a monoplane, and is characterised by several interesting features both in design and construction. There is no tail, and the pilot sits in front of the engine, which is in front of the main planes; he thus has a clear outlook in every direction. In front of the pilot is a leading plane, beneath which is the elevator.

It is interesting to note that the text here refers to Valkyrie 1 being the fifth of Barber's aeroplanes. There was a prototype Valkyrie before Valkyrie No 1, but this only accounts for 4 aeroplanes, unless the heavily modified first machine was counted as a separate machine. Flight, September 24, 1910.

In 1907, Herbert Leno, the son of the famous music hall artist Dan Leno, formed a partnership with brothers Ted and Bert Metzgar to build a monoplane designed by Bert, the "Metzgar and Leno No 1." The construction took four years and was carried out in a garage in the Clapham area of London, adjacent to Battersea.

By Autumn of 1911, the plane was ready for trials. It achieved a fifty-foot hop at a height of three feet. After this point, the partners ran out of money and the project was brought to a premature halt.

Metzgar and Leno monoplane at Shoreham. From Flights of Fancy *by Patrick Loobey*

We will leave the reader to decide who designed the Valkyrie but will mention the following: the garage in Old Town Clapham where Metzgar and Leno had been building their aeroplane since 1907 was less than a mile from the Battersea railway arches where Howard Wright had been established during the same period, and also to where Barber had migrated in 1909. Was it a coincidence that two very similar designs came from the same area independently? We are inclined to think not. Battersea was a small and somewhat unlikely area for the birthplace of aviation. The men working here would have instantly learned of any advances in aviation as discovered by their neighbouring pioneers.

We do not know how much if any input Howard Wright had on the design of the prototype Valkyrie. Some accounts have Wright building the plane, while others suggest that Barber and Wright had fallen out or parted company by that time. It seems logical that by the time the Valkyrie prototype was being built, Metzgar and Leno would have constructed a considerable portion of their machine, and that Howard Wright would have been aware of it. It bears mentioning that neither the Metzgar and Leno machine nor the prototype Valkyrie had a forward elevator. It is our conclusion that the Valkyrie was not Barber's own unique design but rather it evolved through either Howard Wright or Barber's knowledge of the Metzgar and Leno machine.[128]

It was reported that the first flight of the Valkyrie was over one mile in length. We do not know whether it was Barber or Woodrow who first flew it, but certainly Barber was flying it later that year when the ASL decamped to the newly opened Hendon Aerodrome. Several reports, some of which are included below enlighten us about that time:

YESTERDAY'S FLYING.

The Aeronautical Syndicate's new monoplane the "Valkyrie, No. 1" was brought into operation for the first time on the Hendon ground yesterday. Mr. Barber, who has already made some flights on the machine at Salisbury, again gave a very good exhibition and some half a dozen flights of about half a mile in length were made. At times the height of the monoplane was estimated at twenty-five feet. Daily flights Gnome type are also expected next week.

It is stated that Mons. Bleriot, the first flying man to cross the Channel, is likely to make Hendon a rendezvous for pupils, and this week-end one of his machines is expected at Colindale. Two others of the Bleriot-cum-Gnome type are also expected.

We learn with regret that Captain Rawlinson is still lying at the hospital at Boscombe, Bournemouth, as his ankle has had to be re-set. It is stated that he has given up all idea of future flying.

From Hendon and Finchley Times *Sept 23rd 1910*

Woodrow must have taught Barber well, as from this time on Horatio is reported as flying the Valkyrie on a very regular basis. The papers and aeronautical magazines of the time suggest he was a most excellent pilot.

Here is more from *Hendon and Finchley Times* Sept 23, 1910. The article starts with a narrative of the sheds being built at Hendon and continues:

"Looking into one of the sheds one gets a glimpse of an aeroplane. According to the *Aero* magazine, this machine is the property of the Aeronautical Syndicate Limited and is christened the Valkyrie 1. Experiments have been carried out throughout the year with this machine on Salisbury Plain, and the syndicate have now produced a machine with which they are satisfied will fly and give safety and satisfaction to the pilot.

"The machine is what's inaccurately known as the tail-first type, in that it has an elevator in the front of the main planes and no tail behind. Just below the elevator is a somewhat smaller fixed plane which acts as a damper to avoid too quick an action of the machine longitudinally. The engine is placed just in front of the main planes, and in front of the engine, sits the pilot. Twin rudders are fitted behind the central portion of the main planes. With a 35hp Green engine it weighs only 500lbs and although so light, is extremely strong, and is said to be practically unbreakable, judging from the number of rough landings it has had in the course of

---

[128] Note that the Dunne monoplane D7 has a similar structure, to both machines.

experimenting. The whole machine, including the propeller, has been manufactured at the firm's workshop on Salisbury Plain near Amesbury, and even the tyres of the wheels have been built to a special design. Most of the wood used is Honduras mahogany. During the ten days to 14th September, the machine was out about 5 times, and in those 5 trials flew between 50 and 60 miles. It is claimed that owing to the elevator and greatest length of the machine being in front of the pilot he is able to see as well as feel the slightest change in longitudinal balance of the machine. The designer claims that it is possible to descend with safely upon rougher ground than is practicable with any other type of machine. The outer portions of the main planes can be quickly dismounted for packing, a process which is facilitated by the peculiar type wire strainer which is used. The aeronautical syndicate have now sent the machine to the flying ground at Hendon, which will be their London Headquarters, though they will continue to carry out extensive experiments on Salisbury plain.

"An eye witness of some of the recent flights prior to this removal from Salisbury Plain tells us that in spite of a fairly high wind, this machine flew excellently. Getting off the ground straight away and making good flights nine times out of the ten starts on the part of the pilot, so that on the whole the machine has thoroughly proved its worth.

"A big machine is now under construction which is to be fitted with a 60 h.p. Green engine, and will carry two passengers and a pilot. Not counting the weight of the passengers, but including the pilot, oil, water and petrol for an hour, it will weigh only 15lbs to the horsepower. It is expected to be ready in about two weeks. On Tuesday of last week, before transporting the machine to Hendon the machine made eight or ten good flights at a height of 50 to 80 feet, these flights, including two full circles, and averaging 2.5 miles in length. A good show considering the pilot is quite self-taught."[129]

An advertisement appearing in the same journal states that flying will be taught daily and passenger trips will be made at the school of aviation at the Hendon Aerodrome. "We have read with interest Jules Verne's account of a voyage to the moon, and no doubt before long pilots and passengers will be furnishing us with an up to date account of such a journey, or of one as near as they can get to the celestial orb." A tongue-in-cheek remark maybe, but they only had 59 years to wait. It is possible some of them could have seen that prophecy come true.

The *Scotsman* published an article entitled *Aviation as a British Industry*.[130] "Another enterprising firm is the Aeronautical Syndicate, which, besides giving tuition at Hendon Aerodrome and Salisbury Plain, undertakes all descriptions of aeronautical work. This is the firm which has designed the Valkyrie monoplane, which to the casual observer would appear to be flying tail first, but as a matter of fact, is a tailless machine."

---

[129] This notion that the pilot was self-taught is up for discussion and Bertie Woodrow would have had something to say about that, but this is just Barber being Barber.
[130] *Scotsman* October 13, 1910

Flight magazine published frequent updates of Mr. Barber's achievements and fine flights and in December, they published a photograph of the "Valkyrie 2" in flight.

In the same issue, *Flight* reported that Valkyrie 3 was out on Thursday morning, but as the wind was dangerously gusty, the pilot decided to return to his shed.

The Valkyrie 2, a 3-seater flying at Hendon. From Flight *December 3, 1910.*

Some obvious improvements from Valkyrie 1 can be seen in the photograph above. Rudders are much further back on outriggers, and vertical planes have been added to the very front of the machine, both to increase lateral stability. These improvements were also added to Valkyrie 1 after removal to Hendon.

The *Daily Telegraph*[131] reported on the newly opened Hendon Airfield: "The Aeronautical Syndicate have their sheds and factory here. It is satisfactory to note that the last-named firm, who built the all-British Valkyrie machines invented by Mr. Barber, seems to be doing well. If the motors are not yet all that can be desired, the odd-looking monoplanes do their work well enough, being very steady in flight and easy to manipulate. The rather cumbrous under-frame gives security and protection to the aviator in case of a rough decent."

Barber submitted a letter[132] to the *Standard* in praise of that paper's financing of aviation competitions. The article is a reciprocal self-congratulation of the industry. The paper applauded the advancements in aviation by the likes of Barber, and Barber went into detail of what future competitions should and should not be. He warned of competitors building "freak" racing machines as a way of winning competitions, and asked that the competitions also consider reliability and safety, as that being more likely to encourage genuine sportsmen. He then suggested what upcoming competitions should be. The article finished with thoughts about the future of aviation:

"The opinion of many people is that the successful aviator is an acrobat[133] and when the public are tired of watching acrobatic feats, aviation will die a natural death! When a machine has flown from Paris to Berlin, from Berlin to Brussels, from Brussels to London and from London back to Paris, arriving there after a tour of over 1600 miles, the *Standard* will have done its share

---

[131] *Daily Telegraph* February 4, 1911
[132] The *Standard* March 22, 1911
[133] This is the point when Barber thought about coining the term "aerobatics," a portmanteau word made up from aero and acrobatic.

in convincing the world that aviation has left the exhibition stage behind and has become a practical thing which will revolutionize the locomotion of the future."

An article titled "Probable Flight of OBGs to Bedford" (see right) announced that two aviators including Barber were preparing to fly from Hendon to Bedford Grammar School of which they were "Old Boys." There appears to be no evidence that this flight actually took place.

In March 1911, two Valkyries appeared at The Aero and Motor Exhibition at Olympia, these being the Valkyrie 50hp B cross-country racing model, and the 60hp type C three-section passenger-carrying monoplane.

Two months later, in May 1911, accounts of an event at Hendon describe the personalities and abilities of the pilots involved.

The Parliamentary Aerial Defence Committee, of which Mr. Arthur Lee, MP was chairman, hosted an aviation demonstration to illustrate flying as applied to military purpose. Several airmen, including Barber were not permitted to fly at this event.

There seems to be no satisfactory explanation why the organizers refused Barber the chance to demonstrate except perhaps a certain rivalry between Barber and the owner of the aerodrome, Mr. Grahame-White.

Bedford and County Record   March 7, 1911

Howard Pixton's account[134] of the event is enlightening. He wrote in his diary, "The demonstration came to an end. Not until many of the people were leaving were we invited to fly. It didn't matter so much to me but Cody, he was furious, he resented this slight by Grahame-White and took it to heart. He had a great deal of flying experience, more than Grahame-White, having been employed by the government, and had already displayed military uses of kites for reconnaissance at the beginning of the century and he had built the famous Army Aeroplane No. 1. He complained, to Grahame-White that he [Grahame-White] intended this to be a one-man show with himself [Grahame-White] as the star turn, and it is a personal insult to us, having us standing impressively by our machines and then ignoring us.

"I [Pixton] agreed, so did A.V. [Roe]! Grahame-White's name was mud for the time being where Cody was concerned, but our bad treatment did not go unnoticed by the *Aero* magazine:

---

[134] *Howard Pixton: Test Pilot and Pioneer Aviator*, by Stella Pixton

THE AIRMAN'S PROTEST.

Explanation of the Refusal to Allow Mr. Barber to Fly.

Some discussion has arisen concerning the refusal of the aerodrome authorities to allow Mr. Barber, the designer of the Valkyrie monoplane, to take part in the tests. Mr. Barber, who had prepared his machine, stood up and announced, "This is the only all-British machine here, and they have refused to let me compete."

The Times expert says to-day that Mr. Barber is a very experienced airman, who has flown 8,000 miles, made eleven machines, and instructed thirty pupils.

A representative of Mr. Grahame-White's firm informed The Evening News to-day that the committee issued invitations to the airmen who took part, but not to airmen in general, and Mr. Barber's name had not been included.

Had he been allowed to exhibit his machine there was no reason why any other aviator should not have brought a machine and commenced a demonstration.

Mr. Barber was one of the tenants of the aerodrome but there were other tenants who had no part in the occasion.

Mr. Barber, who had prepared his machine, stood up and announced, "This is the only all-British machine here, and they have refused to let me compete." Evening News May 13, 1911.

'The new Roe biplane, which Pixton flew from Brooklands the same morning, distinguished itself by doing a very quick get off in the demonstration of starting, but after that, it was relegated to a corner till the evening when most of the notabilities had departed. S. F. Cody who arrived from Brooklands in magnificent style had to be content to look on till the evening. However, when he and Pixton did fly, their superiority in speed over the ordinary type of biplane was most marked.'

"After a circuit or two Cody had left, disgusted with the whole performance, but we were not the only two who suffered. Barber's machines, the Valkyrie's, similar to the Farman, had white-coated officials standing in front of them to ensure they would not fly. It would have been better if we hadn't been invited at all."

It appears that Grahame-White wanted the whole demonstration to be about his aeroplanes and that although others were invited, they did not have the chance to impress the Parliamentarians. It further seems that Barber was completely ostracised, presumably because Grahame-White thought he would be out-performed by Cody, Pixton, and Roe, and especially by Barber. We can conclude that Barber was a capable airman, and he could impress the crowd with his flying.

THE HENDON AERODROME :— A hitherto unpublished photograph taken during the Parl'amentary Demonstration. On the left is a racing Bleriot. Next is a Valkyrie, the white coats in front of it being the "guards" sent to prevent it from flying. On the right is Cody's big biplane. In the centre is a Bleriot, just landing, and beyond it marked out in chalk, is the deck of the Dreadnought, on which bombs were dropped.

The white-coated guards in front of the Valkyrie from Areo magazine

Mr. Lee, the event Chairman issued a statement about the oversight a couple of days later.

> Mr. Lee added that the unfortunate misunderstanding by which the Valkyrie all-British machines made by the Aeronautical Syndicate were not allowed to compete in the tests was not made known to him until the demonstration was over. The committee had not the slightest idea of favouring one machine more than another and is entirely unconcerned with the disputes between makers. Perhaps if the matter had been mentioned to him during the progress of the tests something might have been done even at that late hour to include the Valkyrie machines.
>
> At Hendon on Saturday several Valkyrie machines gave a splendid exhibition of flying. They performed every evolution known to aviation, rising to a height of 1000ft, gliding down with the engine stopped, in the mode of descent known as the vol-plane, and making left and right turns. One machine also ascended to a height of 500ft in a corkscrew spiral of only 120yds in diameter, the width was measured by the length of the battleship outline marked on the grass for the tests of the day before. About 2000 people were present, including a large number of members of Parliament, which suggests that Friday's demonstration has raised a lively and permanent interest in aviation amongst politicians.
>
> The *Standard* May 15, 1911

Reading between the lines, there seems little doubt that Grahame-White and Barber did not always get on with one another. In his books of the time such as *With the Airmen* and *The Aeroplane*, Grahame-White never mentions Barber, although he writes a great deal about his other contemporaries. This is most likely because he regarded Barber as his main competition or rival.

Further problems befell Barber later in May with the tragic loss of one of his pupils, Bernard Benson. The student died in a fatal accident in a Valkyrie at Hendon.

"Shortly before eight o'clock Mr. Benson, who was a learner in the Valkyrie School, commenced a flight with one of these monoplanes. He had travelled about a mile from the hangars and had reached a height of about 100ft when he attempted a vol-plane. He appeared to lose control, and the machine descended rapidly and struck the ground very violently. The monoplane overturned and the aviator was crushed beneath it. Mr. Bishop, the manager of the Aeronautical Syndicate, who witnessed the accident, stated that Mr. Benson, who was one of their most promising pupils, had covered about four circuits of the aerodrome, when he did what was much too difficult a thing for him to attempt: a vol-plane, which only an expert airman could do. He came down half the way and then lost control."[135]

Because this accident was only the third British aviation fatality, it generated an extraordinary amount of coverage in all the national newspapers. Barber made several statements extolling the virtues and safety of the Valkyrie in what we would today refer to as "damage limitation." From the *Courier* of May 30, 1911: "...the machine used was one of the best [Barber] had manufactured. [Barber] had used it himself a fortnight ago, and he had flown three continuous circuits with his hands above his head, thus showing its stability.

"At the inquest, the jury returned a verdict of misadventure. Mr. Du Parq, counsel for Mr. Benson said he was quite satisfied that no blame could be attached to Mr. Barber. As a witness, Barber said he thought that perhaps being emboldened by the ease and steadiness with which he was flying Mr. Benson was tempted to mount higher than a beginner should do. Possibly he became panic-stricken and lost his head. From his own experience [Barber] could say that when a height of 200ft is reached it seems to be at least 1000ft. When he first reached that height himself, he experienced that panic. And descended as quickly as possible. At the second venture the same height did not seem so bad. If Mr. Benson had followed all instructions, he would have turned off a little of the power, pointed the nose of the machine a little to the ground, and descended gradually."

> **FUNERAL OF MR. BERNARD BENSON.**
> The funeral of Mr. Bernard Benson, the young aviator who was killed whilst flying at Hendon, took place on Wednesday at Brookwood. Among the large number of mourners were Mr. and Mrs. Benson and Miss Benson, Mr. Medlicott (representing the Royal Aero Club), representatives of the Aeronautical Syndicate Company, the aviation school at Hendon, and the City and Guilds College, South Kensington. Many wreaths were received, including one from the students of the City and Guilds College.

The Jarrow and Tyneside Advertiser *of June 1911 reported on the funeral of Bernard Benson.*

Yet more negative publicity was to follow. At the opening of the Shoreham Aviation Ground in June of 1911 Barber was due to give an exhibition flight, but was prevented from doing so by

---

[135] The *Globe* May 26, 1911

high winds. After waiting for some days, he was threatened by a breach of contract suit. The case took some time to come to court and in May the following year, the following appeared in the *Sussex Gazette*:

"In a legal action at Brighton the other day Mr. H. C. Barber, the aviator…said that last summer he waited at the Aerodrome at Shoreham from June 26th to July 5th for a suitable day to make a flight back to Hendon.

"But did not the aviators taking part in the European circuit fly on July 3rd?" he was asked. Yes, replied the inventor of the Valkyrie but they were all regular dare-devils, induced to risk their lives by a bait of £10,000. And now comes news of a terrible accident to Védrines[136] who was one of those regular dare-devils."[137]

Again, as so many times with newspaper article of this nature, we get only the first part of the story. There appears to be no other reference to this case or its resolution. It appears that in this situation, Barber was being perfectly sensible by not flying in the less than perfect weather. Today this would be applauded, but at that time when everyone was most keen to see an aeroplane flying, it may have been considered differently.

In July of 1911, Barber gave four Valkyrie planes to the military. *Flight* reported that "…with remarkable generosity, Mr. H. Barber in his presentation to the British nation of four of his military monoplanes has in a practical way come to the rescue of the British nation in making it possible for practical work now to proceed in the Navy, in addition to the Army."[138]

The machines presented were as follows:
1. One Valkyrie military monoplane fitted with 30hp Green engine. To carry one person. Speed 45mph. Built especially strong, and particularly adapted for use of beginners. In flying order.

2. One Valkyrie military monoplane to carry pilot and passenger (or two light passengers) fitted with 60-8hp Green engine. Speed 40-50mph. Especially suitable for pupil passenger work. In flying order.

3. One Valkyrie military monoplane to carry one person. Latest design of this type. Fitted with a 40-50hp Green engine. Speed 45mph. In flying order.

4. One Valkyrie military monoplane. Latest passenger-carrying type. Built to carry 50hp Gnome engine. Speed50-55mph. Just finished.

---

[136] Jules Védrines was trying to win the Pommery Cup awarded for the longest flight in a straight line in one day. While he had already travelled 200km, travelling at speeds of 160 kph, his journey was disrupted by engine failure, forcing him to make an emergency landing. Compromised by telegraph wires, he came crashing down on a railway line, seriously wounding his head and narrowly escaping the arrival of a train.
[137] *Sussex Gazette* May 2, 1912
[138] *Flight* July 8, 1911

"Not only has Mr. Barber presented these machines to the nation, but he has also offered his services as designer, constructor and pilot, to the governments as much as his time permits. Although no conditions were attached to the gifts, he suggested that two machines be allotted to the Navy, as they are particularly adapted to being fitted with combination floats[139] and wheels to allow them to arise from or descend upon either water or land. This suggestion was accepted, and two accordingly will be allotted to the Navy."

However, in *The Birth of Military Aviation*, author Hugh Driver puts a slightly different slant on the story.

> "The short-lived Hendon-based Aeronautical Syndicate Ltd also presented the war Office with at least one of their peculiarly spartan Valkyrie canard monoplanes. However, this philanthropic gesture served only to hasten the firm's imminent demise. In fact Horatio Barber, stung by his company's unaccountable disbarment from the Parliamentary Aerial Defence Committee's Hendon display in May 1911, had initially offered 4 Valkyrie monoplanes to the military and Naval authorities, and two used models were duly forwarded to Lieutenant Samson of Eastchurch; but documentary evidence survives for only one such aircraft, a newly built two-seater model, being accepted by the War Office in August 1911 - and even then, the army was to provide the engine. Indeed, Lieutenant [Reginald Archibald] Cammell supervised the troublesome installation of a 50hp Gnome motor at Hendon the following month. On Sunday 17th September 1911 he took the aeroplane out for a trial flight, with the intention of flying it on to Farnborough that same day. A fatal crash resulted."
>
> *The Birth of Military Aviation*, Hugh Driver

Eleven days later, on 28th September 1911, Samson reported that both aircraft in his care were also in a potentially dangerous condition, the woodwork being old and strained, and the fabric had worn thin and perished. Moreover, the wire work had had to be renewed, and he described the aluminium fittings as unsuitable for aeroplanes. The engines - in this case presumably the original Green engines, although he does not specify - he acknowledged as being in fair condition, but inherently unreliable anyway, and thus useless for extended flight. Bearing all this in mind, and also perhaps being affected by Cammell's death, he dismissed the worth of either machine to the Royal Navy, concluding that they held no practical value for either experimental or instructional work.

---

[139] No evidence of a Valkyrie ever having been fitted with floats has come to light to date.

Only one week before Cammell's accident, Captain Fulton had complained to the War Office's about their acceptance of undeveloped machines as part of its utilization of what was called private enterprise.

Most of the national and regional newspapers carried coverage of Barber's gift. The article right is typical.

Through July and August, Barber's assorted flying activities were widely reported. Of particular note was his cross-country flight from London to Brighton and back[140] and with his passenger Miss Eleanor Treyhawke- Davies, with whom he had made other flights.

The trip was newsworthy owing to several factors. Firstly, she was the first lady passenger to make such a long cross-country journey. Further, the trip was punctuated with stops for fuel and repairs due to a hard landing. Secondly, on the return leg, the machine was said to have reached 95mph. Thirdly, Miss Trehawke -Davies wrote an account of the event whilst in flight, a copy of which appeared in the press.

> **FOUR AEROPLANES PRESENTED TO THE GOVERNMENT.**
>
> **CROSS CHANNEL FLIGHT POSTPONED.**
>
> The Secretary of the War Office announces that the well-known aviation expert, Mr. H. Barber, has generously offered to present to his Majesty's Government four "Valkyrie" military aeroplanes, with a view to encouraging aviation in the Naval and Military Services. His Majesty's Government have gladly accepted Mr. Barber's public-spirited gift, and, in accordance with the donor's suggestion, two machines will be allotted to the Royal Navy and two to the Army. Mr. Barber's offer was accompanied by no conditions, and his Majesty's Government highly appreciate his generous and patriotic act.
> Mr. Barber's Valkyrie machines, as now perfected, are the result of two years' experimental work. The machine is a monoplane, but it combines several of the features of the biplane, and was specially designed for military work. It is so constructed as to be easily transportable. It is also claimed that the Valkyries are very easily controlled, and Mr. Barber, who is himself an experienced airman, has on several occasions flown considerable distances without putting his hand on the control. Mr. Barber has spent a large sum on experimental work.

Birmingham Daily Mail *June 30, 1911*

> I'm in a Valkyrie monoplane-Pilot Mr. Barber, 300ft high at moment of writing - going higher - never been so high in my life - exhilaration intense "own the earth" feeling.
>
> 500 feet high, Harrow well in sight, White City on left hand. Crossing stream North London on right. Smoke haze obscuring - wind always in front - imagination or fact?
>
> Sheep appear stuck on the ground like cows- Noah's Ark look
>
> 2000ft higher, joy going down. Landing 7.10 pm. Speed over 60 miles an hour.

On his return, Barber had time to give exhibition and passenger flights, the proceeds of which were given to a local hospital. These and other similar flights which had been pre-booked with Barber could be said to be at the forefront of scheduled plane travel, another aspect of aviation in which Barber was a pioneer.

---

[140] A very good account of the London to Brighton trip was written by Chris Tod of the Steyning Museum. See Resources.

Barber refuelling at Steyning after repairs, following a forced landing. Terry Grace collection

This clipping from the Daily Express *July 28, 1911 documents Barber's involvement with aerial photography. From his scrapbook in the Hendon RAF Museum.*

In August of 1911 Barber was to fly to Paris with a lady passenger but the flight was postponed. The *Evening Standard* of August 19, 1911, covered the story: "Ariel Bookings, Hundred percent more passengers at Brooklands and Hendon".

"Within the past few weeks the number of aerial journeys booked at Brooklands and Hendon, and other aerodromes has increased to the extent of 100 percent." Barber's heavily publicized long-distance trips no doubt contributed to this increased popularity.

The *Evening Standard* continued: "The growing reliability of machines and increasing skills of the airmen have mainly led to the popularity of flying. Mr. Barber the pilot and inventor of the Valkyrie monoplane, whose headquarters are at Hendon, has booked £800 worth of passenger flights, and his "fares" require to be taken to all parts of the country."

Tragedy struck again in early September 1911. Another British aviator, Lieutenant Cammell had been killed while he flew a Valkyrie. At the height of about 90ft, the machine tilted and fell to the ground with a terrific crash. He was rescued from the wreckage and taken to the Central London Sick Asylum where he was found to be dead, having succumbed to his terrible injuries. Witnesses said that on reaching Cammell, he had bones protruding from his legs, and one of the planes stays was piercing his back.

The machine was the new Valkyrie which Barber had donated to the military and on which Cammell had spent time supervising the installation of a Gnome engine prior to this flight. It was the first time he had flown an aeroplane of this type, although he had previously been a passenger with Barber.

"Death by misadventure was the verdict of the coroner on Lieutenant R. A. Cammell R. E. Mr. Horatio Barber, technical advisor to the Aeronautical Syndicate, said he had presented to the Government three Valkyrie machines with engines and one without. The machine concerned in the accident was the latter. He had thoroughly tested it.

"In reply to the coroner, Barber said he accounted for the accident by the fact that Lieutenant Cammell was accustomed to a Farman machine. When he made the turn, the machine banked up. In a Farman, this would have been rectified by moving a lever. In the Valkyrie it was necessary to push the right foot forward to adjust the rudder. This he thought Cammell had omitted to do. Had he done so even at the last moment it would have righted the machine." I think the accident was caused," Mr. Barber added, "by Lieutenant Cammell using his control as he would on a Farman machine." He considered Lieutenant Cammell attempted too much."[141]

The First Airmail Flight

The representation of a Valkyrie flying on the occasion of the first aerial postal delivery was depicted on this Will's Cigarettes card. But, in fact, the Valkyrie was only used for the rehearsal for the main event.

---

[141] *Hendon and Finchley Times* Sept. 22 1911

In the image[142] shown right, the "undress" rehearsal shows a Valkyrie being used. However, a Bleriot was flown on the actual first aerial mail.

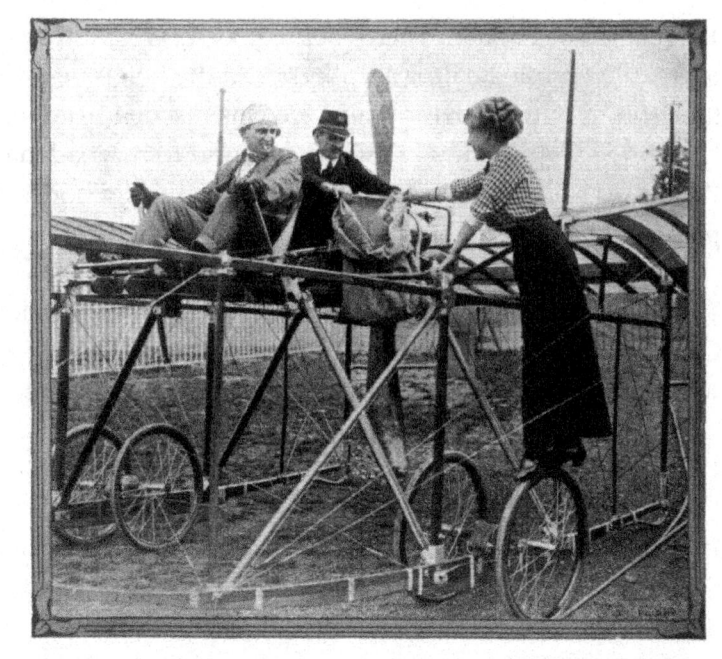

Front page of September 2, 1911 Flight *magazine. The aeroplane is a Valkyrie.*

The May 2007 newsletter of the British Airmail Society published a query from one of its members, wondering why there were two signatures on a postcard commemorating the first air mail flight. The member recognized Prentice's name, but wondered, "Who was this H. Barber?"

The screen capture right is the newsletter editor's answer to the query.

Horatio Barber taught himself to fly, passing his "Brevet No. 30" at Hendon on 22nd November 1910 on a Valkyrie monoplane, and is known to have been flying on Salisbury Plain in 1909. He went on to build over twenty of these Valkyrie pusher planes and is well known in Shoreham as he carried the world's first commercial freight by air from Shoreham to Hove on 4th July 1911 (Osram light bulbs). Barber went on to set up at Hendon the Aeronautical Syndicate Ltd. This was prior to Graham White arriving at Hendon. He decided to retire from aircraft manufacturing in 1912 due to financial pressures. When the company was dissolved it was sold to Handley Page. Part of the Aeronautical Syndicate Ltd.'s enterprises at Hendon Aerodrome was a flying school, in which Ridley Prentice was an instructor. Hence the reason why both signatures appear together on the card.

Ridley Prentice had passed his "Brevet No. 66" also at Hendon on 4th April 1911. He had been a pupil of C. Hubert (of Hendon-Windsor flight fame due to his crash). He also went on to set up a company in 1911 at Hendon, the General Aviation Contractors, who were an agency for the Anzani Aero engines. In all event, a lot of very local enterprise.

The reverse of a postcard commemorating the first airmail flight with autographs of two instructors at the flying school at Hendon. British Airmail Society newsletter Vol 50 No. 197 May 2007

---

[142] *Flight* September 2, 1911

115

In late September Barber took a short holiday on the continent and on his return, announced that he was constructing a new biplane with many novel features. The design was fairly orthodox although possibly slightly ahead of its time. The pilot would be seated behind the main plane in a boat-shaped body. It would have a 50hp Gnome engine driving two propellers by means of chains. Note that Barber made no use of the co-axial contra-rotating propellers as he did on his first plane. On the face of it, this doesn't sound too revolutionary, although his patented balancers were incorporated and proved successful. This plane eventually was known as the "Viking."

In October came the news of the latest Valkyrie incarnation, the new Valkyrie racer.[143] This machine, although little different from its predecessors, was praised for its detail and care of construction. Barber used copper and nickel-plated steel fittings in this machine for the first time, possibly in response to the criticism of the aluminium fittings used on the Valkyries he gave to the Navy.

Also in October, Barber was interviewed about flying on Sundays. His response was recorded in the *Northern Whig* article entitled "Vicar and Aviators".

> "The vicar of Hendon approached the Home Secretary to say that Sunday flying interfered with praying and preaching at the parish church.
>
> Barber replied that it was "A rather high-handed course of action on the part of the vicar." He continued, "If any grounds for complaint exist, I wonder why the reverent Gentleman did not first communicate with the aviators. Personally, I would have willingly refrained from flying during the hours of divine service, and no doubt other aviators would have done the same."
>
> The vicar also complained of people travelling through the churchyard to be able to spectate at the aerodrome."

A new School for Aeronautical Engineers opened late in 1911 at the Hendon Aerodrome.[144] It was the first of its kind. "Judging from the number of young engineers who have joined, the experiment will succeed at once. Its technical chief is Mr. H. Barber, the well-known aviator, who has done so much to promote the science by experiment. A complete course in practical construction and design is given."

This school seems to have been relatively short-lived, as apart from a similar article about its opening, little further appears in the press. The facility remained open after ASL closed.

---

[143] *Flight* October 14, 1911
[144] *Sheffield Daily Telegraph* December 15, 1911

Barber tested the new Viking biplane in January 1912. As reported in *Flight,* "Wind and fog prevented any flying until last Thursday, when Mr. Barber took the new Viking biplane off the stocks and subjected the machine to numerous exhaustive tests. Mr. Barber first ran the machine over the ground at high speed in order to thoroughly prove the strength of the landing chassis. He then let the machine have its way into the air and made many very successful flights. She got away from earth after a remarkably short run and appears to have extraordinary climbing powers. The patent balancers proved enormously effective, the slightest movement of the control wheel instantly combatting any wind gust. Altogether the initial trials were an unequalled success.

"The next day, Barber made several more flights in the Viking, each of over half an hour. In very disturbed air conditions, he took the Viking up to several hundred feet. It was felt the Viking would make an exceptionally comfortable passenger carrier, and Mr. Barber found very little wind pressure in his face, due to the protection of the torpedo-shaped housing around the pilot."

ASL Viking

Flight magazine wrote a long article on the Viking, on 20th January 1912, with many pictures of the plane including details of the novel warping balancers and of the controls and landing gear arrangement. The article ends with a glowing tribute to the work of the ASL: "The Viking biplane undoubtedly represents a considerable advance on the admittedly sound work of the ASL establishment, and if sheer merit goes for anything these days, it should pave the way for an exceedingly prosperous business year."

Unfortunately, these predictions were proven inaccurate.

Meanwhile, in February 1912 Barber became the first Associate Fellow of the Aeronautical Society, and in so doing became the first person in the UK to gain an aeronautical degree. Others included at that time were J.W. Dunne, W.O. Manning, F. Handley-Page and Horace Short. For Barber to be named was a significant honour, as many high-profile aviators and aeronautical engineers were not considered at that time.

Various reports of ASL in the next couple of months detailed their progress, including new Valkyrie models with wing warping instead of wing flaps, but the end was in sight.

On 9th April 1912, we find one of the first notices of the demise of Aeronautical Syndicate in the *Western Daily Mercury*, right.

Many reports from that period speculated about why the ASL collapsed and several claimed that Barber spent too much money on experimentation. If this was true, then the belief is at odds with the *Mercury's* report that the ASL was "plentifully supplied with capital", and that it was the refusal of the War Office to consider or respect the ASL machines which led to Barber becoming disillusioned with this area of the industry.

A few days later he announced in *Flight* magazine that he intended to give up flying and construction of aeroplanes, citing the steadily increasing cost of keeping to the forefront of advancements and technology. He said that it was necessary to build a new plane every two to three months and that, needless to say, a hobby on those lines was pretty expensive. Interesting use of the word "hobby" in Barber's remarks.

Lieutenant Samson's criticism regarding the donated Valkyries may have also contributed to Barber's decision to sell the business. Likewise, although being exonerated from blame in both cases, the deaths of both Benson and Cammell occurred while flying his machines.

We do know by now, however, that Barber often changed direction in his career choices during his life, so perhaps he was ready for something different.

When interviewed about his plans, he stated that he was undecided what he would do in the future. He had intended to go on an extended cruise in the Mediterranean, but owing to several advances he had lately received from aeronautical firms, he suggested that he might possibly continue his connection with aviation as a consulting aeronautical expert. He told *Flight* that, "A book on his experiences and on the possibilities of aviation will probably soon appear."

Flight magazine also commented with the following:

"The ASL which has ranked high among the pioneering firms of aeroplane constructors in England, is going out of business owing to its main supporter, Mr. H. Barber having decided to give up flying, and to the disinclination of the directors to go to the expense of equipping the kind of factory necessary to enable the firm to hold its position.

"The ASL was formed early in 1909, and the principal shareholders are Messrs Battersby, Fergusson, Schmetiau and Ridley-Prentice. Nearly thirty[145] machines have been constructed all of which have flown, and one of which was the first British monoplane to carry passengers, a record which was held for nearly a year; and a great many long-distance cross-country passenger flights have been accomplished. A flying school and also a school of aeronautical engineering has been maintained. The work of the company has been distinguished for the soundness and excellence of construction details, and the staff of mechanics has certainly ranked amongst the best in the country."

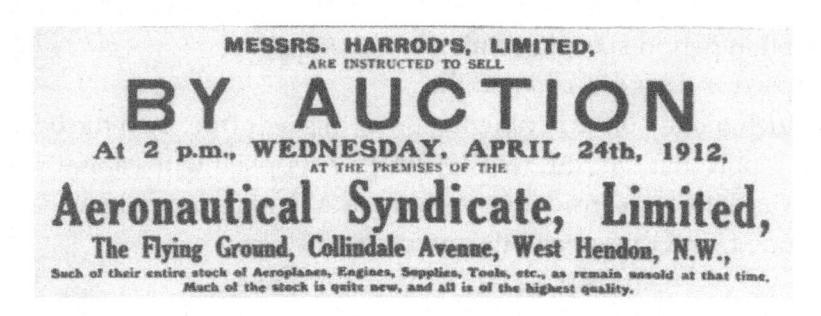

> **MESSRS. HARROD'S, LIMITED,**
> ARE INSTRUCTED TO SELL
> # BY AUCTION
> At 2 p.m., WEDNESDAY, APRIL 24th, 1912,
> AT THE PREMISES OF THE
> **Aeronautical Syndicate, Limited,**
> The Flying Ground, Collindale Avenue, West Hendon, N.W.,
> Such of their entire stock of Aeroplanes, Engines, Supplies, Tools, etc., as remain unsold at that time.
> Much of the stock is quite new, and all is of the highest quality.

On April 4, 1912, an announcement appeared in *The Aeroplane* detailing an auction of the ASL stock by Messrs Harrods Ltd.

Before this auction was held, Messrs Handley-Page stepped in and bought the entire stock. This was proclaimed to be an altruistic gesture by Handley-Page to prevent a quality business enduring the humiliation of a public auction. Others, however, thought it a purely astute business move, in which he bought the entire stock at a fraction of its worth.

The auction included four aeroplanes and a large number of aeroplane engines. In his book *Bloody Paralysers*, Rob Langham wrote that Handley-Page wanted the Gnome engines and aeroplane spares and after having selected these, he sold the remaining stock to George Holt Thomas of what was to become Airco. Handley-Page is said to have made a fortune from this deal and in so doing was able to enter the industry at another level and push forward his illustrious career.

On April 18, 1912, Barber flew farewell exhibition flights, in a Valkyrie at Hendon.

Never one to stay still for long, Barber announced he was to become an aeronautical consultant and took up offices at St. James' St. London. His work was to include drawings, design and construction. Immediately, the Farman brothers retained him to supervise construction of their planes. Later, Barber built at least one Farman type plane in which he replaced the mahogany components with spruce which made the plane much lighter without compromising any strength.

---

[145] It is difficult to account for this number of machines. Other sources put the number at 20 or so.

Flight magazine gave him a glowing valediction:

> "A pioneer indeed is Mr. Barber. Connected with the Aeronautical Syndicate, since deceased, he was the first constructor in England to produce a totally original monoplane - the Valkyrie - and fly it, while a larger machine of the same type was the first all-British monoplane to carry passengers.
>
> Today as an independent consulting aeronautical engineer with a suite of consulting chambers at 59 Pall Mall, he holds an equally unique position in the aviation world.
>
> As for the value of the service, who else over here can boast of three years crammed full of designing constructing and piloting."
>
> June 8, 1912 *Flight*

By July of that year, there was news of another design from Barber. Although details were secret, it was reported that this machine was to be a monoplane specially designed for the military or an "engine of offence" as it was termed, virtually an "aerial destroyer."

Details of the original design are uncertain, but plans may have actually developed into the Grahame-White Type V1, which appeared in 1913, shown below.

Grahame-White type V1 Flight *magazine*

This strange but innovative design was apparently initiated by Barber and completed by J.D. North an employee of the Aeronautical Syndicate Ltd. The control wires for the tail surfaces were carried inside the upper boom, an arrangement credited to Barber. The somewhat Vickers F B 5 "Gunbus" -like machine had the novel design of the upper support for the triangular section fuselage being a continuation of the propeller shaft.

One of the main features of this experimental Grahame-White plane was that a passenger could lay prone and get an excellent view of the target below. Barber pointed out this advantage of his canards, from an early stage. Furthermore, there have been many successful canard planes since that time. The Saab Viggen and Eurofighter Typhoon come immediately to mind.

In his fine 1933 book *History of British Aviation 1908-1914*, R. Dallas Brett pointed out that should any imbalance or breakage of the propeller occur, then the whole plane would break up. It owes its conception to Mr. Barber, who ought to have known better. After one abortive trial flight, the project was abandoned. It seems that Barber designed two biplanes for Grahame-White, but there appears to be little or no information on the second machine.

Even though Barber declared that he was giving up flying, he performed "hands-off" demonstrations at Hendon in early July 1912.

It is important to note that although Barber was still flying the Valkyrie, its days were numbered. Not just because of the collapse of the ASL, but because of its canard configuration which was seen as unconventional even at that stage. Strange then, that in mid-1913, the Bleriot Company started experiments with "an armoured warplane" which bears a striking resemblance to a Valkyrie.

Late in 1912 Barber travelled to Constantinople, during the First Balkan War. In the December 14 interview with *Flight* magazine titled "Aircraft in Warfare, a Chat with Mr. Barber", he was asked why he had chosen to go to Turkey. Barber replied, "… just to see what there was to be seen and learn what there was to be learned."

On his return, several newspapers ran articles that detailed the trip. Barber described the severe fighting at Chataldja. He also recalled his audience with the country's Prime Minister, or Grand Vizier who was an active old man who waited for Barber to salute before addressing him.

As a result of his tour, Barber had much of interest to tell. "When I got to Constantinople, I had an idea from newspapers reports that there was a lot of trouble in the capital, but I found everything quiet and orderly. Certainly, the Christian population was a little jumpy, but there was nothing in the way of panic. All the same, at the beginning they did not know what was going to happen.

"Directly we got to Constantinople we could hear the guns going at Chataldja. It seemed extraordinary to see the streets the same as usual, and the music halls crowded, with the roar of the guns as the accompaniment to the singers. Wounded men and refugees were arriving in tens of thousands. All the mosques had been turned into hospitals, although later the larger number of the wounded were sent to San Stefano.

"The scenes here were terrible. There were hundreds of men lying about, dead and dying. Before I came away, however, a great improvement had taken place in the Turkish arrangements for dealing with the wounded, and chaos had given place to organization.
"I went to the front at Chataldja several times and must say that the men in the trenches impressed me most favourably. Men were of course constantly getting hit by bullets, and the next man, notwithstanding the hail of bullets, would shoulder his wounded comrade and walk with him to a place of safety."[146]

As for what he learned, Barber discovered that the Turkish military air service was not particularly well organized. The air machines had arrived but had been damaged, and there was no one there to repair them properly. The Grand Vizier recommended Barber to the Minister of War, and consequently he took over supervision of the repair of the planes. Barber proceeded to the scene of action and found the aeroplanes in the charge of two young Turkish officers and a French pilot, and he was largely instrumental in making the planes airworthy. It is said that Barber actually flew the repaired planes, and in so doing became the first English aviator to see active service.

After remaining in Constantinople for ten days and spending almost every day at the battle scene and collecting information which was extremely valuable to the military aviation world, he returned to London to resume his consultancy work.

At the end of the *Evening Telegraph* article is a mention of Barber's interest in dirigibles and that he had taken out patents related to their design and use. (See Appendix 6.) "From certain drawings of which [the reporter had] been favoured with a private view, it seems likely that something extremely interesting in this direction will materialize in the near future." Barber also took lessons on and piloted airships. Indeed, in his account of his trip to Turkey, Barber said, "If the Turks had possessed a dirigible, they could have retrieved their earlier misfortunes by throwing the Bulgarian lines into a state of panic."

In the same issue, *Flight* magazine reported that Maurice Farman visited the Grahame-White works where Barber was supervisor. Farman was exceedingly pleased with the manner in which the construction was carried out.

By December of 1912, Mr. Barber had been acting for some time as the sole consulting expert to all the Lloyd's of London underwriters who handled aviation risk. This post came about as a direct result of Barber approaching Lloyds asking for third party coverage for his flying school. Lloyd's had no experience in this area of insurance at that time and asked Barber to write the policy himself, which he duly did. The policy was accepted by Lloyd's. This was the first aviation insurance issued in England and hence was another first for Barber. It was also to be the first step in another of his many changes in careers.

---

[146] *Evening Telegraph and Post* (Dundee) December 4, 1912

The Barber name appears in the press a few times more regarding his part in the design of the Grahame-White type V1 and is mentioned in *Flight* magazine on January 11, 1913.

Barber had his first lesson towards an Airship Pilot's certificate on April 5, 1913. The school was run by Ernest Thompson Willows, a pioneer of dirigibles. At that time, Willows was the only holder of a private airship licence.

The Willows No 5 in which Barber is thought to have flown

At the Willows Aircraft School, *Flight* reported[147] that "Mr. Willows took off with three pupils, Mr. H. Barber, Capt. Bernal and Mr. R.W. Crocker. The balloon drifted over St. Albans cathedral just as the clock was striking five. Luton was passed over and a landing was effected at Streatly a few miles beyond Luton at 6.30 pm. The weather was hazy with occasional rainstorms."

Barber applied for patent No. 22802/12 Dirigible balloons, in July 1913.

By December of 1913 and owing to the growth of his insurance connections, Barber moved to city offices at Capel house, 54 New Broad Street, E.C. so as to be nearer to Lloyd's. He still retained his office at 25 Ryder Street, St. James, S.W.

Aeronautics magazine of October 15, 1914, published an article entitled "The Deposition of metal upon wood". This article discusses the importance of a metallic coating on propellers of Hydroplanes. "A Mr. Barber we understand was the first to use a metal-sheathed propeller, the covering being obtained by depositing copper in a bath on a wooden propeller, which had been prepared for this by means of the application of finely powdered plumbago [lead] which

---

[147] *Flight* April 26th, 1913

converted the wooden surface into the conducting medium necessary." In other words, the props were electro-plated.

Royal Flying Corps / Royal Air Force

In 1914 Barber was a 2nd Lieutenant in the Royal Flying Corps, first at Upavon in Wiltshire, where he was awarded his Brevet. He achieved the rank without having to undergo the normal examination and this caused him some embarrassment. However, this seems to have been the practice for experienced airmen since it is reported that Busteed was also not required to take the usual test.

In their article, *14 Squadron; A First War History; Part 1* (Cross and Cockade Spring 2011), Mike O'Connor and Mike Napier relate the problems of a massively increasing army and an equivalent requirement in the Royal Flying Corps. Fifty squadrons were initially proposed by HQ RFC, but the Secretary of State instructed that figure should be doubled.

Both pilots and aeroplanes were in short supply. The solution was to form a squadron of semi-trained pilots around a small group of experienced pilots and to build strength as aeroplanes became available. Thus 14 Squadron was born, with three experienced pilots, namely Capt. R.O. Abercrombie, Lt., R.E. Lewis 2Lt., and H.C. Barber, together with two trainees. They used aeroplanes from RFC School Shoreham.

In May, the Squadron moved to Hounslow Heath where it began to receive its own aeroplanes including Martinsydes and BE2c Scouts. Later they received Caudrons and Maurice Farman Longhorn training aeroplanes. Barber was in charge of all flying training in England. An amusing anecdote recalls that although his manner was somewhat reserved, Barber's voice was so loud that when trainee pilots were in the air, he could shout instructions to them from the ground.

During this time, his third wife Bertha was living in Manningford Abbots near Pewsey, Wiltshire. Presumably, this was from the time Horatio was based at Upavon.

During his career in the RFC, Barber was promoted to Lieutenant August 12, 1914, and then Temporary Captain on March 18, 1915, and finally to Captain on September 1, 1915.

Barber suffered periods of ill health. On July 14, 1916, he was declared unfit for any duty for two weeks and on August 19, for three weeks. On September 21, 1916, he was declared unfit for both General Service and Home Service. December 9, 1916, he was pronounced permanently unfit for General Service but fit for Home Service.

Based on information found on his service record, he transferred between units several times. First, he was stationed with 3rd RAS (Reserve Aeroplane Squadron) Netheravon, but on March 15, 1915, he moved to 4th Wing with a view to appointment as Commanding Officer, and then to RAP (Reserve Aeroplane Park?) on November 3, 1915. On 26th October to ASRN(SAD?) as Officer in Charge of Officer Instruction. On 6th July 1916 to 1 School of Aeronautics, and on 20th January 1916 to Central Flying School as I/C Theory and Construction. During his service, he invented a rig for training fighting pilots in gunnery. In the picture, right, Barber is seen demonstrating the apparatus. There seems to be little information on its use or usefulness.

Captain Horatio Barber in his invention used to train pilots. Note the aeroplane wheels. Pioneers of British Aviation, Aeronautics, 1919

In August 1918 Barber travelled to New York from Liverpool. Most of his fellow passengers were members of the British Expeditionary Force or Royal Air Force staff.

On 16th September 1918 he registered at the Central Park Arsenal in New York and indicated that his "permanent home address" was the Savoy Hotel. See image below.

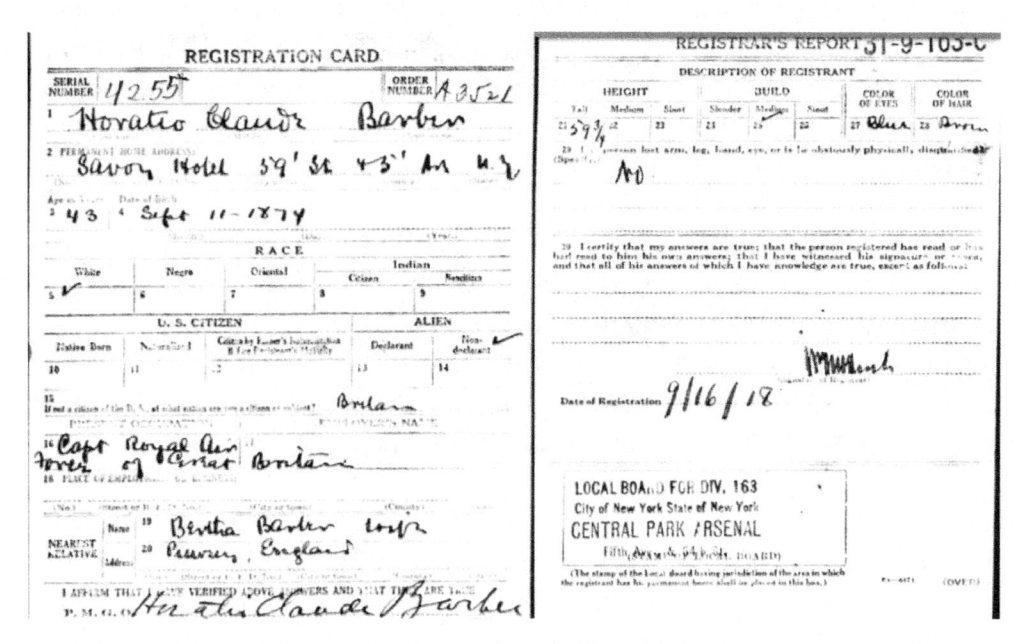

Barber's registration with the Central Park Arsenal, New York, September 16, 1918. One other fact to come from this document is that Barber was not, as suggested by others, to be a tall man, as he was about average height at less than 5 foot 10 inches.

We believe that the purpose of this trip was to consult on the training of Canadian pilots, an effort first carried out by the RFC and then continued by the RAF. Since he was Officer in

Command of all British flying training, likely Barber's visit to New York was in some way connected to this training either in Canada or America.

When England and Germany went to war in 1914, the dominion of Canada was the first to come to England's aid. For the first few years of the war Canada, had no air force and most of its strength lay in its army. But many Canadians wished to join the Royal Flying Corps and become pilots. This was possible only with the consent of their Commanding Officer. The need for Canadian airmen did not become apparent until mid-1916 when Allied casualties need to be replaced. Britain had contemplated using Canada as a source of replacement for airmen as early as 1915. The Corps sent officers to Canada to recruit pilots, some of whom had been trained by America.

Bringing men from Canada to Britain for training as pilots was logistically inefficient, so in summer of 1916, negotiations began to establish RFC training facilities in Canada. Toronto was the headquarters of this training program, with several flying grounds across the country. Camp Borden, west of Barrie, Ontario, was the main training ground. Beamsville near Hamilton, Ontario, was an aerial fighting training school. This facility had accommodation for 400 students and 100 officers. These schools proved to be successful and continued until the end of the war. When the weather became too inclement for flying in the Canadian winter, the schools would decamp south to Fort Worth Texas.[148]

Canadian pilot training in Fort Worth ended in April 1918. It is possible that Barber was in Texas earlier, but more likely he was consultant on the continuing training programme at either Borden or Beamsville.

Barber returned to Britain on October 7, 1918.

The house in Pewsey where Bertha, his third wife was living and presumably the house which had been their home during the first World War was "The Butts" in the village of Manningford Abbots. Throughout his life, Barber seems to have had a great taste in architecture and this house pictured here is no exception. The Arts and Crafts house was built in 1906 by the architect MH Baillee-Scott.

The Butts, Manningford Abbots, home to Mr. and Mrs. Barber during WW1.
www.onthemarket.com/details/3925949/

---

[148] *Royal Flying Corps Borden to Texas to Beamsville*, 1979 William E. Chajkowsky

> The final RAF report on Barber gives a good account of his skills and experience and his valuable contribution to aviation.
>
> - Resigned
> - Built and flew 28 aeroplanes on various engines during 1908-1912.
> - RAC pilots' certificate No. 30.
> - Some experience as an aeronaut and airship pilot, and in airship design.
> - Consulting aeronautical engineer 19/12/14 acting for Lloyd's [of London] among others. Made a special study of aeroplane risks for three years before the war, fixing all premiums and policy conditions and reporting upon losses.
> - Travelled extensively.
> - Since joining RFC, flown Farman, B.E.2c, Gnome-Avro. 3 years' experience in technical training and discipline of Officers and Men, designing instructional material and preparation of technical data.

In 1919, as part of a series entitled *Pioneers of British Aviation*, Aeronautics magazine published a two-page biography of Horatio Barber. The author, although not named, mentioned that he had taken very many flights with Barber in late 1910 and so was familiar with him.

This piece is not without criticism of Barber's skills and achievements, but is certainly written by a man who had a hero-like fondness for the aviator. The article offers interesting insight to the times and Barber's work in aviation.

We record it here, nearly in its entirety, by way of closing this chapter of Barber's life. Author comments are within square brackets.

Captain H. BARBER, R.A.F., with some of his staff of instructors

From Aeronautics *magazine.*

Pioneers of British Aviation: Barber's Biography

Ability to fly in 1910 is almost sufficient, in our estimation, to entitle a man to be counted with the pioneers of aviation. To have flown at that early date on a machine of his own design and construction, and at a period when the number of successful British designers could be counted on the fingers of one hand, is more than enough. Mr. H. Barber did all this and more. He introduced structural details that were afterwards universally adopted. He set a standard in structural soundness. He contributed to the solution of the problem of stability.

Mr. Barber is a remarkable man, with a very peculiar temperament. At the time he began to fly, the average passenger would have regarded him as almost the exact opposite of the intrepid airman or birdman type. He struck one as extremely nervous and altogether too studious for such chancy work as airmanship was in those days. Nor could one see him revelling in engine oil, glue and shavings.

It is not very likely that he thought of anything of the kind much before 1908. He had been residing for some time in Paris and had also been travelling a good deal in Eastern Europe. He was fond of exploring the places that were unknown to the average tourist, and he did a lot of motoring where at that time motor cars had never been seen.

During 1908, the year that saw the Wright Brothers' first flights in Europe, and concluded with that remarkable Aero Show at the Grande Palais, Mr. Barber felt the call. He then had to decide whether to remain in Paris and work there or to come to England. His own country pulled strongest, and the next act opens with Scene 1: A Railway Arch in Battersea.

How many tens of thousands of Londoners on their way to work or going home, by the countless trains crossing the hundreds of railway arches in that remarkable riparian resort, Battersea, suspected that below the rumbling wheels, in a murky cave, worked one of the magicians of the air who was soon to be heard of as the creator of the Valkyrie monoplane, a portent perhaps of the decline of the railways? [Quite an accurate prophecy for 1919!]

THE NEW AND THE OLD

But not for long was the magician content with his cave. Early in 1909, he sought the great spaces of land and sky on Salisbury Plain; and there on Lark Hill, in full view of Stonehenge, and between that strange work and midsummer's rising sun, Mr. Barber set up his workshop. Here among other things he built a Maurice Farman biplane, using for the first time spruce instead of mahogany, which largely owing to Sir Hiram Maxim's enthusiastic advocacy had been regarded as the last word for aeroplane construction. When Mr. Farman saw this machine, he was astonished and not a little troubled. This was certainly not to the designer's plan. However, Mr. Barber was soon able to demonstrate that while a saving in weight had been effected nothing of strength had been sacrificed. And from that day spruce it was. Mr. Barber built his first Valkyrie monoplane on Salisbury Plain.

[No documentary evidence exists to prove that Barber built a Farman plane at Lark Hill. All we know is that he is said to have had five aeroplanes in all during his time here but only four are accounted for. Much more likely is that this is a reference to him supervising the construction of a Farman biplane much later at Hendon, where it is documented that he was retained by Farman Brother to do just that.]

By the way, he was the first to use butted and threaded wires instead of the treacherous loop. Also, he very early on, electrically deposited metal on propeller blades; and he used steel instead of aluminium in the Valkyrie monoplane. [But not before the aluminium fittings had been criticized!]

The Valkyrie was a wonderful machine from the constructional point of view, but its author will agree that in stability it left something to be desired. It appeared to one passenger, at any rate, to be slightly deficient as regards to directional stability. This, of course, is merely a personal view. Briefly, it needed good piloting.

[Barber went to great lengths to show that the Valkyrie was stable in the air, and would repeatedly give exhibition demonstrations of flying the Valkyrie with both hands high in the air. Barber was a very good pilot and especially in his own machine. This criticism of the machine persisted and the two fatalities in the Valkyrie at the hands of inexperienced and over-enthusiastic pilots did nothing to alleviate it.]

As a pilot, Mr. Barber, although skilful was not reassuring. He did not in a filmy style saunter up to the machine as if he had not a care in the world, and nonchalantly puffing at a gasper, vault into the pilot's seat, and soar into the blue. It never occurred to him that the eye of the journalist and the lens of the camera were upon him and that it was up to him to set the standard of the intrepid airman. Well, thank heaven for men like Mr. Barber.

DESIGNED AN AIRSHIP

It must have been in 1912 that he gave up Hendon, Mr. Holt Thomas taking over from him. He then set up as an aircraft consulting engineer, and Lloyd's were among his clients. He designed a big airship, of which one would like to hear more.

But to go back a little, Mr. Barber's interests had been known by the title of the Aeronautical Syndicate. There was a happy band of budding pilots, male and female, at Hendon in those days. Ridley-prentice, Miss Meeze, Capt. Fulton, Capt. Board, Lieut. Dimmock, Mrs. Palmer, Cambers, Valentine and many others. We quote from a report of the time, "At times the height of the monoplane was estimated at 25ft!" That was considered good in those days! As a matter of fact, Mr. Barber often exceeded 2000-3000ft.

There was a Valkyrie 3-seater driven by a 50hp Gnome engine, and Mr. Barber it should be stated, even in those early days gave demonstration flights with his hands off the controls. The machine was really not that bad from a stability point of view, but it needed understanding, and the ordinary R.A.F. pilot of today would at first by no means find it simple. The landing carriage was excellent and contained features that might with advantage still be cultivated.

PAGE & MILES, Ltd.

Electrical Engineers
And *ELECTRICIANS.*

CONTRACTORS FOR
LIGHTING POWER

The Britannia Trophy

The year 1911 was an eventful one for Mr. Barber, as it was for many of us. In June he presented four complete machines (but one less engine) to the War Office. In the following month, he was commissioned by a Page & Miles, electricians of Brighton to carry a consignment of Osram lamps from Shoreham to Brighton (Hove) which was the first goods traffic by aeroplane. [This story is very well documented. The flight was basically a publicity stunt and was extremely newsworthy.]

He was paid a fee of £100 for this trip, and being keen to keep his amateur status as a pilot, generously used the money to present the Britannia Trophy, which is still awarded almost every year to a pilot who has achieved something special. He also stated that any further such monies he might make would also be donated to similar causes. Mr. Barber presented the Britannia trophy to the Royal Aero Club for a challenge competition.

From about this time he went into research and development but did make a remarkable flight with Miss Trehawke Davies.

The Viking biplane followed the Valkyrie.

Nowadays we must consider him chiefly as an aviation insurance expert, indeed the originator of aviation insurance. He is the director of this section of Lloyd's, Eagle and British Dominions and the Excess Insurance Co., under the name of the Aviation Insurance Association, thus opening a new and most romantic chapter in the history of insurance, taking almost every imaginable aircraft risk. For many years he has been working out averages and risks, and in the nature of things he has acquired unique knowledge of the circumstances in which accident occur and the resulting damage.

During the war, he served in the Royal Air Force [mostly RFC in fact] as an instructor in theory. He was a remarkably painstaking instructor, and he embodied his work in a book called *The Aeroplane Speaks* and had a very large sale here and abroad. A most original work, which was recommended by the training department of the RAF. [Barber also wrote a much less well-known training manual entitled *How to Fly a Plane*. See Chapter 15.]

He followed this up with *Aerobatics*, a full explanation of stunts and the way to execute them. This book is a remarkable one, for it is the result of practical experiments made at an age when few men think of flying let alone trick-flying. Mr. Barber moreover is of a nervous temperament, not, one might imagine, suited to this kind of thing. However, he was determined to write on aerobatics from knowledge obtained first-hand; and so he went through the painful process of studying them in the air.

There you have the man! Truly a remarkable man: simple, likeable, inquiring, sensitive, original, alert. One does not regard him as Wilbur Wright, but emphatically he belongs to British aviation and has made notable contributions to the mechanics of the aeroplane, besides being an inspiring figure at a time when aviation sadly needed it.

Who can measure the worth of men like this? Had the nation as a whole been more alert, more intelligent in the period 1908-1914, then assuredly, the subject of this sketch would have achieved greater fame. Like other aviation leaders, he has been diminished by his country's faults. We are speaking of the pre-war period. The war has made us great in aeronautics. Not all the men who laid the foundations receive adequate recognition: official and other opportunists reap the recognized reward. Happily, there is something more precious than money and O.B.E.'s and that is scientific renown and the esteem of fellow workers.

Chapter 12: Barber's Aeroplanes

This chapter provides more technical information about Horatio Barber's flying career and the aeroplanes he had built from 1909 to 1912.

Two factors contribute to the confusing lack of information about Barber's planes at Lark Hill. The site of Barber's first aeroplane shed was very isolated and the press members who covered the latest advances in aviation did not travel there for some time. Also, Barber experimented in a certain amount of secrecy in order to protect his patent and design.

As a result, we do not know with certainty the number of planes he had at Lark Hill, nor the total number he had built during his time as an aviation pioneer. The best estimate from the information available is between twenty and thirty machines.

The Barber/ Howard Wright monoplane (also known as ASL Monoplane No.1)

Barber has annotated this picture as "Post July 1909 Larkhill" (The word "Post" probably refers to a newspaper rather than meaning "after.") From Barber's scrapbook in the collection of the Hendon RAF Museum.

Barber's first aeroplane, shown here was built by Howard Wright at Battersea in 1909. A tractor monoplane, it was similar in design to the machine Wright made for Cooke. The novel addition of co-axial contra-rotating propellers, which had been patented by Lanchester only a few years previous, seems to have been Wright's idea, as he apparently used them in other aeroplanes. We do not know how much input Barber had into the design of this aeroplane. Certain features, such as the patent stabilizing system for the main planes which is apparent on one of the photographs, is due to Barber's influence. Therefore, it's reasonable to wonder if other features were of his design. Again, there are conflicting accounts of whether Barber worked with Wright in his workshop under the railway arches of Battersea, or if in fact he rented his own workshop there.

This aeroplane it seems, never really flew due to the heavy steel tubing construction and cart spring landing gear.

The Barber/Wright monoplane No. 1 was powered by a 50-horsepower, water-cooled, Antoinette V8 – image from Kraków Aviation Museum wwi-models.org

Barber has annotated this picture as "Post July 1909 Larkhill" (post probably referring to a newspaper rather than meaning "after.") From Barber's scrapbook in the collection of the Hendon RAF Museum.

However, a later photograph of the same aeroplane (above) shows changes to the design, such as a larger tail and rudder area, and an additional area of tailplane just behind the pilot's seat. It is difficult to understand the additional fin and rudder additions unless the pilots encountered problems with directional control during taxiing trials, or perhaps when the plane hopped into the air momentarily. The additional forward tailplane, which appears to be fixed rather than controllable, may have been added in an attempt to coax the plane into the air with additional lifting surfaces. This aeroplane is said to have been later sold and then it crashed on its one and only escape from the ground.

Barber has annotated this picture as "Post July 1909 Larkhill" (post probably referring to a newspaper rather than meaning "after.") From Barber's scrapbook in the collection of the Hendon RAF Museum.

- powered by a 50 h.p. Antoinette engine
- Length 27ft
- Span 32ft Wing area 200 sq. ft (but this was later increased)
- Weight 1000+ lbs.

The ASL monoplane. (Sometimes referred to as ASL monoplane No.2)

Horatio Barber at the controls of the ASL monoplane. Annotated by Barber in his scrapbook as "Flight March 6, 1910. (i.e. the day after the first flight by Bertie Woodrow)

This plane was the first of the Syndicate's own design, and the first canard style aircraft to fly in the British Isles. "Canard" refers to the elevator in the forward position rather than at the rear, in what would now be considered a conventional aircraft. This ungainly looking aeroplane was somewhat similar in appearance to that of Santos-Dumont's machine which had freed itself from the ground and into the air in 1906.

The craft was another from the Howard Wright stable with input from W. O. Manning. Many of the design elements are Barber's, discovered as a result of his experimentation with models. This was his first aeroplane to take to the air, flown by his chauffeur and later ASL test pilot, Bertie Woodrow, March 5, 1910. Before the flight, Woodrow taxied for about fifteen minutes and then took off, away from the wind. The very surprised Woodrow, who found himself in the air at a height of about thirty feet, switched the engine off and glided the aeroplane back to earth. The craft sustained some damage to a wing and undercarriage, but was repaired and made further successful flights.

Barber and Woodrow in the ASL monoplane

The ASL monoplane was powered by a Green 60 horsepower engine driving a propeller designed by Manning. Wing warping, similar to that of the Wright Brothers' Flyer was used as the method of control. At the tip of each wing, a small wheel aided with the landing.

- Span 42ft
- Length 31ft
- Weight 800lb
- Speed 35mph

The Valkyrie Prototype.

Little is known of this machine except for the patent illustration, shown right, and the photograph we have included in our book. Some reports indicate that the prototype was built by Howard Wright and this is probably likely, although others say that Barber and Wright were involved in some form of disagreement by this time.

There are some important differences between this machine and the Valkyrie No. 1. Firstly, at the nose of each fuselage frame, the members are joined to a point, whereas on the later model a curved structure was introduced which was later covered with fabric for lateral stability.

From Patent Journal July 19, 1911

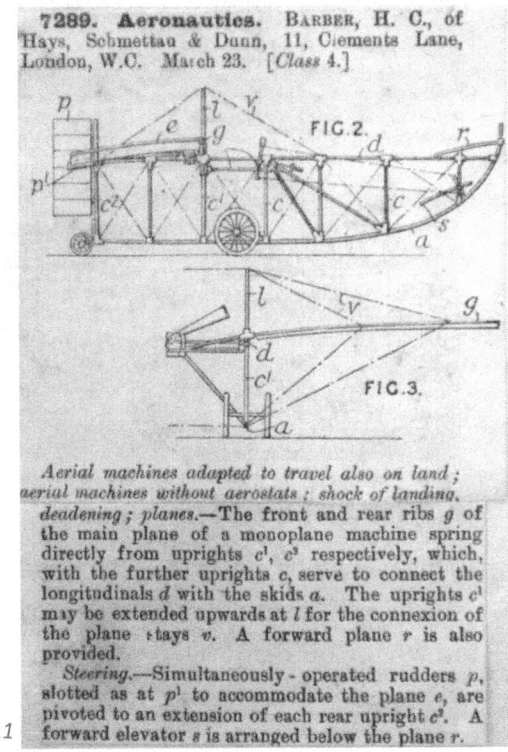

The side frames in the prototype are braced solely with wires, whereas on Valkyrie No.1 wooden diagonal bracing was used. Also on the Valkyrie No.1, a front elevator is added. The wheel spats seen in the prototype attached to the bracing wire are not continued on the No.1. Although not too visible in the above photograph, in another picture, the leading edges of the wings of the prototype are far from straight and look to be ill-tensioned. Whether this was intentional or not, is unknown.

In his book *The Old Flying Days*, Major C.C. Turner relates first hand a story about the Valkyrie; he writes: "One of Mr. Barber's Valkyries had two front skids connected by horizontal bracing wires. Taxiing this machine on the Plain on one occasion the wire caught a molehill, with the result that the two skids closed together and the whole machine collapsed, but with no injury to the pilot. It was certainly an amusing crash to see." (These wires in the prototype photo opposite appear to be extremely close to the ground). "Mr. Barber's chauffeur got into one of the aeroplanes in order to test the engine. He put the engine full on, however and before he realized what he had done the machine was in the air! Another crash but no harm done."

Valkyrie Prototype with Barber's mother Isabella aboard. Barber's aeroplane shed in the background. Note also the Ford motor car licence plate LD7131. Courtesy of Agefotostock.

The Valkyrie prototype with Barber's wife Elsie aboard. Courtesy of Agefotostock

This picture is interesting in that it appears to be the prototype which has had the additional wooden diagonal bracing fitted, which appears lighter in colour than the mainframes, but before the elevator or the Valkyrie 1 logo has been added. This then strongly favours the fact that the Valkyrie 1 was a modified version of the prototype and not an entirely different machine. This photograph appeared in Flight *magazine. Barber's copy is annotated "Flight June 1910. Crashed August 1910. From Barber's scrapbook in the collection of the Hendon RAF Museum.*

ASL Valkyrie No 1, (type A)

From Flight *magazine*

This iteration of the Valkyrie is known as the Amesbury machine because it was entirely fabricated in Barber's aeroplane shed at Lark Hill near Amesbury. It flew for the first time on July 13, 1910, and according to Jane's *All the World's Aircraft*, flew a distance of one mile.

Construction was surprisingly simple. The fuselage consisted of two parallel wooden side members 8 1/2 ft apart. The wings were fabric-covered wooden structures, each made up of leading edge and fourteen shallow cambered ribs, which look as if they were made from ½" square battens. Flying controls comprised wing-tip ailerons, twin rudders and a forward elevator mounted between the side members. An adjustable (on the ground) fore-plane was carried above the nose, supported like the wings, by king-posts and wire bracing. The pilot sat on a small bucket seat amidships, with stick and rudder bar controls, back to back with a 35hp 4-cylinder, water-cooled, in-line Green engine.[149]

- Length 22ft
- Height 8' 6"
- Span 34 ft
- Wing area 190 sq. ft
- Weight without a pilot 520 lb
- Speed approximately 45 mph
- Airframe Honduras Mahogany
- Propeller Mahogany
- Covering un-proofed Egyptian cotton.

---

[149] *Horatio Barber's Canards* by John W. R. Taylor

The Green C 4 on display at the RAF Museum, London. Designed by Gustavus Green and built by the Green Engine Co., this engine was one of two Green designs to win a Government prize. The engine first ran in 1908.

Drawing of Valkyrie 1 from *Pioneering Aircraft 1903-14* by Kenneth Munsun.

This aeroplane was taken to Hendon on September 1910 and is pictured below outside the ASL sheds

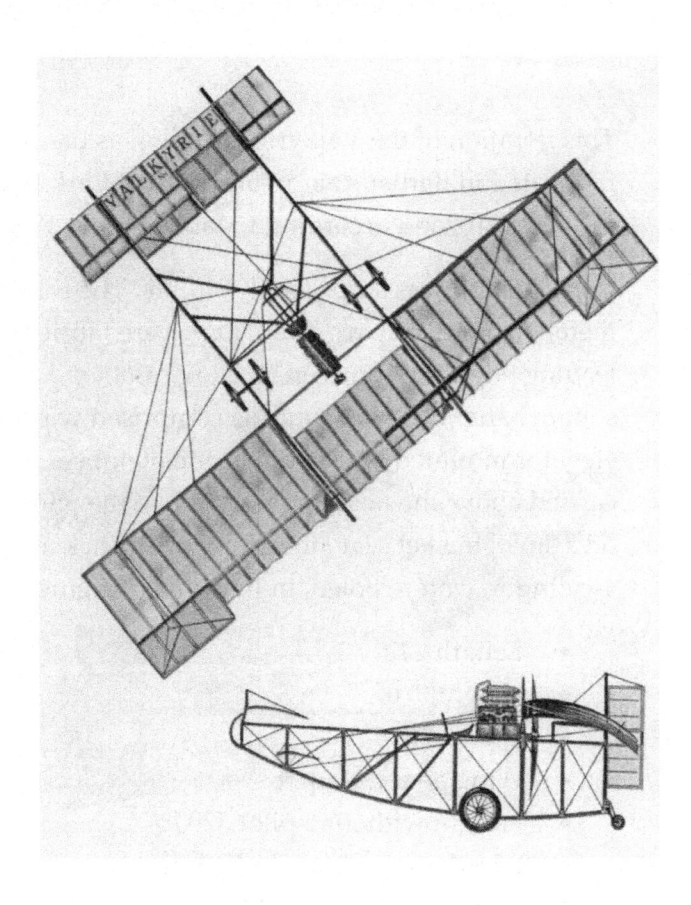

This picture of Valkyrie 1 together with another was published by Flight *and taken on September 13, 1910. This was the last flight at Larkhill prior to being dismantled for removal to Hendon, where the Aeronautical Syndicate Ltd had established a base. A similar picture probably from the same source appears in Barber's scrapbook and is annotated September 1910, Lark Hill.*

ASL Valkyrie No.1 at Hendon. From Flight *magazine.*

Valkyrie type B Racer

The Valkyrie type B racer was first flown on 12th November 1910. It was smaller than the No. 1 but with some rearrangement could carry a passenger. Some days later, the larger type C 3-seater was flown.

The nomenclature is somewhat confusing in that the first type B was sometimes referred to by its works number as Valkyrie III whereas the C type is known as Valkyrie II.

Valkyrie type B racer with Barber at the controls- Hendon.

The Valkyrie II 3-seater was flying at Hendon in October 1910 with a 60hp engine.

- Span 39ft
- Length 29ft 9in
- Weight 800lb
- Speed 50mph

Valkyrie B racer construction and undercarriage details. Note the aluminium brackets and suspension system and rear skids. Colin E. Read photo.

The Valkyrie II (C type) Three-seater with Barber at the controls 1910. The number on the front plane appears more like 8, but must be 3? Flight.

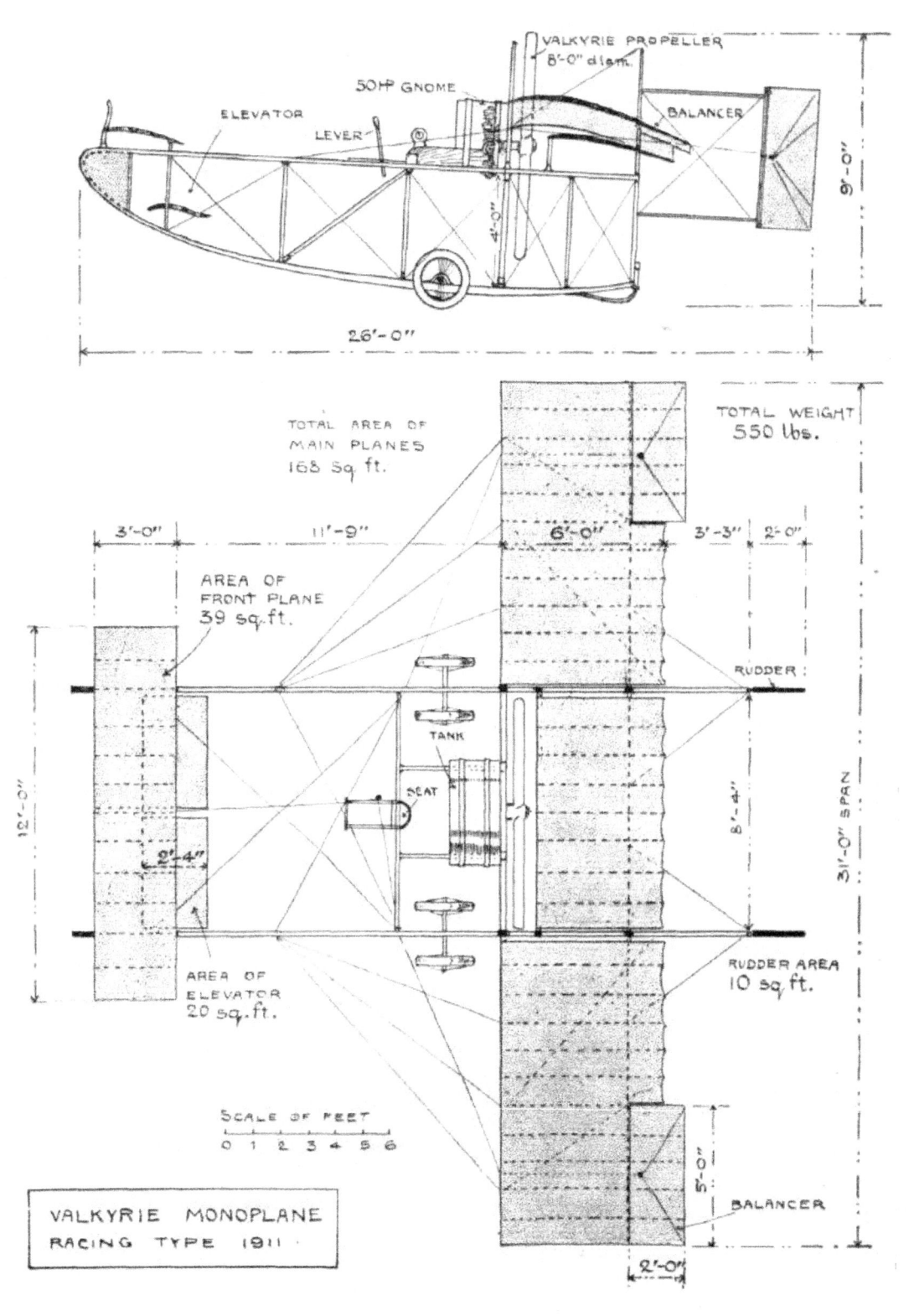

Valkyrie Racer B type, 1911

The ASL produced many more Valkyries. How many of each type were made is not known. Barber said that he built and flew a total of 28 aeroplanes in total, of which 24 would have been Valkyrie models with many amendments and improvements to the structure and flying performance. This figure is impossible to verify so is presumed to be true.

The Aeronautical Syndicate, Ltd.

We have received from the Aeronautical Syndicate, Ltd., the makers of the well-known Valkyrie machines, a very complete and well got-up catalogue in which are explained the various excellent features embodied in the construction of their machine, which is of creditable British design and creditable British workmanship throughout.' We call attention particularly to the excellent landing chassis, the strength and design of which must have saved many a beginner from slight accidents.

Three machines are listed, namely, type A, a single seater, single surface planes of 31ft. 6in. span; type B, a cross-country racing model, single surface planes 30ft. 4in. span; and type C, a three-seater passenger carrier, double surface planes 38ft. 8in. span. A noticeable feature of the list is an illustration, which we reproduce, of the Valkyrie machine, showing all the parts numbered, a list being given in the catalogue of each of these parts together with its price. This is sufficient indication that the makers have great faith in their machine, and therefore have standardised it.

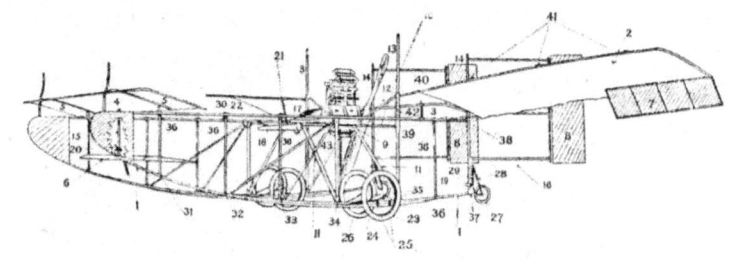

Valkyrie diagram numbered to facilitate the supply of spares.

From Aero *magazine March 15, 1911*

We note an interesting development in the later Valkyries, with Nos. 10 to 12. The dihedral of the main planes was changed to a lesser angle. Curiously, Barber incorporated the earlier style of control using wing warping instead of wing flaps. The later machines flew successfully, although it had been suggested that they were unstable in the hands of inexperienced pilots. As mentioned elsewhere, Barber held public displays to disprove the sentiment.

The ASL stable December 1910 Flight

The following page shows the evolution of the Valkyrie models in approximate scale, highlighting some of the most noticeable changes.

The prototype had no wooden diagonal bracing to the side frames, relying on only wire cross bracing. The nose of the aeroplane was pointed, unlike all of its successors. It appears not to have a front elevator.

The Valkyrie No. 1 incorporated two diagonal braces to the side frames, and the characteristic curve to the nose of each side frame. Note, it is thought that No.1, after being transferred to Hendon from Lark Hill may have been further modified to incorporate the extended rudder assembly as seen on later models.

The Type B Racer had only one wooden diagonal brace to each side frame, the rudders were moved backwards on extended booms and the front section of each nose was covered with linen to improve stability. Skids were used at the rear of the side frames in place of wheels. A Gnome 50h.p. engine was incorporated into this model.

The 3-seater (Type C) was much larger than the other models. The side frames were similar in design to Valkyrie No.1, but the height of these side frames, together with the width apart and wingspan were much increased.

Flight July 1, 1911: AN OBJECT LESSON IN MOBILITY – An all-British Valkyrie military monoplane on its own wheels passing the Marble Arch en route from Hendon flying grounds to Brighton [at the end of June,] where arrangements for exhibition flights have been made. In this manner, the Valkyrie military design can travel anywhere with freedom, and the planes, which are attached to the sides, can be fitted in a few minutes, the machine then being in complete flying order.

EVOLUTION OF THE VALKYRIE

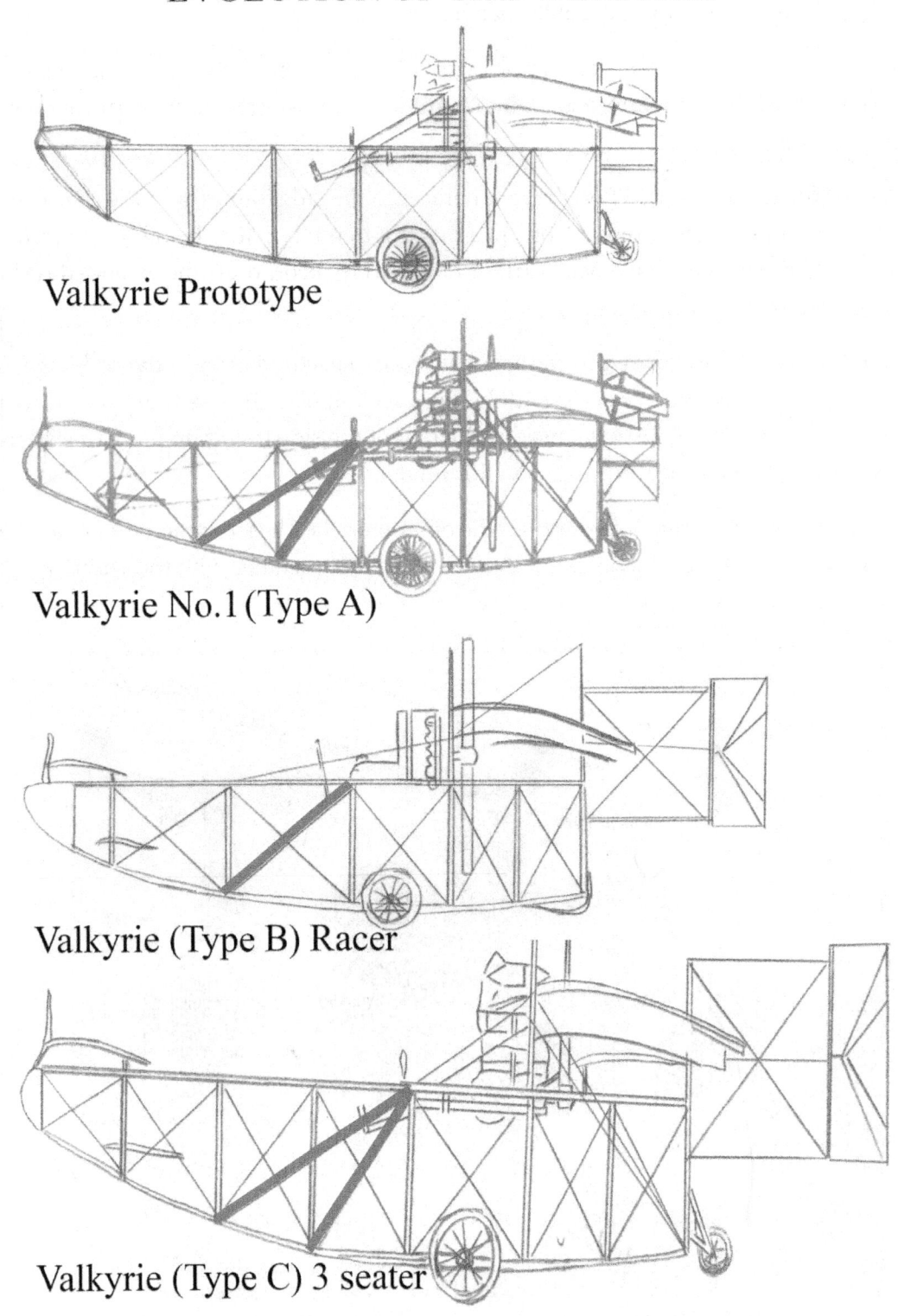

Valkyrie Prototype

Valkyrie No.1 (Type A)

Valkyrie (Type B) Racer

Valkyrie (Type C) 3 seater

Sketches are in approximate scale to show major changes in each Valkyrie type. We have enhanced the diagonal bracing to emphasize the changes in the design. Terry Grace drawing.

The ASL Viking also known as "Mrs. Grundy"

The New Viking monoplane with the balancing ailerons clearly visible between the wings. Flight

Never one to stay still for long, Barber's next design was a significant departure from the Valkyrie design. Until the Viking, all of his success had come about as a result of the canard layout, which is to say with the elevator in the front of the machine.

The Viking, on first inspection, appears to be a standard tractor type biplane. It is difficult to understand why Barber felt compelled to return to the more conventional layout - his first monoplane was of this tractor configuration - unless it was solely for commercial reasons, in that most designs of the aeroplane were of that layout. We know that the Valkyrie had a (possibly undeserved) reputation of being unstable, and the fact that it was fragile-looking did not help matters.

Looking closer at the design, we note The Viking's several very innovative introductions. The power system of contra-rotating propellers on each side of the engine, one being driven by a crossed chain to achieve the rotation in the opposite direction is reminiscent of the Wright Brothers' Flyer. This plane was known to Barber and others as "Mrs. Grundy" because it had been made to demonstrate the fact the Aeronautical Syndicate could make as good a machine in this configuration, like any other constructor. The term "Mrs. Grundy" was popular at that time as representing a conventional or priggish person. It comes from a character in the 1798 play "Speed the Plough" by Thomas Morton. This seems a little contradictory because although as previously stated the aeroplane did at first glance look much more conventional than the Valkyries, Barber was using the machine as a sort of testbed for his innovative flexible balancers for lateral control. At least one of the contemporary photographs shows the machine with temporary balancers, during the time the originals were being modified.

The aeroplane had pleasing lines with a streamlined cowling which protected the occupants who were seated side by side amidships. The cockpit housed a revolution counter and both fuel and oil gauges along with lubrication sight glasses for the engine. The main planes of the aircraft retained a similar structure to that of the Valkyrie. The fuselage tapered significantly towards the tail plane.

The most interesting of the innovations was undoubtedly the balancing ailerons situated on each side between the upper and lower planes. These were of aluminium and steel construction and worked in a wing warping manner in such a way that one outer edge of the aileron would be forced downwards at the front and rear in order to increase the curved surface thereby increasing the lift, whilst on the other side, each edge would be forced upwards producing an inverted curve - that is to say like an upturned wing, which had the effect of forcing that side of the aeroplane downward.

Barber insisted that these additions were purely experimental, but they obviously worked, as the plane first took to the air in early 1912, and by all accounts performed very well. Other improvements included the much more sophisticated undercarriage which incorporated cantilevered telescopic shock absorbers and stick-type controls which were becoming more popular at that time.

Barber continued to test the aeroplane for a while and although it flew well, the Viking was not a commercial success. On the collapse of ASL, the plane was sold to the Chanter Flying School at Shoreham where in much-modified form it continued to fly with the addition of floats. The contra-rotating propeller system was removed and replaced by the more conventional single propeller, and part of the fuselage covering towards the rear was also removed.

A fire on February 29, 1912, destroyed three hangars at Shoreham including that of the Chanter's Flying School. The company lost two Anzani-powered Bleriots and their design of a monoplane in the blaze, but the Viking survived. Chanter's business never recovered and nothing more is heard of the Viking.

Chanter Flying School modified ASL Viking Float-plane at Brighton. Courtesy of the Regency Society. Brighton

Another possibly later photograph in which even more of the fuselage covering has been removed from the modified ASL Viking at Brighton. Courtesy the Regency Society Brighton.

Chanter's had another connection to Barber. In his book *Shoreham Airport an Illustrated Guide*, Peter C. Brown states that the company had lost a court case related to some unpaid fees associated with the cargo flight made by Barber in the previous July. This presumably is Barber's famous flight with the Osram electric lamps, the first commercial cargo flight in the UK. Brown, however, makes no mention of the amount or purpose of these fees.

The Grahame-White Type VI

This was a military biplane project which was apparently initiated by Barber, but finished by J. D. North. The concept "aerial destroyer" was a novel but ill-conceived craft which was not successful and, according to several sources, it apparently crashed during its maiden flight. However, in Graham Wallace's *Claude Grahame-White, a Biography* we find a report that on "Daily Express Day" eight women readers of the *Daily Express* were taken for free rides in the military biplane. This obviously suggests that the plane flew several times after the maiden flight.

This 3-seater biplane had several novel features. For one, the upper fuselage supporting boom was not only a structural part of the fuselage but was also the propeller shaft. The rudder and tail plane control cables ran through this hollow shaft. It was also possible for one of the passengers to lie prone in the cockpit, and peer through a hole in the floor for accurate bomb aiming. This design drew some criticism, especially regarding the propeller shaft setup. If for any reason the propeller became unbalanced in flight, then the whole plane would likely disintegrate.

Grahame-White type V1 which was partially designed by Barber

View of Grahame-White type V1 during construction and clearly showing the unorthodox propeller shaft arrangement and the chain drive from the engine. From an old postcard- unattributed.

The aeroplane was designed to take a 120hp Austro-Daimler 6-cylinder inline engine, but when it was shown at the Olympia Exhibition in 1913, it was fitted with a 90hp engine of the same make.

- 3-seater
- Length 33' 9"
- Wingspan 42' 6"
- Wing area 390 sq. Ft.
- Weight 2,200lb
- Propeller 2 bladed, 10' 9" diameter.
- Endurance 2 hours
- Armament Colt .30 calibre machine gun.

Chapter 13: 1910 to 1915

Another Divorce and Another Marriage

As was the case with most pioneer aviators of the time, only the affluent could afford to take part. Thanks to the considerable fortune he amassed while he was a stockbroker in Canada, Barber was able to join the ranks of the wealthy airmen. Prior to WWI, Barber achieved professional success in aviation – designing, building, and flying aircraft.

A quick look at the 1911 Census of England and Wales shows us that the Barbers enjoyed an equally successful living situation. The family were comfortably well off, with no less than four servants, residing in the affluent surroundings of Kensington. The servants consisted of a parlour maid, a chambermaid, a cook, and a domestic nurse. Horatio also employed a chauffeur.

1911 Census of England and Wales – the Barber household at 3 Vicarage Gardens W – a 10-room house with a staff of four. Note that Horatio declares his occupation as Aeronautical Engineer.

On November 9, 1912, Horatio again fell afoul of the law, but this time for a speeding offence. The *Dorking and Leatherhead Advertiser* reported that Horatio C. Barber of 59 Pall Mall was fined 30 shillings for breaking a 10mph speed limit. We know that the Pall Mall address was his office. It was at this address where he granted the *Flight* magazine interview, "A Chat with Mr. Barber" in December 1912.

In spite of the outward appearance of a successful career and home life, Barber's private life was, once again, far from happy.

Another Divorce

By 1913, Horatio was no longer living with his wife Elsie. At first, she tried to compel her husband to return home under the law that allows an abandoned marital partner to seek "restitution of conjugal rights." When that failed, Elsie filed for divorce.

The contents of the divorce petition are very enlightening and include correspondence between the two. It's interesting to note that he is addressed as "Claude."

> 48 Queensborough Terrace,
> 16th November 1913
>
> Dear Claude,
>
> I have now been in London three weeks and I object extremely to being left to live alone like this. It causes me the utmost humiliation and I am writing to ask you to come back and live with me and if you will do this, I promise to let bye-gones be bye-gones and will do my best to make you happy.
>
> Yours
>
> Elsie

Barber did not reply to the first letter. Was he punishing Elsie with the "silent treatment?" Perhaps *he* was not yet ready to let "bye-gones be bye-gones." Was he the guilty party and avoiding contact? See later in the chapter for an explanation as to what those "bye-gones," or transgressions were.

Elsie sent another message dated November 24, asking that he respond to her earlier request to return home. On the 19th December 1913, she received the following note from her husband:

> 1 Durward House
> Kensington Court, W.
> December 18th, 1913
>
> Dear Elsie,
>
> In reply to your letters of the 16th inst. and November 24th I am unhappily forced to say that, having regard to the difficulties which have arisen between us, I cannot live with you again.
>
> Yours sincerely
>
> Claude

In the divorce petition, Elsie declares that the letter from "Claude" is indeed her absent husband. "The original of such last mentioned letter is now produced and shown to me as [Elsie Mabel Porter.] The said letter is in the handwriting of my husband the said Horatio Claude Barber who has not returned to co-habitation with me and still withholds from me Conjugal Rights."

Addressing the court, the divorce document continues:

"YOUR PETITIONER THEREFORE HUMBLY PRAYS that your Lordship will be pleased to decree that the said Horatio Claude Barber do return to cohabitation with your petitioner and render to her conjugal rights that she may have the custody of the said Claude Percy Barber and Conrad Hope Barber and that your petitioner may have such further and other relief in the premises as to your Lordship seems just.

Signed Elsie Mabelle Barber."

"Claude" never returned home.

A Decree RCR was signed on April 23, 1914, and they were divorced.

DIVORCES H. C. BARBER.

Former Miss Porter of Jersey City Obtains a Decree in London.

Special Cable to THE NEW YORK TIMES.

LONDON, Jan. 14.—Mrs. Elsie Mabelle Barber, formerly Miss Porter of Jersey City, obtained a divorce in the Divorce Court here today from her husband, Horatio Claude Barber, a well-to-do stock broker.

The marriage took place in Jersey City on May 27, 1903. The couple lived in America and Greece. The wife obtained a decree for the restitution of conjugal rights last April, with which the husband failed to comply.

A private detective testified to watching the respondent with another woman in London.

New York Times *January 1915*

Barber's celebrity was great enough that the news of the divorce eventually made it to the press in the United States.

Elsie had hired a private detective in order to secure a divorce. It seems that proof of infidelity was required, and Barber had been spotted with another woman.

The reader will note that Horatio was still being described as a "stockbroker" when in fact he had been out of the stock market business for some time. At the time of the news item, he was involved in military and aviation work and consulting for Lloyd's of London.

The detail about the couple living in Greece is noteworthy as no information about that time has come to light, apart from Barber's musings about Corfu in *Airy Nothings*. How did the reporter know that titbit? Who issued the media release? Did someone provide the *New York Times* with a copy of Elsie's divorce petition? In it, she lists the assorted places where the couple lived, including Greece. (See image below.) Knowing what we know about how frequently Barber moved about the globe, Elsie's phrase, "… and at divers [sic] other places" seems understated.

> 2. That after the said marriage your Petitioner lived and cohabited with her said husband at various places in the United States of America Canada and Greece at No. 3, Vicarage Gardens in the said County of London at Oakwood Court in the said County of London at No. 4, Rue Benjamin Goddard Paris in the Republic of France and at divers other places and that there is issue of the said marriage two children, to wit, Claude Percy Barber born 29th October 1904 and Conrad Hope Barber born 19th January 1906.
>
> 3. That your Petitioner is at present residing at No. 111, Iverna Court aforesaid; the said Horatio Claude Barber is an Engineer and is at present residing at No. 1, Durward House, Kensington Court in the said County of London and both your Petitioner and the said Horatio Claude Barber are domiciled in England.

Barber v. Barber divorce petition – Elsie's declaration, listing the assorted places where she and Horatio lived during their marriage.

The Paris address of No. 4 Rue Benjamin Goddard [sic] is significant as to where and when the Barber's lived after leaving Canada in 1907. This street was constructed in 1908.

Bertha Louise Alexandre Hildenbrand

A year and a half later, October 16, 1915, Horatio married Bertha Louise Alexandre Hildenbrand. They were wed in the district of Kensington, London.

According to the 1911 census, the Hildenbrand family lived at 10 Cambridge Terrace, Paddington, a posh neighbourhood. Mother Hildenbrand, also a Bertha, was head and householder. Daughter Bertha L. was twenty-one and a photographer.

The couple may have been in a hurry to tie the knot because on March 25, 1916, John Worthington Barber was born.

Horatio and Bertha had four more children:

- Bertha Marie Louise Barber was born in 1918. Bertha and presumably Horatio were living in Pewsey, Wiltshire at that time, possibly from when Horatio was based at the Central Flying School, Upavon in England.
- Robert Cecil Hildendrand Barber was born in 1919. He joined the Army and on his death in 1986 was listed as Brigadier. He was nominated for the Military Cross in 1945.
- Suzanne Alexandra Barber was born in 1921 and married on January 20, 1945.
- James C. Barber was born in 1927, registered in Eastbourne England, and died in 2012.

> SHAW : BARBER.—On Jan. 20, 1945, quietly, in London, GEORGE ANTHONY THEODORE, second son of Mr. and Mrs. G. E. SHAW, of Jersey, C.I., to SUZANNE ALEXANDRA, younger daughter of Mr. and Mrs. H. C. BARBER, of Jersey, C.I., and Bermuda. (care of Crown Agents, Millbank.)

Suzanne Barber marriage announcement 1945.

The Authors Speculate

We include here unconfirmed details that may or may not be related to Horatio and the two women in his life during 1912 and 1913.

We know that in March 1912, Barber announced that he was giving up flying and in April, he performed farewell flights. He was quoted as saying that he was taking a long cruise, possibly in the Mediterranean if his business dealings allowed.

Did these business dealings involve aviation insurance, or something else? Perhaps colonial development? In a letter to his son John, Horatio wrote that while in Paris in 1908, he thought about "doing something in Kenya."[150] According to the Yearbook[151] of the Royal Colonial Institute, a Horatio Barber joined up in 1913 as a non-resident fellow attached to Nairobi, British East Africa. With that in mind, we wonder if the Mr. H. C. Barber and wife who left Liverpool on May 2, 1912, bound for Sherbro in West Africa was our couple? Either Elsie, or his future wife Bertha may have joined him on this trip. The destination, a former British colony, was an island just off the coast of Sierra Leone, on the west coast of Africa. If this was Horatio, perhaps this was his Mediterranean cruise, or his business trip – or both.

We also found a record of a later trip. On April 21, 1913, an H. C. Barber, travelling solo, returned to Liverpool from Sierra Leone.

Switching focus to Bertha's story, we found an obituary for Matthias Hildenbrand. The *Feuille d'Avis de Neuchâtel*, Switzerland, July 2, 1913, reported that Madame Hildenbrand and her

---

[150] See Appendix 7
[151] archive.org/details/1916yearbook00royauoft/page/96

children, Mademoiselle Bertha Hildenbrand and her fiancé of London attended the funeral. The names and circumstances fit, as we know that Bertha married Horatio two years later. Technically, though, at the time of the funeral, he was still married to Elsie. But we also know that later in 1913, Elsie wanted Horatio to return home, and if he did, she'd let bygones be bygones.

We also know that Elsie had hired a detective and the results of the investigation revealed that Barber had been spotted with another woman. A discovery that may have been made when Mr. H.C. Barber and Mrs. Barber sailed to Africa either in 1912 or on a return visit in July 1913.

July 24 1913 passenger list from Liverpool to Sherbro Mr. and Mrs. H. C. Barber – note his occupation is "Trader's Agent"

As for 1913 and the divorce petition, Elsie had endured "loss of conjugal rights" almost from the start. Barber was rarely home, although, like father like son, Barber was home often enough to sire two children. However, a husband's absense was the norm for the period. The men were exploring at the frontiers, looking to enrich their country, and more importantly, themselves. They returned home only occasionally. The wife and mother, meanwhile, was at home with her staff. She and the children were well-cared for financially. Likely the humiliation of infidelity was the real reason that Elsie wanted rid of him. She had her suspicions or knew outright that he was involved with someone else, possibly as early as 1912 when he made that first trip to West Africa.

Chapter 14

Barber as Aviation Insurance Broker

In England, during his early days at Hendon, Horatio pondered the idea of third-party insurance coverage for his flying school. He approached Lloyd's of London, but since aviation insurance was a brand-new concept, no such policy existed. Lloyd's asked Barber to write the contract himself, which he did, and his work was accepted. This was, according to several documentary accounts,[152] the first aviation insurance issued in England: another first for Barber.

It was also to be the first step toward another change in career. Lloyd's offered Barber a consultancy post as a result. *Flight* magazine first mentions Horatio's work as an aviation advisor with the insurance company late in 1912. According to the article[153], he was the "sole consulting expert" to all of Lloyd's underwriters.

Several years later in 1919, *Flight* magazine commented on the newly formed Aviation Insurance Association.

> According to an official communication forwarded to us, a corporation to be known as the Aviation Insurance Association has been formed to undertake the covering of aircraft risks. It intends to accept at home and abroad all risks in connection with heavier and lighter than air craft.
>
> A committee has been appointed, consisting of some of the best known men in the insurance world, and this committee has been fortunate enough to secure the services of Capt. Horatio Barber, RAF who has been a well known figure in aviation for many years.
>
> He was the first man in England to receive an aeronautical degree and has had long experience as pilot, designer and constructor, and built the first all British passenger carrying machine.
>
> Before the war he was engaged as a consultant on aviation and had a large practice which included Lloyd's whom he advised on all questions relating to aircraft insurance. Aircraft insurance is a branch of the business which will require very careful initial handling combined with close knowledge of the subject and considerable breadth of outlook. These qualities Capt. Barber possesses in marked degree and we congratulate the Association on their choice.
>
> *Flight* March 13, 1919

---

[152] See later in the chapter for discussion of an earlier company that offered insurance coverage
[153] *Flight* magazine December 14, 1912

Cuthbert Eden Heath

Visionary underwriter Cuthbert Heath started the Aviation Insurance Association.

Heath had started work at Lloyd's at the age of eighteen on a salary of £100 a year, but by the age of twenty-one, had become an underwriting member. He wrote Lloyd's first reinsurance policy for a fire insurance company, which provided coverage for financial losses due to a fire. Heath also wrote some of the first burglary policies and he was the first person to develop retail insurance.

Cuthbert Eden Heath

Heath is chiefly remembered for how he managed the insurance claims after the 1906 San Francisco Earthquake. He sent a telegram to his claims representative in the US, authorizing him to pay in full "irrespective of the terms of their policies." He is also said to have insured a chimpanzee against death. He paid up in full on the death of the animal and had it stuffed and displayed in his office as reminder of his folly.[154]

Heath was astute enough to secure Barber as manager of the Aviation Insurance Association, knowing that he had more experience in risk assessment relating to aviation than any other at that time.

During Barber's time, the Society of British Aircraft Constructors asked Lloyd's Register to undertake aircraft inspection. This continued until the general committee appointed specialist aviation surveyors around 1930. This group eventually became the Civil Aviation Authority.

The other member companies of the Aviation Insurance Association, besides Lloyds' were the Eagle Star and British Dominions Insurance Company Ltd. and the Excess Insurance Corporation Ltd.

AVIATION INSURANCE ASSOCIATION.

On Monday the first aeroplane-bus, designed to carry twenty passengers, was placed on exhibition, and the time is evidently very near when these aerial machines will be as common to our view as the ubiquitous motor omnibus now is. To-day, very close upon the announcement of Monday's ceremony, comes the news of the formation of a powerful insurance association composed of the majority of Lloyds' Underwriters; the Eagle, Star, and British Dominions Insurance Company, Ltd.; and the Excess Insurance Corporation, Ltd.

The new undertaking will be known as the Aviation Insurance Association, and the Committee of Management consists of Messrs. Cuthbert E. Heath (chairman of the Excess Insurance Association); J. R. Duder, George Simmons, and W. C. Campbell, of Lloyds; and Sir Edward M. Mountain as chairman, with Mr. Horatio Barber, A.F.Ae.C., F.R.G.S., as manager, and offices at 1, Royal Exchange Avenue, London, E.C.3.

The operations of this important undertaking will embrace every class of insurance necessitated by the world-wide exploitation of all classes of aircraft.

The Northern Whig March 12th 1919

In 1920, *Aeronautics* magazine published a column entitled "Insurance for Pilots" and the writers praised the Aviation Insurance Association for designing a scientific formula that allowed pilots to reduce risk.[155] Before the Association, there was no insurance protection for

---

[154] *Cuthbert Heath Maker of the Modern Lloyd's of London*, Anthony Brown.
[155] Barber advocated for health and safety and he compiled a checklist for pilots to use before taking flight.

pilots who through incapacitation were unable to continue in their profession. The editorial claimed that Captain Barber, with his long service experience preceded by his experience in building and flying aeroplanes, had solved the problem. The new insurance covered total incapacity as well as nervous or temperamental causes -- illnesses which may have prevented a pilot from continuing his duties. The company had no fixed fee schedule for this type of coverage. Instead, the premium or tariff paid for was based on the pilot's particular situation. Applicants were encouraged to write to the Association regarding special circumstances; with their unique experience and background, the Aviation Insurance Association would be able to advise.

However, in his fine biography *Cuthbert Heath: Maker of the Modern Lloyd's of London*, author Anthony Brown suggests that Heath's retention of Barber's services was not so successful. "The underwriter of the British Insurance Aviation Association, ex-RFC pilot Captain Barber has much experience in technical aviation problems." [156] Brown then goes on to say that possibly Barber was more expert on these problems than on underwriting, because the business had not been a success.

Classic British aviation advertisements 1909 - 1980

Brown's criticism of Horatio seems somewhat harsh. After all, Barber went on to base the rest of his career in underwriting aviation insurance with success. Perhaps any mistakes he made at that time were lessons learned and put him in good stead for his future business in America.

Remarkably, in 1921 when aviation in general and passenger service in particular were enjoying increasing popularity, the Association stopped accepting risks because they felt there was no future in aviation insurance. (Although the company did insure Charles Lindbergh and his aeroplane the *Spirit of St. Louis* for $18000.) Lloyd's of London stopped providing aviation insurance in 1921 after bad weather caused a series of crashes. This was likely the impetus that compelled Barber to venture into the insurance business on his own.

The story of how Barber was the first to write a policy for third party aviation risk is cited in several references about the history of British flying. However, both Brown's writing about Heath and Lloyd's, and Ian Ormes' book *Leading Edge* mention Barber only in passing.

---

[156] According to Brown, Barber's salary was £1500 plus 5% of profits

Ormes' chronicle of the pioneering years of aviation insurance is less than complimentary about Barber's Valkyrie aeroplane. He suggested that the craft resembled a large sled with a pair of wings and although it flew successfully, the plane had little in its favour and was discontinued. Ormes goes on to say that Horatio Barber was regularly consulted by [Lloyd's] underwriters in the early days, and his recommendations concerning the aircraft to be insured and the pilots flying them were mostly accepted without question. On this note, the same book states that the insurance firm Car and General were covering aeroplanes for accidental damage with its "Empyrean Policy for Aviators" as early as August 1910. Perhaps Barber wasn't first after all?

Barber and Baldwin, Inc.

By 1922 Barber had returned to the United States and together with Robert H. Baldwin, J. Brooks Parker, and Archibald Black, he organized the firm of Barber and Baldwin Incorporated. This was the first underwriting agency in the United States to specialize in aviation insurance. Barber was also President of Aero Underwriters Corporation.

At this time, Barber was an underwriter for Hartford Insurance Company[157] which offered aviation insurance. In 1913 Hartford began to offer automobile coverage and then eventually aviation coverage.[158]

The announcement, right, appeared in the press in early 1923

Barber & Baldwin, Inc.

Barber & Baldwin, Inc., have issued a very interesting booklet detailing their activities and the purposes for which the firm was organized. Their office is at 30 East 42nd Street, New York.

Horatio Barber, senior member of the firm, will be remembered as the author of "The Airplane Speaks", and one who has been identified with aviation the last fourteen years. With Mr. Barber the directors include Robert H. Baldwin and J. Brooks Parker, assisted by Archibald Black, the aeronautical engineer. The firm is listed as aeronautical consultants, underwriters and fiscal agents.

In 1925 Barber wrote a financial analysis and proposal for an airline between New York and cities to the west. The paper[159] studied both domestic airmail revenue and also the European airlines of the day. The first route proposed was from New York to Chicago with connecting legs to St. Paul and Kansas City. By flying at night, he proposed that a saving of one day could be achieved when flying mail to Chicago, and two days to cities further west.

This report was quite thorough. Barber had hired agents to meet with banking officials in the eastern cities. Their job was to gather information and to encourage the banks to use airmail for business.

Barber proposes several ways to save or make money by using airmail or air freight. For example, banks could reduce the time it required to forward cheques if airmail was used. With

---

[157] The Hartford Company began in 1810 when a group of Hartford merchants got together to offer fire insurance. They provided fire insurance for Abraham Lincoln in 1861.
[158] Hartford Insurance Files relating to Horatio Barber from the Smithsonian Air and Space museum Archives
[159] *Aviation* May 15th 1925

low user fees, Barber calculated that banks could earn $4,000 a day. By sending aerograms, financial institutions could earn $920 a day.

Barber also suggested that other business could benefit and therefore profit by using air services to transport goods such as newspapers, merchants' samples, films, jewellery, machine parts and so on. Consulting American Express, it was thought that 500lbs of such cargo could be carried each way, at a rate of ¼ cent per pound, per flying mile, which would secure a revenue of $3,000 a day. Passenger travel would eventually be considered as part of the service.

From these projections, Barber proposed that a yearly revenue of $1,995,840 could be achieved.

The paper continued with a detailed analysis of capital costs including the construction of hangars, purchase of landing fields, radio and night flighting equipment, and of course, the cost of planes. The bottom line: $2,732,500 in expenses.

Barber's calculations included an airline schedule of 3,500 miles per day or 807,000 miles in a flying year of 252 days, using 26 aeroplanes, 34 engines and 16 pilots.

After yet more detail, Barber concludes his analysis with an invitation to write to H. Barber at 30 East 42nd Street, New York City.

It is not clear from reading this paper how serious Barber was when he put forth this proposal for an airline. Certainly, he went to great lengths to prepare what was essentially a business plan. There is no evidence that the proposal went any further.

> Horatio Barber of Barber & Baldwin, Inc., is organizing two insurance companies for the purpose of caring for aviation risks. The first company, the Aero Insurance company, will insure planes against the hazards of fire, and the second, the Aero Indemnity Insurance company, will take care of the liability problems.

Chicago Tribune *September 28, 1928 – Barber organizes two insurance companies*

In 1928, using a model that worked well for him when he was a stockbroker in Canada, Barber organized his companies, advertised in the papers, and wrote on the subject, this time, an article entitled "Insurance, Underwriters and Aeronautics." In order to avoid the "language of insurance men," he began with an analogy – a writing technique similar to that he used in *Airy Nothings*. (See Chapter 15)

He wrote how he was a one-time designer, builder, and a pilot of aircraft and also captain of a small aerial fleet. (Presumably, here he is talking of the Valkyries rather than his time in the RFC.) At the time, he was overwhelmed with the experiences, problems and difficulties of this most fascinating game. "All pilots, mechanics, designers, manufacturers and operators were my brothers, and so I regard them now."

He continued, "Since that time the Gods have seen fit to burden me with a much greater fleet consisting of many thousands of craft, these being policies of insurance. They are captained by pilots out of my direct control and on whom I rely to follow their directions as specified in the "ship's papers," i.e. the Schedule of Warranties. Each vessel carries a precious cargo of risks for which I am responsible, and these risks can be $1,000,000 and over. I am responsible to my admirals, who are the presidents of the insurance companies whose fleet of policies I command, whilst also having a moral responsibility to the aeroplane operators. I have to follow the fleet's sailing orders which often involve opposing principles which must be balanced with niceties if my fleet is to prosper. I warrant that no one will envy me in this task of interpretation and managing of such business."

Barber acknowledged that he must not make excessive profits from the premiums paid by his clients. When considering the money paid by the company to cover claims, he said, "On the other hand, I must not make a loss for the insurance companies or they will withdraw from the commission, and then everyone, including myself will be on the rocks."

The paper continued in this flowery manner, strange, and yet eloquent. Barber described in detail all of the factors which must be taken into consideration. On several occasions, he bemoaned the lack of profit, whilst at the same time advocating for cheaper premiums. Since he was in the insurance business before and after World War I and in some capacity right up to 1947, one assumes that his profits would have been more than adequate, but possibly not so lucrative as one might think.

Early in October 1928, the Hartford Courant wrote a column updating the readership on the latest in Hartford stocks. A large portion of the column was devoted to news about Barber's two insurance companies, Aero Insurance and Aero Indemnity. Apparently, plans had changed, and a public offering of stock was no longer in the works. However, the article advised that some of the stock of the directors' qualifying shares would be offered shortly.

The piece goes on to provide a biography of the man in charge: Horatio Barber, who had a long experience in aeronautics and in aviation insurance… that dated from 1908 and his actual flying experience "embrace[d] the years 1908 to 1912."[160]

Later that month, the newspapers published advertisements promoting the public offering of shares in Aero Underwriters Corporation. To the right is a quarter-page ad from the October 23, 1928 edition of the *Star Tribune*, Minneapolis, Minnesota – again, Barber spared no expense.

Accompanying the ad is a media release that explains that "the rapid expansion of commercial aviation is making history almost daily, and as a result, the necessity for the absorption of its hazards is becoming more apparent." To meet the need, two companies owned and managed by Barber's Aero Underwriters Corporation were organized: Aero Indemnity Co. and the Aero Insurance Co., Inc., the latter having a fire and marine insurance charter. The two companies were to cover fire, accidental damage, tornado, theft, public liability,

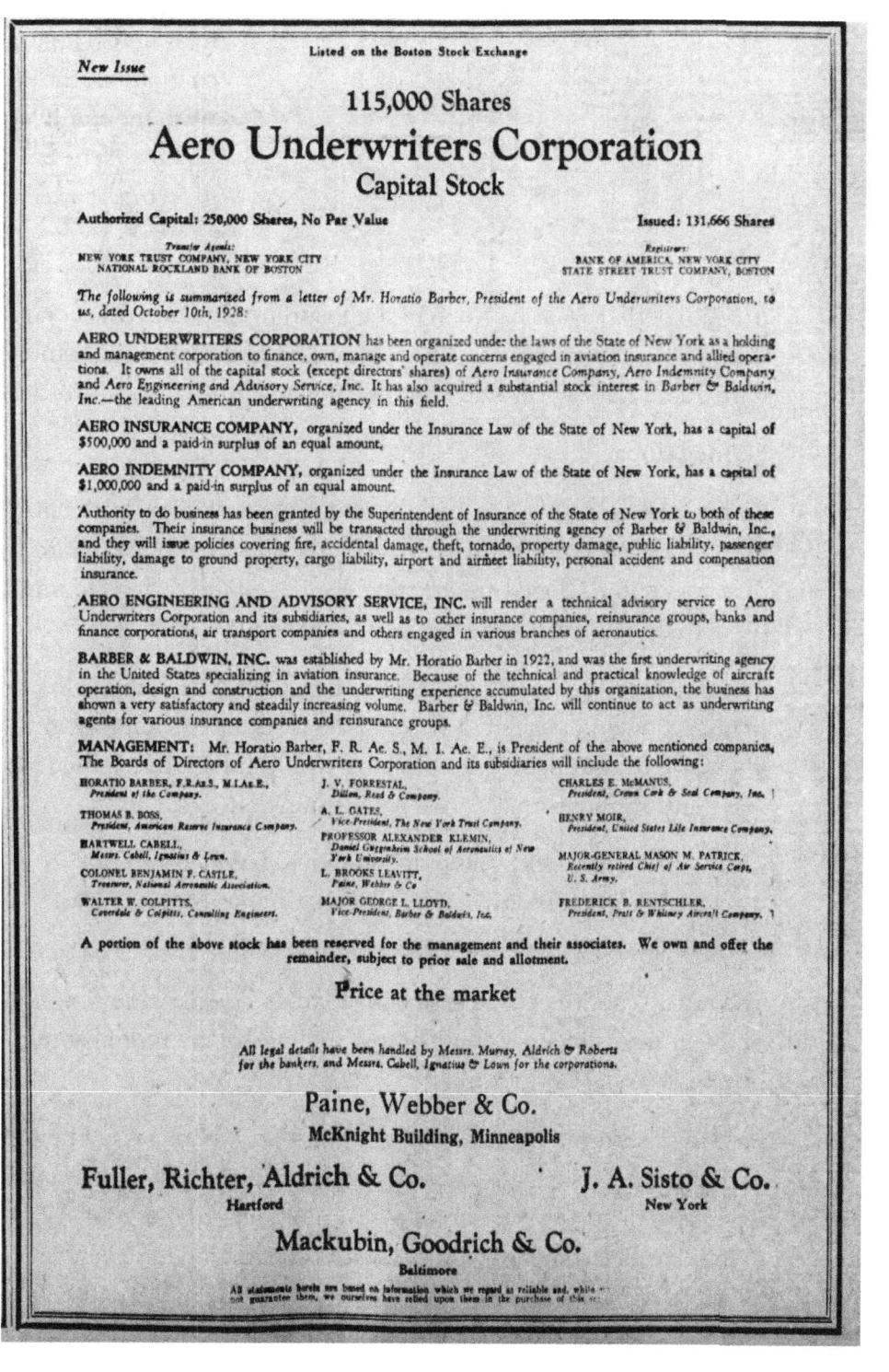

---

[160] We cannot confirm that Barber was involved in aviation as early as 1908. He attended the Paris show December 1908, and as far as records show, his work in aviation in Britain commenced in 1909. However, he applied for patents some two weeks after the Paris show, which suggests he had started working sooner.

passenger liability, property damage, personal accident, compensation and cargo. Underwriting for the companies was undertaken by Barber & Baldwin, Inc. of New York.

In 1929 Barber sailed back to Europe[161] in order to establish an organization there. His several companies, the Aero Insurance Company, the Aero Indemnity Company, Barber and Baldwin, and the Aero Engineering Company were growing. It was time to expand overseas.

Aviation *Feb 16 1929*

In 1929, Barber was chairman of the Insurance Brokers division of The Aeronautical Chamber of Commerce of America Inc. By this time, he had parted company with Baldwin, but the firm of Barber and Baldwin would continue in name until the mid-forties.

Going Global

Barber had made it to the top – his enterprises were now global. The March 1929 news of Barber sitting as president of the board of directors of the Globe Underwriters Exchange Inc., brings to mind his activity in Cobalt and his Open Call Mining Exchange.

The headline news, right, described the Globe exchange as already in operation and partnered with Rossia Insurance Company in Hartford, Connecticut. The company would function as a holding company and investment trust for insurance stocks.

The names of the stocks involved in the exchange could not yet be disclosed, however, it was "believed that shares of the several companies closely identified with the Rossia will be included."

Rossia Takes Big Part In New Company

Local Insurance Interests Identified With Globe Underwriters Exchange, Holding Concern

Stock Issue Will Raise $12,500,000

President Horatio Barber, of Aero Underwriters Association, Heads Directors List

Hartford Courant, *March 15, 1929*

The article continues to describe Mr. Barber's qualifications as one who was "recognized as one of the pioneers in aviation insurance and one of the foremost underwriters of this class of business."

Less than a year later, in February 1930, several directors of both the Rossia and the Globe exchange boards resigned, citing irreconcilable differences. Apparently, the Globe Underwriters Exchange company did not follow through on original plans. Rossia intended to organize its own securities company which would function in "the manner originally anticipated for the Globe." Barber's name was not mentioned in the reports, nor, as a matter of fact, in any press after the original 1929 announcement.[162]

---

[161] *Aviation* November 30 1929 entitled "Barber Underwriters to Conduct sales Survey"
[162] *Hartford Courant*, Connecticut February 12, 1930

In 1930 Barber made public the second annual report of the Aero Underwriters Corp., for which Barber and Baldwin Inc. was the subsidiary underwriting agency. Excluding premium income which went to reinsurers, the gross income was $1,051,402 and after expenses, the company reported a net income of $204,432.

Also in 1930, Barber & Baldwin issued a booklet describing the development of its aviation insurance service and the various facilities it offered in that field. The firm at that time was affiliated with The Aero Insurance Co., Aero Indemnity Co., Aero Engineering and Advisory Service Inc. and the Aero Underwriters Corp.

Still in 1930, Barber devised a method of ranking pilots, similar to the system used in the Merchant Navy. He sponsored a policy of "moral suasion" in order to exhort pilots and airline operators to greater efforts in safety and regulation. He suggested there were two possible methods for reducing the number of air accidents: either close bureaucratic supervision or a practical and effective campaign to provide efficient and responsible direction among pilots and operators themselves. He favoured the latter as being cheaper and less restrictive to the growth of flying. He suggested a system of honorary ranks which would become automatically substantive in accordance with the position of the individual. This would act as a stimulus to better professional ethics and conduct. He went on to conclude that such a practice would improve the morale and safety of flyers and flying and would establish a superior confidence among foreigners in American air transport. He also pointed out that such trained personnel, with its high morale, would be of unusual value in cases of national emergencies.

In 1931 Barber resigned his position of President of the Aero Underwriters Corporation in order to become Chairman of the Board.

By 1932, Barber had left America to settle in Jersey, one of the Channel Islands. This was now his home base when he was not abroad, and he would eventually retire here. The Aero Underwriters Corporation ceased trading in the mid-forties, along with the name of Barber and Baldwin. It is not certain how much involvement (if any) Barber had in the insurance business from 1932 onwards.

Chapter 15
Barber the Author

Of all of his self-anointed professions, Barber never identified himself as a writer. Which really was his strong suit.

In 1896 and 1897, as Secretary of the Kalgoorlie Hospital in Western Australia, it would have been Barber's remit to write notices and announcements. It is possible that he was the author of the regular newspaper notices that detailed the number of people admitted to hospital, the number who died during that period, and letters of thanks to the donors for their contributions to the hospital fund.

During Barber's days as a stock promoter, he wrote two pamphlets. Both were a means to present himself as a practical mining man and consultant. As well, he used these brochures to advertise his brokerage company, Canada Mines Ltd., and to float two wildcat mines. These schemes are discussed elsewhere in this book.

Cobalt, the Mining District is a careful blend of truth and fiction. Barber describes the geology of the Cobalt region and the major producing mines by including geological reports credited to Prof. WG Miller.

Elsewhere, he includes uncredited accounts by "others" or "officials" that rave about the riches to be encountered and wonderful opportunities not to be missed. These portions, the fictional component, are long on hyperbole and short on fact.

How to Fly a Plane was Barber's first entry into aviation authorship. This book and his more well-known variation *The Aeroplane Speaks* were used as flight training aids during WW1.

Not only the plane, but the surfaces, forces, and angles talk as if in the first person. It is more a book of theory than practical tuition but is written in a very understandable manner. Certain editions include many drawings and illustrations. The novel, clever way in which it was written has made it a classic which is still in print.

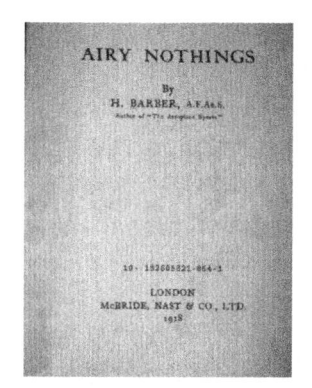

Airy Nothings is a small book of six chapters and a poem. A strange volume, it was written by Barber in 1918 whilst on a fortnight's leave in a Torquay hotel. Most of the chapters are lightly disguised accounts of Barber's own aviation adventure, but one chapter looks into the future and is quite prophetic.

It would be easy to dismiss it as rambling jottings, and indeed *Flight* magazine, which throughout his flying career had given Barber only praise, on this occasion criticized the publication, saying it was a rip-off of Kipling and was frankly a disappointment. The editors also came down on him for appropriating the title from a book of humorous verse by Jesse Pope, who in turn, probably lifted it from Shakespeare's *Midsummer Night's Dream*. There is little doubt that had Barber not had such success with his previous publication, this book would not have been published.

However, the text is compelling in the way it conjures up a certain atmosphere of the time, and if what he writes is based on his own experience, some hidden facts are revealed. We suggest, therefore, the book should not be dismissed lightly.

The first chapter is written in a Betjemanesque style with phrases such as "cool sandy roads of Sunningdale and Blackwater, bordered by sweet-smelling pine woods." Barber starts with a sketch set in 1909, and a gentleman (obviously Barber himself) and his chauffeur (Bertie Woodrow) motor down from London to the west country, through Berkshire and through Basingstoke – Whitchurch - Andover, before ending on Salisbury Plain, where they stop by an obviously new, and to the gentlemen's eyes, "extremely ugly building" quite near the road. The building is made of unpainted corrugated iron and "its extraordinary garishness is utterly at variance with its surroundings." The chauffeur suggests that his employer might like to see this, as "…it belongs to one of these new flying gents as reckons motor cars'll be out of date in a few years." The chauffeur eventually persuades the gentleman to take a look inside the shed. The gentleman concludes that it is a "horrible affair and that if this flying gent succeeds, we may find our lovely countryside entirely spoiled by such abominations."

We have Barber the author looking in on himself, and judging himself, perhaps harshly. The tongue-in-cheek description of the flying machine is interesting. Was Barber reflecting on what he had achieved and had he concluded that his contributions to flight were something less than desirable?

The story continues and describes the gent taking the machine out of the shed, taxiing it around the ground and it actually hopping into the air. Further, there is an account of a photographer laying on his back and taking a shot of the plane off the ground. The ending of this part is again reminiscent of Betjeman, with the gentleman telling his chauffeur to "Drive on to Devizes now. We may still get there in time for tea."

The chapter continues with a sketch set in 1913 in which the gentleman is persuaded by his nephew to take him to "some new Aerodrome as I think they call it" to see some flying machines. Before they go, the gent is reflecting that several hundreds of mad-brained fellows [aviators] whose concentration should be on preparing themselves for life's useful work are pandering to "the mob's" love of adventure and risking the lives of innocent passengers. Again, this seems to be a somewhat critical reflection of Barber himself, as he was perhaps more than anyone the aviator known for taking very many passengers on some of the most adventurous flights.

The gent then suggests that it will be necessary "to send one of my well-known letters to the Times." Incidentally, the phrase "my well-known letters" is one which Barber used repeatedly in his communications from Cobalt and Larder Lake.

The gent then goes on to discuss with his nephew the fact that an aerial post at a shilling a letter from Hendon to Windsor has been set up, and how it can't possibly compete with the beloved GPO. Could this be another reflection on himself as the first aviator to carry commercial cargo?

The man explains to his nephew that he too had been interested in aviation and went through the whole thing on Salisbury Plain not three years ago. Trying to persuade his nephew against becoming an aviator, the gent asks, "Why fly when you are made to walk?"

They proceed to Hendon in the car and the gent reflects on how reliable his chauffeur is and how smart in his blue livery and cap. We can assume from this that Barber and Woodrow had a good working relationship. Further, although Woodrow would have "known his place," Barber was a good employer and had there been any friction, Barber would have vented about it in this book.

On arriving at Hendon, the nephew sees that pleasure flights are available for two guineas. The gent suggests it is too dangerous for his nephew to go up, and in the end, it is he himself who is persuaded by the owner of the machine to take a flight. The gent asks the pilot not to go too high but when the pilot asks if he should descend or go higher, he answers the latter. Whilst at a great height, there is a metallic crash from behind the gent and sudden silence from the engine. The machine dives towards the ground. The pilot says it may be all right, so there is still hope. The gent observes a big hole in the wing where the linen has torn and it gradually gets bigger and that wing starts dipping. The pilot then orders the gent to crawl out onto the opposite rising wing to try to achieve some balance and this he eventually does. He looks back at the pilot who appears to be amused at his plight, and he comes to the conclusion that airmen are all mad and that he had learnt that at Salisbury Plain years ago and as usual he was right. They eventually land safely and the gent is shaken but unhurt and he and his nephew return home. We can perhaps deduce that Barber actually went through this experience when taking a passenger up, and only express regret that he did not write about these things more directly, as there is little evidence.

At home, the nephew enthuses about the future of aviation, with the country studded with good landing grounds and how flying may become safe, pleasant, and useful. The gent declares that it is all about money and that no account has been taken of accidents such as the one he was involved in, to which the nephew says, "Well what about insurance? Anything can be insured nowadays." The gent then goes on to explain underwriters have to make a living and that they are not charitable institutions, and that premiums charged must be more than their losses or there would be no business. Here once again is Barber reflecting on his involvement in aviation insurance, and although that was to become his main business from the time of writing the book (1918), he on more than one occasion stated that the rewards of the industry were not great.

After these arguments against aviation, the nephew brings up the subject of the possible usefulness of the aeroplane for reconnaissance in warfare and that it might change all military strategy and tactics, to which the gent has to concur, and of which Barber as an instructor, was well aware. It seems that in this chapter, Barber feels that the aeroplane will be more important in warfare than in commercial applications. However, in another chapter, he sees the future in air transport.

In the next chapter called "Dream or True Vision" Barber takes us to the future. He talks about travelling in an airliner at 300mph and 70,000ft, of flying over the channel to the Seine and Paris and on to Swiss meadows and Geneva and to Italy and the Mediterranean, and then over Corsica, Bosnia, Albania and the Isles of Greece. While supposedly flying over Corfu[163] he wishes he could descend and lunch on pilaf and wonderful Greek confectionery, and then afterwards stroll along the marina admiring the Corfiote belles (now that sounds like Barber!) They fly over Athens… and the story ends when he feels a dig in the ribs from his wife's parasol as he comes out of his dream to the realities of 1918 Torquay.

A short chapter describes the attractions of ballooning and a flight over London. It is of little consequence other than that it mentions ascending from the prosaic surroundings of Battersea gasworks which he claims to be a drab and uninteresting place to all but a balloonist. However, we must remember that it was the gasworks that attracted the Short brothers to the area, in search of cheaper fuel. They stayed at Battersea after their interest turned to heavier-than-air flight, and their presence attracted other aeroplane builders, including Barber himself.

The penultimate chapter is perhaps the most interesting from our point of view as it illuminates facts about Barber's first plane. Although somewhat ambiguous, we can learn from the narrative. He writes this chapter in a lighthearted, almost humorous style as he attempts to convey his engineer's Scottish accent.

The opening lines set the scene of a solitary shed in the middle of Salisbury Plain in 1909. The term solitary gives us a clue to approximate the date. *Flight* magazine of 17th April 1909 reports

---

[163] Horatio and Elsie may have first landed in Corfu after leaving Canada in 1907 and staying there before relocating to Paris, as suggested by her divorce statement. See Chapter 13.

a site had been allotted on Salisbury Plain close to the Packway and that consent had been given for private aeronautical experimentation. It states that a member of the Aero Club was the first to avail himself of the facility, and this we know to be Barber. The shed was solitary for only a very short time, as by May 29th, 1909, *Flight* reports that the construction of two sets of buildings on Knighton Down for the Army and Navy is proceeding apace. Barber's shed was known to have been completed before the end of May, and at the beginning of June, *Aero* magazine of June 2nd states that the ground has been marked out for two more sheds adjacent to it.

The narrative continues with the description of a weird looking machine of monoplane type within the shed. The first part of the description is concerning its weight which is said to be heavy, far too heavy due to its all-steel body, and with a complicated arrangement of five wheels which were intended to make landing easier should it get off the ground. Therein lies the ambiguity, for all the pictures that we have seen of this plane it would appear to have only 3 wheels to the undercarriage. Is Barber forgetting the details here? Or, as may be the case, were two wheels removed before these photographs were taken in an attempt to lighten the load?

Interestingly, in Jane's *All the World's Airships of 1909*, there is a sketch of what is called Barber's Monoplane. This sketch clearly shows five wheels, three making up the undercarriage (as in the photographs) and one each under the near tip of each wing. Perhaps that was the original configuration which reached Lark Hill, and as he wrote *Airy Nothings*, Barber recalled this original set up.

This sketch in Jane's *Airships of 1909* has been seen by some to be inaccurate, and certainly, the tail plane is different from any photographs of the aeroplane, but it is quite likely that the craft had five wheels at the time the drawing was made, presumably in Howard Wright's workshop in Battersea. Certainly, the drawing illustrates and the text refers to the co-axial rotating propellers; as well, *Airships* states that the wings were fitted with Barber's patent automatic lateral stability system. Also, the sketch clearly shows a system of rotating wing tips rather than the whole wing warping system which seems to have been chosen for the version which Barber took delivery of.

We know this was Barber's first aeroplane because of the description of the all-steel body, and the further description of its two propellers connected to the best French engine, an Antoinette. It is worth noting here that both the EVN powered monoplane and the Avis monoplane had five wheels so it is certainly possible that Barber's plane either started life with five wheels or acquired them during the time at Lark Hill.

Back to the chapter: The pioneer aviator was gazing ruefully at his very expensive first effort. Beside him stood the foreman. This foreman concludes that the heavy construction will have to go and that this flying game calls for something much lighter. The airman replies that he is perfectly right and that they had better scrap it and build something new. The foreman, who is called Harry in the narrative, asked if he could first take a photograph that he wished to send to a friend in the North who is getting interested in flying machines.

This "Harry" is probably the thinly disguised Herbert Henry Bannister who became Barber's assistant/foreman during his time at Lark Hill. Herbert was a local tinsmith with a business in Durrington, and it is thought his wife provided accommodation in a house near the Stonehenge Inn, Durrington. Of note is the fact that in *Kelly's Directory* of the area for both 1901 and 1911 he is listed simply as a Tinsmith, whereas in the 1911 census he enters his occupation as the grander "Aeroplane Constructor."

By 1920, Bannister was listed as a shop keeper in *Kelly's*. It is known that he built wheels for some of Barber's aeroplanes, but the 1911 census suggests he was much more involved and was most likely the constructor for Barber when the first Valkyrie model was being built at Lark Hill.

The narrative continues and Harry takes a picture of the aeroplane in the hangar, including some guests who had arrived at the shed to take tea with the pioneer. Just ten days later, the pioneer is at work on his second machine.

There is no suggestion here that they have moved back to Battersea for the building of this machine, which if true is at odds with most accounts of Barber's second machine being the ASL monoplane which is believed to have been built by Wright and Manning under Barber's supervision. This is interesting because when he was interviewed during the period of the ASL collapse, Barber suggested that he had five aeroplanes at Lark Hill, but only four are documented: the Wright monoplane, the ASL monoplane, the Valkyrie prototype and the Valkyrie No.1.

The question could then be asked – was some machine built at Lark Hill, in between the Wright monoplane and the ASL monoplane? The answer is probably no since no information has come to light. However, it should be remembered that Lark Hill was very isolated at that time.

Journals such as *Flight* have no entries other than to broadly report that experiments are being conducted on Salisbury Plain. In spite of the fact that local people were drawn to the site in hundreds, the two local newspapers of the day make no mention of Barber's experiments.

According to *Airy Nothings,* the second machine is a lighter, all-wood machine with a more powerful engine and that the builder is unable to make use of any part of his first machine. Consequently, it is relegated to just a bad memory that cost him £1000. The description of this aeroplane certainly fits that of the ASL monoplane in that it was built of wood with a more powerful engine, so perhaps that is what he is describing in the story.

But how to explain this following anomaly? Records show that the ASL monoplane came about after Barber conducted a prolonged study of model aeroplanes, but in the narrative, he was again busy building another machine after only ten days.

The second part of the narrative gives us more clues as to what happened to the Howard Wright machine.

The pioneer finds Harry reading a letter from an aviation enthusiast in the North. The author of the letter explains that he wishes to buy the Howard Wright machine and get it into the air without delay, in order to start an aerial passenger line. He suggests that he could improve the machine with time. He enquires if it is for sale and the price required. The pioneer then turns to his secretary, Donald and instructs him to write a reply to the writer of the "mad epistle."

Donald, being a Scot, is dismayed at the losses made by his employer, but had termed "the new and improved machine a feckless contraption," decides to recoup some of the pioneer's losses. He thus replies to the letter, that the machine can hardly be called a liner, because its flights have been somewhat limited owing to its metal construction, and yet it has actually left the ground and might perform fairly well if a light wooden body were substituted. The total cost of manufacture has been about £1000 but the owner is building another machine and would take a reasonable offer.

So: we have more clues. The machine has been modified and there are photographs to show this, but most importantly we can say that it did actually get airborne.

Three days later, the secretary enters the drawing office with a telegram. The communication is an offer of £800 for the feckless contraption. The secretary is very excited and apparently astounds the mechanics with a flow of pure Gaelic. The pioneer exclaims that they can certainly not take advantage of anyone, but the secretary responds with a quick retort, "Well sir yo'll no forget that you thought it worth spending a £1000 on it." The secretary then explains that he told the fellow that the machine barely got off the ground and would need a new lighter body and so forth and said he was very precise in his description, and that it would be sinful for the pioneer to refuse the offer. The pioneer lets the secretary have his way and returns to his drawing board.

The aeroplane that was the subject of the correspondence was of course Barber's machine that was built by Howard Wright.

In the last part of the sketch, called the sequel, the secretary is seen coming back into the drawing office and presents the pioneer with what he calls an interesting communication. This is a prospectus for an airline company called the Trans-Continental Aerial Navigation Company of Great Britain Ltd., with a capital of £50,000. The document describes the vast wealth to be made with the conquest of the air and the intention of putting the British Empire at the fore of Aerial Superiority. It states that the men who are now interested in forming this company have for some time been investigating monoplanes, biplanes, multiplanes, helicopters, ornithopters and dirigibles, and that after much research they have been fortunate enough to secure, without doubt, the most bird-like and therefore practical flying machine yet invented. The machine [aerial liner] has been built and proven in free flight. It was produced on scientific lines under conditions of the greatest secrecy in the wilds of Salisbury Plain. The owner is an airman of extraordinary brilliance, a mechanician rather than a mechanic, an inventor rather than an engineer, one who is more interested in scientific research than money and has granted an option of purchase for the very reasonable sum of £3000 in cash and 25,000 £1 shares.

How Barber must have enjoyed penning those few lines about his own brilliance!

The pioneer only realizes this when he gets to the end of the prospectus, turns over the page and there is the picture that "Harry" took with some passengers on board enjoying tea.

Barber tells us that this is all true and that readers should scan the press of the time to verify it.

From this sequel, we know that the machine was sold "to a man in the North," likely H. Hales, judging from an advertisement that appeared in the *Aero* magazine on 12th October 1910:

"Magnificent passenger-carrying Wright monoplane with a 50hp Antoinette engine, not used, cost £1,000 a Bargain. H. Hales, Burslem.

This man, this H. Hales was Harold Keates Hales. (See Appendix 3, for more about H. K. Hales.)

At the end of the book is a poem entitled *Flight - a Rhapsody* which was inspired by the memory of the late Wilbur Wright. This is Barber's first venture into poetry and fortunately seems also to be his last. Not the worst poem ever written, certainly, but not worth commenting upon here.

Airy Nothings is a book with hidden depths, one which could easily be dismissed on first reading but is worth a second glance to any person wishing to get closer to the man and the times.

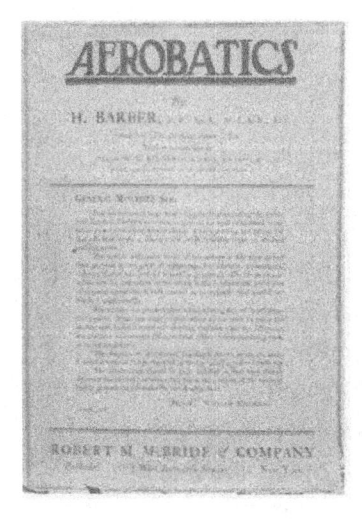

Aerobatics is a remarkable work for several reasons. Barber has been credited for coining the term, a plural noun meaning loops, rolls, and other feats of spectacular flying performed in one or more aircraft to entertain an audience on the ground. The word has remained in use in the English language.

Barber is also famous for being the first to execute several of the manoeuvres described in the book. For example, he was able to demonstrate exactly what was going on when a plane gets into a tight helical spin in terms of air currents, eddies, forces on the surfaces, and so on. Although aviators such as Parke showed by accident how to get out of a spin, it was Barber who first applied theory to this and many other manoeuvres.

Again, this book is still being reprinted and is freely available, so no in-depth discussion of this book is required here.

In 1932, Barber's name was included in *Who's Who of American Authors Vol IV 1929 - 1930*.

BARBER, HORATIO: aeronautical underwriter; b. Croydon, Eng., Sept. 11, 1875; s. Charles Worthington and Isobel (Loughborough) B.; educ. Bedford and Oxford Univ.; m. Bertha Louise Alexandra (von Hildenbrand), 1914. AUTHOR: The Aeroplane Speaks, 1917; Aerobatics, 1918; Airy Nothings, 1919. General character writing, aeronautical; began building and flying aircraft, 1908; designed, built and flew the first all-British airplane; qualified as airplane and airship pilot; organizer of works of Aircraft Mfg. Co., officer of Royal Flying Corps during World War; organized Aviation Ins. Assn. of Lloyd's came to U. S. 1922; pres. Aero Underwriters Corp., Aero Insurance Co., Aero Indemnity Co., Barber and Baldwin, Inc., Aero Engineering and Advisory Service, Inc., Avbar, Inc., Aviation Syndicate, Irc., Fellow Royal Aeronautical Soc., Royal Geog. Soc., member Inst. of Aeronaut. Engrs. CLUBS: Army and Navy (New York), American Yacht Club, Royal Societies (London), Royal Air Force, Royal Aero. OFFICE: 122 E. 42nd St., New York, N. Y.; HOME: East Portchester Conn.

Entry for Horatio Barber in Who's Who Among North American Authors Vol IV 1929 – 1930.

Note the conflicting detail regarding his education at Oxford. The University has no record of his attending.

Also inaccurate is the notation that "he began flying aircraft in 1908." He first flew in the UK in 1909.

Chapter 16

On Jersey and the Travel in Retirement

In the early 1930s, Barber and his family moved to the Channel Island of Jersey. This island is a tax haven, and this is the most likely reason for his moving there, except of course it is a very agreeable place to live. He eventually retired there. Unlike in his previous existences, there are very few records of his life on the island and what little we have was difficult to retrieve. It appears he went into semi-retirement, keeping a much lower profile than in his former years, although he was still an avid traveller and crossed the Atlantic many times to Canada, the US, Bermuda, and St. Kitts and Nevis.

On December 30, 1933, Barber bought a fine house called "Belmont" on the northern outskirts of St. Helier in what is now the junction of Oaklands Lane and Rue Mont Neron. The cost at that time was £4,100. Belmont is a rather grand yet attractive affair in a Gothic Revival style. Today, nearly unchanged, the property would be worth several million. No doubt Barber would have stayed here in retirement had it not been for the events of 1939.

Belmont St Helier ca 1930 www.theislandwiki.org

Belmont St Helier 2108 Terry Grace

On September 3, 1939, Britain declared war on Germany, but there was little change on the Channel Islands. The residents carried on with their lives in the usual fashion for six months or more. Only at the last possible moment did anyone consider thoughts of evacuation.

Either Horatio had great foresight, or he was very lucky. December 23, 1939, he sold Belmont for the princely sum of £9,950. The unfortunate buyer lost his new home to the Germans when their army invaded just six months later.

The Barber family told Norman Parker the story about how Horatio and presumably his family drove their car down to the docks in St. Helier, immobilized it and managed to catch the very last boat out of Jersey. Of course, this may be factual. However, when we spoke with a member of the Jersey Historical Society, she suggested that it was probably apocryphal. She said, "If I had a pound for every time I heard that story…"

Horatio and family returned to Britain and stayed briefly at the charming residence of Basset Manor, Checkendon, Oxon.

September 1940, Horatio, his wife, daughter Suzanne and son James sailed to Bermuda from Liverpool on the *Pacific Steam Ship Orbita*.

Bassett Manor, Checkendon, www.geograph.org.uk

The passenger list informs us that Bermuda was to be their permanent place of residence. Barber often made this declaration on his travel documents, but he rarely stayed for very long. We also learn that by this time his occupation was listed as "retired." He was 64 years of age.

During May 1941, Horatio and Bertha sailed on the *SS Evangeline* to New York to visit Horatio's son from his first marriage, Conrad Hope Barber. It is interesting to note that Barber has a broken forefinger on his left hand. Horatio's calling is given as "nil."

Two years later in April 1943 Barber and his wife are aboard the aircraft *Atlantic Clipper* and land at La Guardia Field in New York. It is possible that this was the first time he flew on a commercial flight. According to the manifest, the couple travelled to 15 E. 60th St. New York. Again, under the heading "Purpose of coming and time remaining", the term "reside permanently" is entered.

Two months later, we find the Barbers in Vermont. On June 21, 1943, a bit from the society pages in the *Burlington Free Press* reports that Mr. and Mrs. Horatio Barber are staying at Porter House.[164]

> mer at the school. — Mr. and Mrs. Horatio Barber of England are in Porter house to remain till October first. — Alexis Alfred Den-

Here again, we see that Barber is not one to stay still for very long, even during wartime.

A year later, on June 28, 1944, Horatio and Bertha returned to the United States from Canada. The border crossing document includes several notable entries.

Barber has been described as being a tall man but this entry has him at 5'10". His WW1 records indicate 5'9¾ ", what we would consider an average height. Perhaps this is quibbling, but one cannot help but wonder if Barber gave the impression of being taller by his demeanour, as would someone who had a personality that was "larger than life."

This time his occupation was recorded as "executive." The reverse of the document is more revealing.

---

[164] The name Porter here is intriguing since that was his second wife Elsie's maiden name! Was he perhaps staying with his ex-wife's family? More likely, Porter House was the name of hotel.

MANIFEST — Port of ROUSES POINT, N.Y. Date JUN 28 1944 Serial No. 795

B-616

Family name	Given name	Accompanied by
BARBER	HORATIO CLAUDE	Wife Bertha L.A.

C.T.V. No. 2320 Place and date: Montreal, Can. JUN 27 1944 Section and subdivision: Act of 1924, 5 Quota country charged: GT. BRITAIN

Place of birth: Croydon, Surrey, England Age: 68 Yrs. Sex: M Occupation: Executive Read: Yes

Language or exemption: English Race: England Nationality: Eng. Last permanent residence: Warwick West, Bermuda

Name and address of nearest relative or friend in country whence applicant came: Son, James C.

Ever in U.S.: Yes, 4/23/43 To: New York, N.Y. Passage paid by: self

Destination: 15 E. 60th Street, New York, N.Y.

Money shown: $200 Ever arrested and deported: No Purpose in coming and time remaining: Reside Permanently

Head tax status: NJ 9212b Height: 5 ft. 10 in. Complexion: Med. Hair: Gray Eyes: Blue Distinguishing marks: Lt. fore finger broken

Seaport and date of landing: N.Y. (LaGuardia Field) 4/23/43 Atlantic City N.C.18804 Registration card No. ARY-102-103

Records by N.Y. Primarily examined at 4/23/43 LA.3(2)6Mos.

U.S. Department of Justice, Immigration and Naturalization Service. Form I-448 (Ed. 1941)

DISPOSITION BEFORE B.S.I. / **VISITORS OR TRANSITS**

MEDICAL CERTIFICATE

Afflicted with: DEFECTIVE VISION
PRE-SENILITY
CLASS "B"

Part of body afflicted: —

Born 9/11/75

Joseph Markel, Surgeon, U.S. Public Health Service

REMARKS AND ENDORSEMENTS

99578/831 FX-19245 AR-7591042
P.P.C-111718 Great Britain, valid to 5/29/45
Letter 5/16/44 An. Cons. Montreal, Canada
PX 6/14/44 at N.Y. P.A. McGlynn, Imm. Inspector

Under the heading, "Medical Certificate" it states that he was "afflicted" with defective vision and pre-senility class "B", a condition that today we would call "early signs of dementia."

After the war, Barber returned to Jersey and on October 15, 1945, he purchased another property, 4 Balmoral Terrace on the Trinity Road. This home was also situated on the northern outskirts of St. Helier, but nearer to town, and somewhat more modest than Belmont. The house is a large, four-storey Victorian end unit of a terrace house, with a small garden, but good views. The exterior today looks the same as it did in the 1940s, but the interior has been sub-divided into apartments.

4 Balmoral Terrace, 2018 Terry Grace

It is not known why Horatio bought this smaller property, whether for practical or financial reasons, but this is where he would be based and spend the rest of his life, except for travel and an extended stay on Nevis in the Caribbean.

> The Britannia Trophy was put up for competition in unusual circumstances. In 1911, Mr. Horatio Barber, a founder-member of the Royal Aero Club and designer of the Valkyrie tail-first monoplane and Viking biplane, was given £100 for making a commercial flight. He was anxious to retain his status as an amateur pilot and gave the money to the Royal Aero Club for the trophy. Mr. Barber is the holder of aviator's certificate No. 30, issued in November, 1910. He now lives in Bermuda. Until now, winners of the trophy have merely held it for a year and have had no permanent memento of their achievement. The plaques to be presented in February will remedy this.

Horatio was living in Bermuda in 1952 according to an announcement in the Times *from December 22nd of that year.*

Primarily, the information in this chapter has been culled from travel documents and one or two notices in the society pages. By 1952, when Barber was living in Bermuda, he was in his late 70s. Toward the end of this period, he generally identified himself as retired, or without an occupation. Naturally, he had slowed down somewhat, and perhaps in his case, any undertakings he wished to pursue were hampered by his "pre-senility" diagnosis. His name or his business interests were no longer deemed newsworthy if we are to judge by the lack of headlines in the papers. Until, that is, he travelled to Nevis.

On the Caribbean island, once again Barber created a stir when he took on the role of "Colonial Development Officer."

Chapter 17

On Nevis, Mr. Barber Causes an Earthquake

To say that Horatio Barber was a man of legend may sound like hyperbole, but in this case, it is a fact. In their book *Caribbean Folk Tales and Short Stories*, Ophelia A. Powell Torres and Victor M. Torres tell the story of "A Mysterious Phenomenon"[165] in which our protagonist plays a starring role. The setting is on Nevis in the West Indies in the early 1950s.

One night, so the story goes, the folks of Nevis were startled from their sleep. "Loud roaring noises like rolling thunder" came from the mountain, and heavy earthquakes caused avalanches of dirt and rocks to cascade down Nevis Peak. Since the locals knew it was a volcanic mountain, they feared it was about to erupt.

> The monkeys fled from the mountains to find refuge, protection and companionship with the people in the villages.
>
> Many of the monkeys never returned to the mountain and have taken up residency in the villages until today.
>
> What would have caused such earthquakes and roaring noises from the mountain to cause people and the monkeys to flee in despair?
>
> What could have caused the mountain to sound so angry, irritable and frustrated like a mad man?

What caused the commotion? A better question would be, "Who?"

The answer, of course, is Horatio Claude Barber, Colonial Development Officer.[166]

The Bath House

In 1947, Barber travelled to St. Kitts and Nevis where he purchased an old hotel, formerly known as The Bath House, from Mrs. Edmund Branch.[167] He lived there with his family.

---

[165] *Caribbean Folk tales and Short Stories*, Ophelia A. Powell Torres and Victor M. Torres, 2005
[166] In 1949 Barber and his wife Bertha departed the UK for Bermuda, via NY – his occupation was Colonial Development Officer.
[167] Horatio Claude Barber testimony, quoted in *The Union Messenger*, Friday April 4, 1952

The Bath Hotel, as it became known, was originally built by Mr. John Huggins. Some sources say such notables as Horatio Nelson and Samuel Taylor Coleridge stayed there.

The hotel was built above a naturally occurring hot spring which was said to have healing properties. The Nevisians had been using the waters for both therapeutic and practical purposes for generations. In later years, after colonization, the site was a tourist attraction.

An advertisement from the 1843 Guide to the Madeiras, Azores, British and Foreign West Indies, Mexico, and Northern South-America, etc *by John Osborne*

The 1843 illustration[168] above appeared in a guidebook published in Britain and produced by The Royal Mail Steam Packet Co. which started regular services to St. Kitts in 1835. The image was part of an advertisement for "Mineral Spa, Bath House, Nevis" the text of which declares that "the extraordinary powers and unfailing efficacy of the NEVIS BATHS have been long well known in the medical world, and have been celebrated in every treatise descriptive of the colonies."

The hotel passed through several hands over the generations and underwent cycles of decay and ruin followed by renovations and rebuilding.

Neal Ferris of the University of Western Ontario in London, Ontario, conducted archaeological fieldwork at the bathhouse site in 2018. Based on his research, published online in April 2019, the date of the original construction of the building remains uncertain, though the records suggest it was between the 1780s and early 1820s."[169] Ferris reported that today the local people still consider the hot springs as vitally important and they use the site frequently.

Leeward Islands Development Company

Also in 1947, Barber purchased additional parcels of land adjacent to the hotel, and he organized the Leeward Islands Development Company Ltd. He envisioned a luxury hotel as a destination for rich tourists. According to Ferris, this was an ambitious undertaking similar to earlier proposals from the 1880s. The local government was receptive to Barber's plans and

---

[168] Screen capture from Google Books

[169] A note from author Maggie Wilson: Again, serendipity played a big part in our research. As we prepared to put the book together, we had little to go on regarding Barber's time in Nevis. When I searched online one last time, I came upon Neal Ferris' just published research paper, *Aspirational Heritage: The History & Archaeology of the Bath House-Hotel and Bath Stream-Spring Landscape, Nevis. Report Prepared for the Nevis Historical & Conservation Society (NHCS)* April 2019.

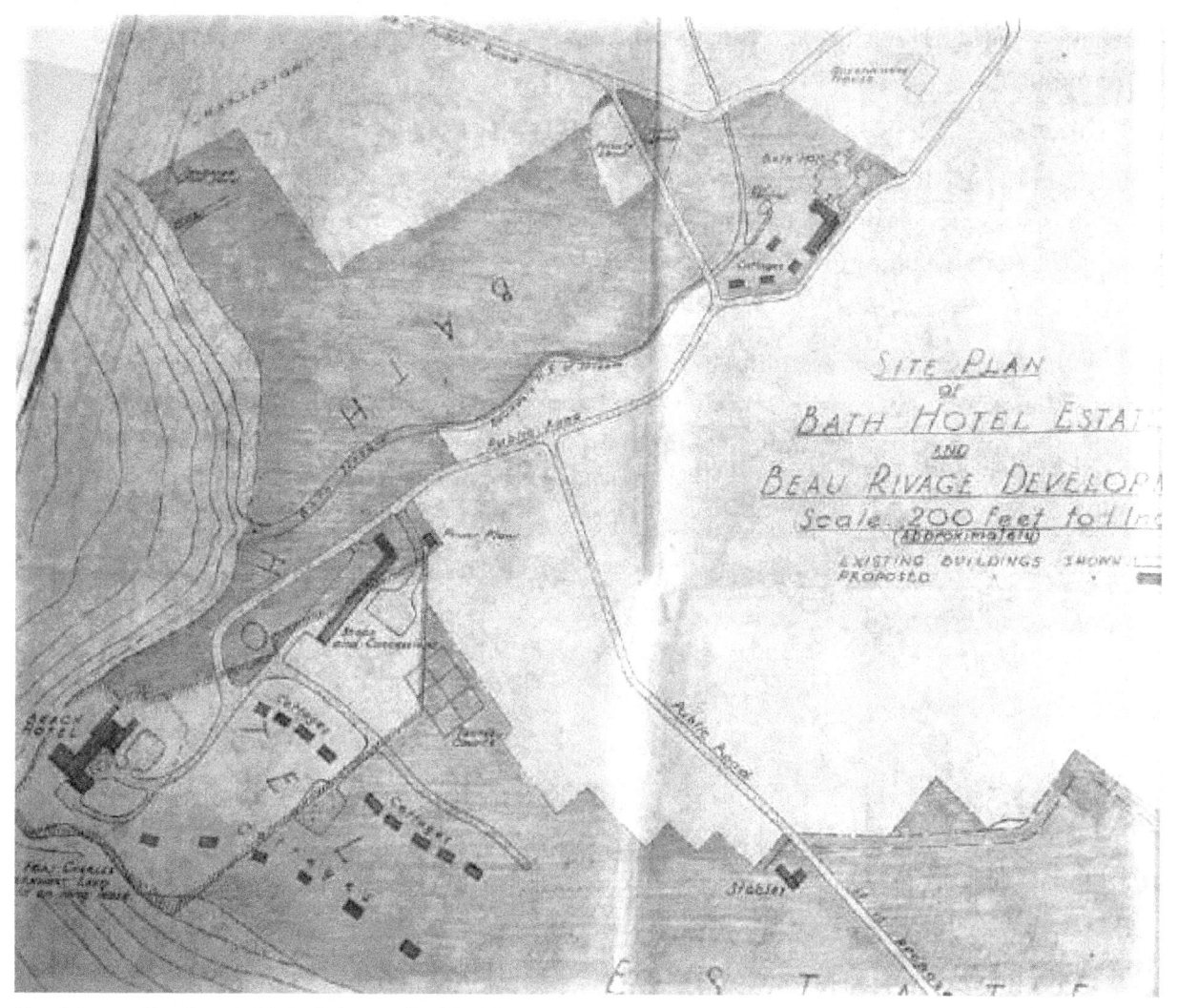

Development Plan from 1948, including Barber's holdings in darker grey, and public lands encompassing Fort Charles, to be leased by the Colonial Administration (Presidency of St. Kitts, Nevis and Anguilla) to Barber. Note the absence of Bath village and local residences from the map. Nelson Museum Archives, Bath Hotel Folios, D2.3. Used with permission by Neal Ferris

agreed to cooperate with his development company on the condition that Barber allowed the local residents to have their customary access to the site. Ferris writes that "Mr. Barber agreed to do this and even undertook to build shelters for the use by the people."

Barber was slow to get the project underway. At first, the tourist business consisted of renting out the existing hotel units and providing the bathers with access to the springs. When the economy took a downturn in 1949, Barber put his development plans on hold. By 1950, the local Nevis administration was under the impression that Barber had given up the project, although Barber denied the assertion.

In 1950 Horatio and his wife Bertha were living in the hotel. From their balconies, the Barbers and their paying guests had a full view of the pathway which the local people used to access the traditional bathing site. Barber repeatedly claimed that he had no problem with the people using the springs. However, he did find it troubling that those bathers were often noisy and often naked. Barber protested, and the relationship between him and the Nevisians turned confrontational.

Horatio's name was in the local newspaper headlines after he tried to stop the offending parade of nude bathers. He filled in the source of the spring, planted cacti around the bathing pool and erected barbed-wire fences. As the property owner, he felt that he was within his rights to refuse access to the bathing site. The local government and the local citizenry, of course, felt otherwise.

Nevis council considered a resolution to acquire the necessary land to ensure public access to the hot springs but withdrew the motion when Barber said that he was willing to compromise. He reiterated his claim that he did not want to prevent people from using the springs. But he did want a view that was unsullied by naked bathers. To solve the problem, he proposed that the offending bathing pool be relocated out of the way of the main hotel.

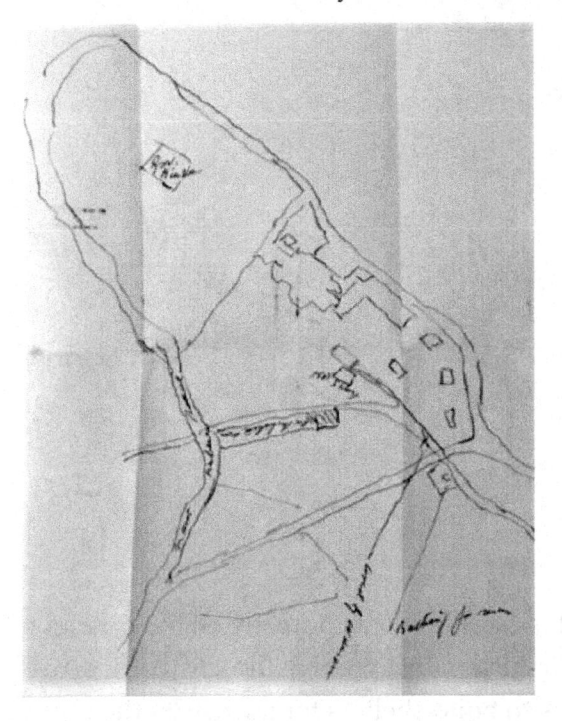

Barber's sketch plan accompanying a letter from G.P. Boon to Administrator Burrowes, August 11, 1950 (NASKN COMP, S29/00001 A185/50). The sketch depicts the location of the Women's bathing place, and "C", in the lower right, the proposed new location of the Men's bathing place. It also marks a prohibited area (path from the "Main Island Road"), including a diagonal box depicting where men had been bathing (and generally where most Stream-bathing occurs today). Used with permission by Neal Ferris

Ferris tells us that in December 1950, "on his own initiative, Barber constructed a concrete pool downstream and out of sight of the [hotel] in the hopes of encouraging people to bathe there." According to Barber, the building was destroyed in the dark of night by local people.

Fact and folklore intersect at this point, as illustrated in this passage from the Torres and Torres folk tale, "A Mysterious Phenomenon".

> **A Mysterious Phenomenon**
>
> The people of Nevis proved to be very wise. They immediately connected the little concrete house built by Mr. Barber in the middle of the hot spring with the earthquakes and loud roaring noises of the mountain.
>
> Nevisians, having diagnosed the ailment of the mountain armed themselves with their prescription sledge hammers and demolished the little concrete house.
>
> Naturally, believe it or not, when the little concrete house was demolished, the hot spring flowed freely again and the earthquakes and roaring noises from the mountain ceased.
>
> *Caribbean Folk tales and Short Stories*, Ophelia A. Powell Torres and Victor M. Torres

Anti-Colonial Sentiment on Nevis

In 1951, Nevisians continued to agitate for total independence from British colonial rule. Unwittingly, Barber had played into the hands of those who lobbied for a free nation. "From the beginning of the [bath house] episode, local officials were expressing concerns that …interested parties are making as much political capital as they can out of the affair."[170]

Proponents of an emancipated Nevis looked upon Barber's refusal to allow unhampered access to the hot springs as an "act consistent with [past] British colonial injustices."[171] They referred to Horatio's efforts to secure a semblance of privacy in his own home, on his own property as colonial domination.

To demonstrate their objections, protestors organized a "bathe-in."

On the morning of June 10, 1951, about 150 people congregated at the hotel hot springs. They brought along a gramophone and speakers. Disturbed by the racket, Horatio, with the assistance of a policeman, confronted Robert Bradshaw who was president of the Labour Union and the protest leader. Barber demanded that Bradshaw and his gang depart at once.

About an hour later, at their leisure, the group moved across the street to attend a rally hosted by the Labour Union. There, they listened to Bradshaw's speech. It the newspapers, Bradshaw was quoted as saying, "I told [the rally attendees] we had gone to bathe and had a very nice time in our waters. I told them… they could continue to go to the stream & bathe as they have been accustomed to bathe from time immemorial and, further, that if Mr. Barber misbehaved himself… they should pay him no attention whatsoever because he could do nothing about their going to the stream and bathing in it… I reminded them that Mr. Barber was an alien to these shores, but that as one of His Majesty's subjects he had a right to live in any part of the

---

[170] NASKN COMP, S29/00001 A185/50: Letter from Warden, Evelyn to Administrator Burrowes, June 15, 1950, as cited in Ferris' *Aspirational Heritage*
[171] *Aspirational Heritage: The History & Archaeology of the Bath House-Hotel and Bath Stream-Spring Landscape, Nevis. Report Prepared for the Nevis Historical & Conservation Society (NHCS);* Neal Ferris, April 2019.

Empire; but that if Mr. Barber continued to make a nuisance of himself… then it would be necessary for my government to do something positive about it…. more aliens to these shores will come, but so long as they behave themselves and realize that they have come to live with us, everything would be all right."[172]

For a week after the bathe-in, people harassed and threatened Barber, hurling insults at him and throwing stones at his hotel. Barber complained to the authorities.

Correspondence between Barber's lawyer and colonial officials indicates that the police took the complaints seriously and they investigated Barber's claims. However, one official felt that Barber was a man who was prone to exaggeration and who had "not the faintest idea of dealing with the people of Nevis; that he was tactless and irritable… and that "his nature is such that he does little to improve his relations with the local people."

The governor's office investigated whether charges of sedition could be laid against Bradshaw, the leader of the bathe-in. While the authorities found that Bradshaw had acted in an inciting and seditious manner, they felt it more politically prudent to let him off with a warning.

Back in Court

Barber sued for damages in April 1952. He claimed that because of the trespass his business lost money, and he personally suffered. The defendants admitted to being on the property, but that it was a public space and that they were within their rights, since partaking of the therapeutic baths was a custom since "time immemorial." The judge ruled that Barber had not proven financial loss. However, the judge did find that the protesters organized "an aggravated trespass, in which over 100 people invaded Barber's property as if it were a public park." Barber was awarded $1500.[173]

Views of the Bath Hotel Verandah and ramparts, ca. 1952. NMA Photo folio, D1 Bath Hotel (one of a series identified as originating from the Bath Hotel & Assoc.). It was perhaps from this verandah that on June 10, 1950, Horatio Barber came out to first see the start of the Workers League's "Bathe-In." Used with permission by Neal Ferris.

After the court case, Barber made it known, once again, that he had never intended to prevent the use of the springs, as long as the public bathed where and when he deemed appropriate. But then, no doubt tired, frustrated, and perhaps somewhat mystified, Barber took the usual next step when he met conflict. He fled.

---

[172] *Union Messenger* 1952, as cited in Ferris' *Aspirational Heritage*
[173] *St. Kitts - Nevis Daily Bulletin* April 15, 1952 as cited in Ferris' *Aspirational Heritage*

The Leeward Islands Development Company was just another grand project in Barber's long list of endeavours. He was used to success. Unfortunately, the contentious issue between Barber and the Nevisians served to energize and strengthen the drive for independence from British colonial rule. The timing of the tourism enterprise was terrible. He had not anticipated this outcome, being "tone deaf" to the social and political climate in which he chose to live and conduct business.

We close this chapter of Barber's time in the Caribbean with a paragraph from Ferris's archaeology report:

"In 1952, Barber hired Philippe de Froberville to be his property manager. Correspondence between Barber and de Froberville indicates that Barber only rarely returned to Nevis after 1952, though kept a keen oversight on his business affairs on the island at least until 1961. Over that decade, de Froberville regularly undertook to meet and communicate with prospective purchasers of Barber's property, kept the books for the Leeward Islands Development Co., and managed the Bath Hotel Estate and Hot Springs as a subsidiary of Barber's larger corporation."[174]

As of April 2019, Ferris also notes that it is unknown if Barber was able to sell the hotel before he died in 1964.

Explosive Postscript

Correspondence with the Nevis Historical and Conservation Society yielded this tantalizing bit of ephemera related to Horatio's time on the island. The Society referred to it as an "Interesting Fact." Of course, as per usual, we are left wondering…

> **Interesting Fact**
>
> Barber was given a license under the provisions of the Explosives Ordinance No. 11 of 1951 giving him permission to import and store 200lbs of gelignite and 500 detonators at Montravers Estate, Nevis on 9th March 1955.
>
> The license stated that he must use the gelignite within four months upon arrival, store it in a separate building from detonators, securely locked, and at least 200 yards from nearest dwelling or thoroughfare.
>
> Warning notices suitably posted to satisfaction and licensee shall comply with any instructions issued from Superintendent of Police or anyone designated by him (Superintendent of Police).

---

[174] *Aspirational Heritage: The History & Archaeology of the Bath House-Hotel and Bath Stream-Spring Landscape, Nevis. Report Prepared for the Nevis Historical & Conservation Society (NHCS)* Neal Ferris, April 2019

Chapter 18

The Story Ends

Horatio Barber died July 6, 1964, bringing to an end an extraordinary life of exceptional achievements, scandal, and outrageous swindles.

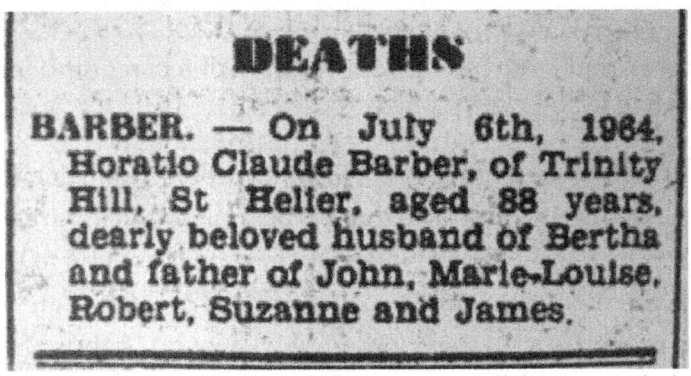

DEATHS

BARBER. — On July 6th, 1964, Horatio Claude Barber, of Trinity Hill, St Helier, aged 88 years, dearly beloved husband of Bertha and father of John, Marie-Louise, Robert, Suzanne and James.

Jersey Evening Post *July 7, 1964. It has been reported that Horatio died from cancer, but we are unable to confirm.*

Previous accounts of Barber concentrated almost entirely on his aviation career since little was known about his life before or after that time. The aviation magazines of the day, and especially *Flight* depicted him and other aviators as superheroes, which of course they were during that embryonic stage of aviation.

Our research has cast light on Horatio's other less-illustrious activities. The character who is revealed, a down-to-earth human being, is an equally fascinating man.

Conclusions

Before our research project began, Terry was in the process of compiling an updated history of the aviation pioneer Horatio Barber and his contribution to flight in Great Britain. Terry knew that Barber made his fortune from mining in Canada, but what mines? Where? Was Barber a mine owner? An investor? When Terry found references to a Horatio Barber associated with Cobalt, Ontario, a silver mining town, he contacted Maggie of the Cobalt Historical Society, and the rest, as they say… is history. We agreed to combine forces and to write a more complete account of Horatio Claude Barber.

We are satisfied that we have answered the question about Barber's wealth: he made his fortune as a speculator and stockbroker. His most lucrative period was 1906 to 1907 when he facilitated the sale of shares in wildcat mines, first in the silver camp at Cobalt, then in the goldfields of Larder Lake.

Another of our goals was to fill in the blanks in existing Barber biographies, before and after his time in aviation. Most of those timelines have a great gap from the date of his birth in 1875 to 1909.

While we have shed light on portions of that mysterious time, much still remains hidden. Due to the nature of the man and the nature of his businesses, his name was often in the news. Frustratingly, and by the same token, his name was often *not* in the news. These were usually the episodes when he landed himself in legal tangles and the headline stories ended abruptly, without follow up reports.

As far as we can tell, after he arrived back in the UK in 1909, his time as a stockbroker was never mentioned again, apart from the small line in Elsie's divorce notice in 1915. One almost wonders if Mrs. Barber, in a moment of retaliation, tried to disgrace her ex-husband.

Speculator and Speculation

Which brings us to the definition of the word "speculator." As an occupation, Barber's job as a stockbroker was to encourage and facilitate investment in mining.

Our job as researchers is to present the details we uncovered in newspapers and literature. While these reports help to sketch in Horatio's life, we get only a superficial outline. The stories passed along by the Barber family offer tantalizing clues, but they do nothing to clarify the story. So many questions remain unanswered, not only during his time before aviation but all through his life. We can only speculate.

For instance, how did Barber manage to escape the negative press after his time as a stockbroker in Canada? Barber was an excellent self-publicist and he spent great sums to promote himself, his brokerage and his associates' mining companies. How could his mining involvement which generated so much copy in the newspapers not be remembered just two years later? Especially when you consider the number of people from all over the world who lost money by investing in his schemes. If he took steps to suppress the stockbroker story, he did a very fine job indeed. If he was a "fugitive from justice" as described by the *Canadian Mining Journal*, perhaps he knew people in high places who would, for a price, keep the news out of the press.

Then again, perhaps he wasn't wanted by the police since the authorities had their sights set on "larger game." At the turn of the 20th century, extradition treaty laws were ineffective. Con-artists regularly used loopholes to escape arrest, and they fled from the scene of the crime to take cover in a neighbouring country. This included men who swindled others for far greater amounts than did our Mr. Barber.

Perhaps it was simply the case that people have short memories, something that every good promoter of a mining company knows.

Many books have been written about pioneer aviators and only a few give Barber the briefest of mention. Most omit him altogether. His aviation career is only a degree more memorable than his time in mining. Although some of his flying achievements have been documented, he remains under the shadow of the likes of Samuel Cody or A.V. Roe.

More questions surface when we think about his personality and how that affected the people in his life. What was it about Horatio that compelled him to start up in one direction and then move so abruptly to another? He strikes us as a "twitchy" sort of personality, loud, abrasive, impulsive, restless. What was it like working with or being married to a man like that?

For at least the last twenty years of his life he had apparently lived with dementia. But was pre-senility the correct diagnosis? Today, would his condition be characterized as obsessive-compulsive, or attention deficit hyperactivity disorder? He still managed to organize and run the Bath House business on Nevis. Perhaps his intellectual impairment, whether from ageing or some other medical ailment, contributed to the failed venture.

What about his relationship with his children? It appears that he and the two boys from the first marriage were estranged. Only the children of Barber's third marriage are listed in his death notice, shown above. In Horatio's will, he bequeathed the house at Balmoral Terrace and two-thirds of his personal property to his wife Bertha, and the remaining one-third to his five children divided equally between them. As for the two sons from his second marriage to Elsie, Claude Percy Barber had died in 1960, but Conrad Hope Barber was still very much alive in 1964.

Sadly, no obituaries have come to light. Perhaps when Horatio Claude Barber died on July 6, 1964, aged 88, he had grown to enjoy his privacy.

Horatio Barber was a man of the times, one of the thousands who set out on great adventures to explore the new frontiers and to strike it rich. He was a man who made up for his limited education with self-confidence and resourcefulness, "base guile and unrighteous shrewdness." If gardening skills were required, he claimed to have them. If the job called for a mining engineer, then that was his occupation, or so he wanted people to believe.

Of his three marriages, at least two seem to have been impulsive and ill-advised, but Barber answered only to his own desires. His restlessness and his impulsiveness were a curse at times, but on other occasions, his salvation.

By 1909 when he began to devote his time and money to aviation, he appears to have outgrown his less reputable habits. It could be that revisions that closed loopholes in investment legislation convinced him to toe the line. After all, January 1909 was when his cohort Frank Law was jailed for defrauding investors using virtually the exact strategies as Barber had done.

Now Barber was legitimately involved in aeroplane design, building and piloting. He taught others to fly – this time, his school was bona fide.

Nevertheless, he did not stay long in aviation. He gave up flying after three years and retired his RAF commission prematurely. Was this more impetuousness? Was this self-preservation or simply his restlessness steering his life? We do not know.

Perhaps more detail will surface in future years. However, even if we found a long-lost memoir written by one who knew him intimately, we shall still have unanswered questions.

Horatio Claude Barber 1911 Catherine Evans collection

Appendix 1

Horatio Claude Barber – A Timeline

Below is a list of the key dates in Horatio Barber's life, with an emphasis of his career prior to 1909 when he was involved in aviation in the UK.

Born September 11, 1875, Thornton Heath, Surrey, England

Educated 1891 to 1892 at Bedford Modern School

Appointed Secretary to the Kalgoorlie Hospital Western Australia 1896 to 1897

Married to Edle Annita Margarete Pippe at St. Michael's York, Toronto, Ontario, April 4, 1898

Married to Elsie Mabelle Porter Jersey City, New Jersey May 27, 1903

Travelled to San Francisco, via New York, Liverpool departure October 1903

"Tutor" H. C. Barber involved in Hale Ranch swindle reported in the news February 1904

Son Claude Percy Barber born York, Ontario October 29, 1904

Manager of Incorporation and Securities Company of Canada at 72 Queen Street W., Toronto, 1905 to 1906

Mr. and Mrs. H. C. Barber lived at 76 Admiral Road, Toronto 1906 to 1907

Son Conrad Hope Barber born, Toronto, Ontario, January 19, 1906

The Cobalt Open Call Mining Exchange, Cobalt, Ontario, was incorporated March 30, 1906, H. C. Barber was director, charter member, secretary.

Canada Mines company was incorporated September 1906, H. C. Barber was secretary-treasurer and manager.

Travelled to Larder Lake, Ontario to set up Canada Mines brokerage office in March 1907

The Barber family (without Horatio) returned to the UK in July 1907

Attended the Paris Salon de L'automobile where, for the first time, aeroplanes were on display in France, December 1908

Howard Wright built Barber's first aeroplane at Battersea 1909

Built a shed at Lark Hill for his aviation work May 1909

Organized the Aeronautical Syndicate Limited at Hendon June 1909

Acquired his aviator's certification at Hendon December 1910 – his was number 30

Flew the first cargo flight carrying a box of lightbulbs between Shoreham and Hove July 4, 1911

Technical aviation consultant for Lloyd's of London insurance company ca 1912

Announced his intention to quit aviation in April 1912

Elsie Barber sued for divorce in 1913 which was decreed February 11, 1914

Presented the 'Britannia Trophy' to the Royal Aero Club July 5, 1913

Joined the Royal Flying Corps as Second Lieutenant at Upavon in Wiltshire 1914; was in charge of technical instruction at the RAF Central Flying School

Married Bertha Louise Alexandre Hildenbrand, October 16, 1915, London, England

Retired his military commission, February 1919

Manager of the Aviation Insurance Association, London, England, March 1919

With Robert H. Baldwin, J. Brooks Parker, and Archibald Black, Horatio organized the firm of Barber and Baldwin in the United States, 1922

Moved to the USA and worked in aviation insurance in various companies and capacities to 1932. At the end of his insurance career, he set up a home base on Jersey, Channel Islands.

Purchased the Bath House Hotel and additional parcels of land on Nevis; organized the Leeward Islands Development Company, 1947

Moved to live at the Bath House Hotel in Nevis, 1950 to 1952

Lived in Bermuda 1952

Died July 6, 1964, Jersey, Channel Islands

Appendix 2

Horatio Claude Barber's Family Tree

In this appendix, the reader will find information about Horatio Barber's siblings and additional detail about his second and third wives. A schematic of his family tree is found at the end.

HORATIO BARBER'S SIBLINGS

Parents Charles and Isabella Barber had eight children between 1868 and 1881.

- George Walter (1868)
- Maude (1870)
- Lilian (1871)
- Frederick (1873)[175]
- Horatio Claude (1875)
- Cecil Harry (1877)
- Edith Muriel (1878)
- Percival Charles (1881)

George Walter Barber (1869-1951

The image here, from the Australian War Memorial website[176], is a studio portrait of Colonel George Walter Barber.

He served for a brief spell as an apprentice crewman on board the vessel *The Star of Russia*. He was forced to leave his post due to poor eyesight and afterward he studied medicine at the University of London. This seems like quite a change in direction and is similar to Horatio's tendency to reroute his career. We find it remarkable that his eyesight wasn't good enough for the merchant navy, but good enough to work as a surgeon!

After working at Bedford Hospital in Great Britain, he became the Ship's Surgeon with P&O Steam Navigation Company.

George Walter Barber - Companion of the Order of St Michael and St George (CMG), Companion of the Distinguished Service Order (DSO), Deputy Director of Medical Services (DDMS), Australian Corps.

---

[175] Per email correspondence with Simon Doyle who is George Walter Barber's great-grandson, we include Frederick in the list of siblings. However, we have not been able to find a birth or death registration for Frederick to confirm the information. We include his name in the list, but not on the family tree.

[176] awm.gov.au/collection/C1006202

George arrived in Australia as "unassisted passenger" on the *Valetta* on February 7, 1895. He landed in Sidney New South Wales (NSW).

On August 8, 1896, at the age of 27, he married Janet (Jessie) Watson Salmond in Springwood NSW. He practised medicine in Kalgoorlie, NSW, and later that year he was appointed as the District Medical Officer of the Kalgoorlie Hospital. He worked there until 1911.

In 1914 he enlisted and was appointed Senior Medical Officer in the Freemantle Garrison. He eventually became second in command of the 2nd Australian Stationary Hospital, then was promoted to Lieutenant Colonel in January of 1916. His contributions were instrumental in increasing medical efficiency by introducing new hygiene regulations and improving sanitary conditions.

In October of 1916, he was awarded a Distinguished Service Order and was promoted to Colonel.

In 1917 he was mentioned in dispatches and won the Croix de Guerre.

By 1919 he was back in Australia and became Principal Medical Officer for the 5th Military District in Perth. He eventually became Deputy Director of Medical Services.

In 1925 he became Colonel and temporary Major-General in Melbourne, becoming Major-General in 1927.

He retired in 1934.[177]

Colonel George Walter Barber and Baron von Richthofen.

We uncovered a link between George Barber and the most famous of all aviators. Although brother Horatio was a well-known pilot during World War One, the most renowned of that period, and arguably of all time was Baron Manfred von Richthofen, also known as The Red Baron.

During his legendary aviation career in WW1, Richthofen was reputed to have shot down 80 enemy aeroplanes. He himself was killed while flying in combat. To this day, controversy remains as to who shot him down, and whether the shot was fired from the air or from the ground.

Many books and articles have been written on the subject and most of these writers cite Charles Edwin Woodrow Bean and his book *The Official History of Australia in the War 1914-1918.*

At the time of the crash, Richthofen was flying his famous red Fokker triplane near Corbie in the Somme Valley. His body was removed to a hangar belonging to the Australian Flying Corps, near Poulainville. A group of four doctors conducted a preliminary post mortem

---

[177] George Barber's military career is from *Australian Dictionary of Biography; Barber, George Walter (1868-1951)* by William A. Land

examination. A single rifle bullet had hit von Richthofen in his chest, on the right, and exited on the left after hitting and being deflected by the spine. The pilot also suffered a fractured jaw and bruising was also reported. The examining doctors concluded that the bullet came from slightly in front of the body and from below. This report was signed by Colonel T. Sinclair.

A separate report from two other members of the examination team, Captain G. C. Graham and Lieutenant G. E. Downs, stated that that the bullet could not have come from the ground. In other words, the bullet originated from an airborne gun.

The body was examined a second time, this time under the Presidentship of the Director-General of the Australian Army and Air Force Medical Service - Colonel George W. Barber.

No known report of this examination exists, but in 1935, George Barber wrote to Bean:

> October 23, 1935
>
> My Dear Bean,
>
> With reference to your letter of October 14th asking for information,
>
> I was inspecting this Air Force Unit, and found the medical orderly washing Richthofen's body so made an examination. There were only two bullet wounds, one entry, one exit of the bullet that had evidently passed through the chest and heart. There was no wound of the head but there was some considerable bruising over the right jaw which may have been fractures. The orderly told me that the consulting surgeon of the Army had made a post-mortem in the morning and I asked how he did it, as there was no evidence. The orderly told me that the [consulting] Surgeon used a bit of fencing wire which he had pushed along the track of the wound through over the heart. I used the same bit of wire for the same purpose so you see the medical examination was not a thorough one and not a post-mortem exam in the ordinary sense of the term. The bullet hole in the side of the plane coincided with the wound through the chest and I am sure he was shot from below while banking.
>
> I sent a full report to General Birdwood at Australian Corps. And I have often wondered what became of it.
>
> With kind regards.
>
> Yours sincerely
>
> George W. Barber.

Dr. Barber enclosed a diagram of the bullet wounds on the body. This diagram clearly showed the entrance wound in the left posterior axillary line level with the ninth rib, and [Barber] drew a cross over the right chest internal to the nipple on the AP view.

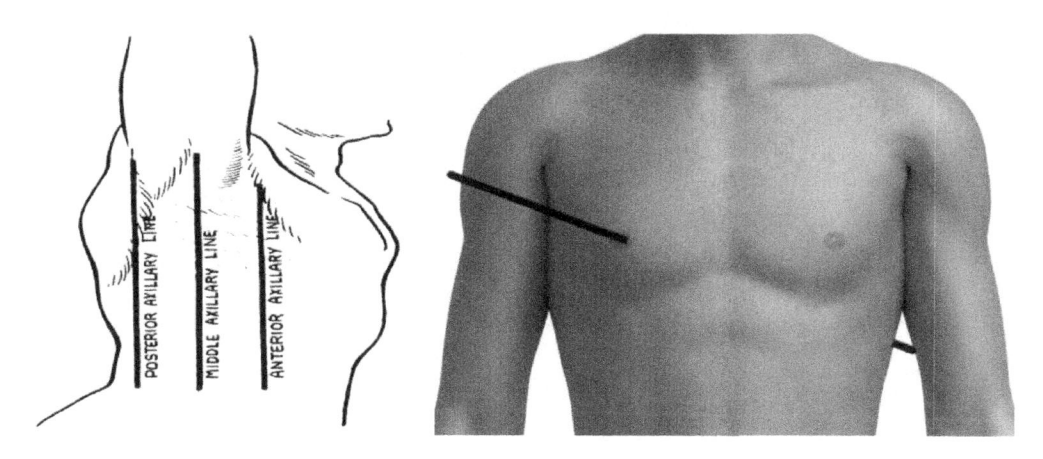

Under the diagram he wrote: "Richthofen approximate sites of exit and entry of bullet. I forget now which was which but think the site of entry was the one in the back, G. W. B." Composite image from Google screen capture and Terry Grace.

Barber's letter suggests that the probe used by Sinclair was not suitable, being prone to catch on and pierce tissue. (Normally a probe with a ball end would be used to prevent this and to ensure it went exactly through the bullet trajectory.) Barber's letter cast profound doubt on the accuracy of Sinclair's examination report. It would have been possible to use the fence wire to determine from the exit wound that the bullet entered the heart, but impossible to determine the track of the bullet to the spinal column from the entrance wound.

Eyewitness reports of what happened that day are on record, but they, like the written reports above, are at odds with one another.

The mystery remains unsolved. Who shot down the Red Baron? Was it from the ground, or from the air? The most favoured hypothesis is that von Richthofen was killed by a machine gun position on the ground, thanks to the crucial evidence that was provided in the letter by George Barber.

HORATIO BARBER'S SIBLINGS, cont'd.

Maude Helen Barber (1870-1955) Maude never married and it is understood that she helped raise Horatio's two sons from his first marriage. She was employed as a governess.

Lillian Isabel Barber (1871-1872) died of acute bronchitis at three months

Frederick Barber (1873) died of whooping cough at two years and nine months.

Cecil Harry Barber (1877 - ?) Cecil was awarded his 2nd Mate Certificate in August 1899

SECOND MATE OF A FOREIGN-GOING SHIP.

To Cecil Harry Barber

Whereas it has been reported to us, that you have been found duly qualified to fulfil the duties of Second Mate of a Foreign-going Ship in the Merchant Service, we do hereby, in pursuance of the Merchant Shipping Act, 1894, grant you this Certificate of Competency.

By Order of the Board of Trade,

this 25th day of August 1899

Countersigned,

Assistant to the Registrar General.

Registered at the Office of the Registrar General of Shipping and Seamen.

Edith Muriel Barber (1879-1966) In 1911, Edith was a novice at the Holy Trinity Convent on Woodstock Road, in Oxford. When she died, her body was buried at Wolvercote Cemetery. A notation on the register of graves indicates she was associated with the Convent of All Saints & St. John's Home, Oxford.

Percy Charles Barber (1880-1970) Percy was Curate of St. Johns, West Bromwich 1906-09 and at Tettenhall from 1909-13. He was Chaplain RFC/RAF 1917-19 and was made MBE in 1919. He was Priest-in-Charge at All Saints, Four Oaks from 1913-19 and Rector of Pembridge with Moor Court 1920-37. From 1936-50 he was Prebendary of Withington Parva in Hereford Cathedral. He retired to Beaminster, Dorset.

MARGARETE, ELSIE, AND BERTHA - Life after Horatio

Regrettably, we found no additional information about Margarete, Horatio's first wife.

Elsie Mabel Porter Barber

After Elsie was divorced in 1914, she remained in England until she met Rutgers Stagg Kasson, a salesman for Hare's Motors. The couple were married and she returned with him to the USA in 1922. There, she changed her name to Barbara. Her son Conrad Hope Barber declared Mrs. Kasson as his mother on several travel documents. She was widowed in 1933. On the 1940 US census, she was the superintendent at Jacob Gould Vocational School in New York. We have been unable to determine when or where she died.

Bertha Louise Alexandre Hildenbrand Barber

Bertha Barber died in 1975. Her death notice appeared in the Jersey Evening Post.

The undertaker's notes state that she died at Bon Air Nursing Home, St. Helier and that her ashes were sent to John W. Barber, 8 Church St., Ewell Surrey, for internment in England. The cause of death was senile cardio-vascular degeneration, bedsores, and pneumonia (terminal).

In her will, Bertha left all the real estate situated on the island of Jersey to her five children in equal shares. Conrad Hope Barber, Horatio's son from his marriage to Elsie, was still alive at that time, but he was not mentioned in the will.

DEATHS

BARBER.—Peacefully in Jersey on October 26, 1975, after a long illness, Bertha Louise Alexandre Barber, of 4 Balmoral Terrace, Trinity Hill.

Funeral private.

Cut flowers may be sent to G. E. Croad Ltd., funeral directors, 89 Don Road, on Thursday, October 30, by noon.

Jersey Evening Post, *1975*

Barber Family Tree

- Charles W Barber (1841-1893) + Maria Walker (1844-1865)
  - George W Barber (1869-1951)
  - Maude Helen Barber (1870-1955)
  - Lilian Isabel Barber (1871-1872)
- Charles W Barber (1841-1893) + Isabella Loughborough (1845-1915)
  - Bertha L A M Hildenbrand (1859-1975)
  - **Horatio C Barber (1875-1964)** + Elsie Mabelle Porter (1886-)
    - John W Barber (1916-1980) + Patricia M Bunbury (1917-2006)
      - Unknown
      - Unknown
      - Unknown
    - Bertha M M Barber (1918-1999) + Robert C H Barber (1919-1986)
      - Unknown
      - Unknown
    - Suzanne A Barber (1921-) + George A T Shaw (1917-1990)
      - Unknown
      - Unknown
  - Edie A M Pippe (1875-)
  - Cecil Harry Barber (1877-)
  - Edith Muriel Barber (1876-1966) + Percy Charles Barber (1881-1970)
    - Claude Percy Barber (1904-1960)
    - Conrad Hope Barber (1906-1981) + Yvonne C Campion (1905-2005)
      - Unknown
      - Unknown
      - Unknown
    - James C Barber (1927-2012)

Appendix 3

The Mystery of Barber's First Aeroplane

We have seen from *Airy Nothings* that Barber sold his first plane to a friend of his foreman "from the North". Snippets of information in the newspapers and aero journals of the time give us insight into the larger story.

Howard Wright Exhibits Bi-planes

In March of 1909 several reports from the Aero Exhibition at Olympia state that Howard T. Wright had taken at least three orders for his biplane which was on display at the event. This was a machine which was partially constructed of welded steel tubing. One such order that may have been placed around that time was from a gentleman from Burnley.

> *The Burnley Express* September 4, 1909
>
> This enterprising Burnley gentleman had given an order to Mr. Howard T. Wright for one of his well-known biplanes. The machine was of the latest type, being constructed of steel tubing, and having the most powerful of engines. The machine which is to carry 3 persons will cost over £1000.
>
> The biplane is already constructed, but Mr. Wright will not allow it to leave until it has been thoroughly tested. A Burnley gentleman has gone to London to receive instructions from Mr. Wright, and he will probably take charge of the machine when it arrives in Burnley. The machine is expected to make three flights every Saturday and that with improvement it will be used for pleasure parties.

William Ellis Cooke Purchases an Aeroplane from Wright

The "enterprising gentleman" was W. E. Cooke who was the managing director of the Burnley Motor Pleasure Co. Cooke had plans to use the plane to establish an Aero Club with Howard T. Wright as the first honorary member. Other plans included a commercial flying operation called the East Lancashire Aeroplane Co., of which Cooke was the head. However, Wright wrote to the *Aero* magazine[178] saying that it was quite untrue that he had accepted the role of president of the Burnley Aero Club.

Many accounts in the press at this time reported on the "Burnley" aeroplane which was to be the first aeroplane in Lancashire. Since each story refers to the machine on order as being a biplane, it is strange that when the plane was eventually delivered, it was a monoplane. This

---

[178] *The Aero* September 28, 1909

fact is confirmed by subsequent news reports. How mysterious, then, that no comment was made in the press about why a biplane was ordered but a monoplane was delivered.

The monoplane was fitted with a 50hp Antoinette water-cooled engine driving a two-bladed propeller. The engine's long condenser radiators were attached along both sides of the fuselage. Petrol sufficient for three hours flight was drawn from a tank suspended above the wings. The fuselage was of tubular steel. The wings were equipped with warping controls and a triangular rudder was fitted. (See image below.)

Unlike the biplane that Cooke had ordered, the monoplane in this configuration had not yet flown and was untested. The craft was transported to Manchester by a specially chartered train, and then on to Burnley, where it was to be displayed on the athletics track.

W. E. Cooke and his daughter in the monoplane – note the triangular rudder. This image also appears in P.D. Stemp's Kites, Birds and Stuff-Over 150 Years of British Aviation

According to Stemp,[179] Cooke's purchase was a co-axial monoplane – a two-seater that was built by Howard Wright for Horatio Barber in 1909. The machine was powered by 50hp Antoinette engine, driving two co-axial propellers, which were later replaced by a single propeller.

While the monoplane acquired by Cooke looks similar to Barber's first aeroplane, we note several very obvious differences. The question has to be asked if this machine was a modified version of Barber's machine.

Let us consider the evidence for and against this hypothesis:

Firstly, in *Airy Nothings,* Barber suggested that the aeroplane was sold to a syndicate which had plans to start what we would call an airline. That fits with Cooke's intention to launch the East Lancashire Aeroplane Co.

---

[179] *Kites, Birds and Stuff-Over 150 Years of British Aviation* by P. D. Stemp.

We've shown this image elsewhere in the book, but repeat it here for comparison to the W. E. Cooke plane. From Barber's scrapbook in the collection of the Hendon RAF Museum.

Secondly, although there is a resemblance to the Barber aeroplane, the Cooke monoplane has been quite heavily modified in several respects. Recall that in *Airy Nothings*, the prospective buyers said that they were intent on improving the machine.

The wings and fuselage appear as per the original Barber model, but the under-carriage has been changed from cart spring to a much lighter arrangement and the automatic stability equipment of the Barber machine is absent. Also, the complex single axle contra-rotating propellers are gone, and the fuselage side radiators are shallower. Even though Barber's first machine got into the air, it was a failure because of its weight. Likely changes were made to decrease the overall weight of the machine. Cooke's plane weighed in at 750lbs whereas the Barber machine tipped the scales at 1000lbs.

Where were these modifications carried out?

Since Barber either worked in Howard Wright's workshop or occupied the premises adjacent to Wright's in Battersea, it is reasonable to conclude that the work would have been completed there.

One of the three known photographs of Barber's first machine at Larkhill shows the cockpit occupied by a man who could be Howard Wright or more likely, the co-designer W. O. Manning. We do know that Manning visited Barber at Lark Hill when the Valkyrie was first being flown, so it is possible he may also have been consulted at this earlier time. In the photo, the plane has undergone its first remodel and has a modified tail and additional plane. It is reasonable to assume that if this machine did eventually re-emerge as the Cooke machine, then either Wright or Manning was responsible for the changes.

Thirdly, both in Barber's book *Airy Nothings* and in the Burnley local press, the machine was said to have been worth, or cost £1,000.

Fourthly, we know from a court case of August 1910 that there were problems raising the money for the original biplane order.

The court case in question was about the small amount of £3 7s for expenses owed. The details reported[180] in the press reveal a great deal about how an order for a bi-plane resulted in the delivery of a monoplane.

Frank Hudson Partners with Cooke

W. E. Cooke had approached solicitor Frank Hudson to help him with matters related to promoting and raising money for his East Lancashire Aeroplane Co. Hudson demurred and said that he could not help with those particulars, but he was interested in putting money into the scheme.

During the court case, it was revealed that to raise the £1,000, Cooke had borrowed £250 from his father-in-law. Hudson borrowed a similar amount from the same man. Cooke had planned to borrow the remaining £500 from a bank and claimed that the funds were assured. However, according to Hudson's testimony, the bank loan was "a fiction". Howard Wright, the aeroplane owner, was reluctant to release the machine to the syndicate without payment in full.

Out of his own pocket, Cooke forwarded £3 7s expense money to Hudson who travelled down to London to see the machine. Once he examined the aeroplane, he found that "it wouldn't work," When Cooke learned the news, he requested that Hudson make a notation on the warranty to reflect that the plane was not in working order. Hudson refused to comply. The two men quarrelled, and the suit for the £3 7s seems to have been an act of revenge on Cooke's part. The judge noted this and he ruled in favour of Hudson.

What came out during this trial was that Hudson had managed to raise the additional £500 money to pay for the aeroplane. He then purchased and then sold the machine without Cooke's knowledge.

To recap:

a) Two men, W.E. Cooke and Frank Hudson were partners in the East Lancashire Aeroplane Co.

b) The syndicate arranged to purchase an aeroplane from Howard Wright. However, the two main shareholders had a falling-out.

c) Even though according to the papers they ordered a biplane from Wright, a monoplane was delivered.

---

[180] The *Burnley Gazette* August 6, 1910

The two men were desperate to acquire an aeroplane for the exhibitions which had already been widely advertised and reported in the newspapers. Did Cooke and Hudson take the cheaper option of a monoplane which just happened to be in Wright's workshop at the time undergoing modification?

We can't be absolutely sure but have discovered more evidence which reinforces this particular view.

On September 11, 1909, the *Express and Advertiser* secured an interview with Howard T. Wright. After addressing the question of who exactly Howard Wright was, and that he was in no way connected to the American pioneers, Wilbur and Orville Wright, a description of the aeroplane ordered by the "Burnley gentleman" was discussed.

Howard Wright described the aeroplane as resembling a large moth (others had described it as looking more like a large dragonfly). The weight of the aeroplane was about 750lbs with a driver, and had 240 square feet of surface. It carried eight gallons of petrol which was enough for three hours of flight. The soaring speed was about 30 mph. The propeller was designed for 35mph and ran at the same speed as the engine, 1181 rpm. The steering in a vertical direction was by a rudder at the back, operated by the driver, and in a lateral direction the steering gear was worked with the feet. The machine has what was called automatic stability, that is to say it was stable fore and aft without any action on the part of the driver. It was stable laterally in still air, whilst the balance was corrected by what was called warping the main planes. The chassis of the machine was shaped like a boat and the driver sat near the end with the passenger in the front.

Therefore, this was an aeroplane with "automatic stability". In other words, it seems that this was the aeroplane which had Barber's patent stability system still attached at the time Wright was speaking. We know of no other Wright machine with "automatic stability", other than that which he built for Barber. It is more than likely that this was Barber's original aeroplane in heavily modified form.

Wright continued to say that because of this automatic stability, his machine was far superior to the Americans' Wilbur and Orville's *Flyer*, adding that the probability of a complete smash with his machine was very slight indeed. Wright said that he was due to go to Burnley to find suitable places to fly the machine, and was to take the mayor of Burnley on a flight.

Now, it seems that when the machine eventually reached Burnley, it did not, according to the available photographs, have the "automatic stability" system installed, so it must have been further modified by Wright before being hastily transported to Burnley to satisfy W. E. Cooke's pre-advertised events. This system may have been removed to further lighten the weight of the machine or perhaps Barber was protecting his patent, or perhaps it just didn't work as designed.

We find it interesting that Wright pointed out that the propeller turned at the same speed as the engine. This was to distinguish the configuration from the Lanchester patent of two co-axial contra-rotating propellers rotating at one-third of the engine speed due to the reduction gearbox as was used on Barber's first machine. In other words, at this stage of the rebuild, the two contra-rotating propellers had been replaced with a single one. Although Wright did build other machines with this propeller system, it was abandoned at an early stage, probably because it was not as efficient as the single propeller system. This was possibly due to under-powered engines of the day, rather than a flaw in the system itself.

The End of the Cooke-Hudson Syndicate

We know that the aeroplane was displayed around the Burnley area, but was only taxied and never flown while it was owned by Cooke and Hudson. Cooke recouped at least some of his investment (which was in fact mostly Hudson's money) by taxiing people around the show grounds for a fee. At Blackburn, the aeroplane was displayed in a large hall with the engine running. Unfortunately, the propeller detached and broke when it flew up and hit the ceiling of the hall. This incident led to the demise of Cooke's other interest, the Burnley & District Aero Club.

Frank Hudson sold the aeroplane to the Northern Automobile Co. of Bradford. This Bradford firm subsequently advertised the machine for sale and it was purchased by a businessman by the name of Harold Keates Hales.

Mr. Hales Purchases an Aeroplane

Hales was a businessman who started his career operating a bicycle shop. He went on to build a shipping empire and become a Member of Parliament. He was apparently known to be the first car owner in Burnley, having bought a 2hp Benz in 1897. As an MP he famously claimed that he never used the horn on his motorcar and he unsuccessfully petitioned to make it illegal to do so. He was the inspiration for Arnold Bennet's novel *The Card*, and, like Barber, he donated a trophy. A much grander affair than the Britannia Trophy, this was the Blue Riband Trophy, presented for the fastest crossing of the North Atlantic by ship.

After attending the Rheims Aero show in 1909 he returned to England, "a man inspired", and he spent many months developing a system of vertical take-off consisting of rotating discs which he hoped to apply to Bleriot type aeroplanes. Because of a lack of funds, this project never got beyond the model stage, but in his autobiography[181], he implies that they were on the right track and that the same principle was used in the invention of the autogyro.

Although this project failed, he was still very much into aviation, and in his story, Hales states that at about the same time that Bleriot crossed the English Channel and Mr. Latham failed in

---

[181] *The Autobiography of "The Card"* by H. K. Hales (Samson Low, Marston Co)

his attempt to do the same thing, he happened to see quite by chance the following advertisement:

"50hp eight-cylinder Antoinette monoplane cost £1,000, unused; will sacrifice for £200 for immediate sale. Box No.-------"

After checking his bank balance he took the first train to Bradford, and in a local garage, he saw for the first time the graceful lines of the plane in which he would eventually make his first flight in a heavier-than-air machine. (Hales had earlier made many flights in lighter-than-air machines).

The wording of the advertisement is ambiguous, as it could suggest that it was either an Antoinette monoplane or an Antoinette-powered monoplane. It seems clear from the wording in the autobiography that Hales understood the machine to be an Antoinette. He writes: "In appearance the Antoinette resembles a giant dragonfly. Constructed almost entirely of aluminium and painted a dazzling white it seemed almost too fragile to bear the strain of landing, but on close examination I found that it was built on very sound lines with cross struts at places where strength was of paramount importance so that my belief in its reliability became confirmed."

Was the body rebuilt with aluminium by Howard Wright, or more likely, did Hales mistake the steel tubing for aluminium?

Hales goes on to describe the eight-cylinder V-shaped engine which they had fired up, as he talks of flames coming out of the exhaust pipes in the darkness of the garage. He states that the propeller was immediately in front of the crankcase and that the pilot was accommodated in a light plywood seat. The moulded wings were covered with wired struts tightened by swivel nuts. Pedals controlled the steering via wires to the tail and the joystick regulated both ascent and descent. (Note that Hales did not write this book until 1936, by which time terms such as "joystick" and "pilot" had since become the norm).

It seems that Hales was told by the owner (who we assume was Frank Hudson) that the "Antoinette" had been imported from France by a local syndicate for the purpose of exhibitions in halls across the country. The businessmen had hoped to make a large profit in a short time. But because of the comparative lack of interest by the British public, coupled with the absence of suitable venues, the syndicate was forced to fold. Hales negotiated the price down to £150 and had the aeroplane transported back to Hanley on the back of a motor lorry. He exhibited the machine for three days in a tent and he charged admission fees. A mechanic was on hand to keep the propeller turning.

From this account taken from Hales autobiography, one is left with the impression that he had purchased an Antoinette, but photographic evidence suggests that this was not the case, as the two images opposite illustrate.

Apparently, Hales was somewhat naïve. For some reason, Hudson wanted to conceal the origin of the aeroplane, perhaps because of its accident when the propeller came off. The seller would have wanted to also hide the fact that it was a "recycled" machine and not brand new as was advertised. The story of its import from France seems also like a seller's tale to disguise its provenance.

From The Autobiography of "The Card" *by H. K. Hales (Samson Low, Marston Co.) Harold Hales sitting in his newly acquired monoplane. As can be seen, the plane is not of the Antoinette type, but appears to be the very machine displayed by Cooke and Frank Hudson. See next image.*

The image of Cooke and his daughter from earlier in the chapter has been reversed horizontally and overlaid with the image above. We believe that the machine is the same aeroplane in each photo.

One of Hales' friends, unnamed, had suggested that he display the machine, and in gratitude Hales offered this chap the first flight in the machine. Reluctant at first, the fellow did eventually climb aboard and was encouraged to taxi around. Either by accident or design, the machine swung to the left and ended up in a hedge.

After the plane was retrieved Hales climbed aboard. As the machine gathered speed, all Hales knew about flying was that he had to pull the stick back, and this he did. With one gigantic leap, the "Antoinette" jumped into the air to a height of about fifty feet. It was, according to Hales, a moment of unforgettable exhilaration. Suddenly the machine swayed and with a deep dive crashed to the ground. Hales sat in the wreckage, assessing the damage to himself and the aeroplane. He had miraculously escaped harm, the wing of the machine had collapsed, but the engine and propeller were undamaged.

The incident occurred on July 10, 1910. Apparently Hales had had enough of flying his own aeroplane for the time being because three months later on October 12, 1910, the following advertisement appeared in the *Aero* magazine:

"Magnificent passenger-carrying Wright monoplane, 50hp Antoinette engine, not used, cost £1,000, bargain. H. Hales, Burslem."

It is noteworthy that Hales refers to the aeroplane as a Wright monoplane in this instance because even as late as 1936 in his autobiography he refers to the craft as an Antoinette.

There seems to be no further reference to the aeroplane, and the trail goes cold at this stage.

Postscript

A letter[182] written to the press in the autumn of 1910 is signed "An Aviator". We suggest it was Barber who wrote to bemoan the lack of faith, enthusiasm, and investment in aviation. He said, "Should an inventor come forward, the first thought of the capitalist seems to be to try to exploit the inventor before the invention is carried out."

As Barber would have done, the writer used an analogy. "Here is an example thereof: An inventor thinks out and constructs an aeroplane of changeable incidence, automatic longitudinal stability, a quite new type and most perfected, and an improvement on anything already in existence. It is constructed of steel with a motor of 35-40hp, 25 metres of surface carrying power and together with pilot weighs 500 kilos." [Now this seems to describe Barber's first aeroplane sufficiently well and the style is certainly very much like Barber's, especially in the description of the perfection of the machine.]

The writer continues: "An agreement is made with a young chauffeur who loyally acts his part [a description that fits Bertie Woodrow perfectly], and a capitalist at whose place the machine was constructed, but who not alone refuses to pay his share, but demands the payment of several hundred pounds sterling before the aeroplane is delivered." [We are aware of at least one such account of an investor being involved with Barber's first machine, so that piece also fits with the example the writer is narrating.]

---

[182] The *Aero* October 12, 1910.

"Result: The aeroplane has been ready for months, but on account of the bad faith evinced by the partner(who still has the machine in his possession), and the refusal of the inventor and another partner to be exploited before the aeroplane is worked, everything remains in abeyance, and the whole will be terminated in the machine being out of date. This is one of the reasons why aviation makes but little progress in England."

This letter fits Barber and his aeroplane so well that we suggest that it was he who used the putative example to express his displeasure not only his with the investor but with the Government, too, who showed little interested in aviation at that time. Throughout his aviation years, Barber and others worked hard to persuade the Government and the armed forces of the importance of aviation in warfare. We believe that this is Barber venting his anger.

The letter generated no replies.

Appendix 4

Horatio Barber's Firsts

1. Barber was the first person in Great Britain to be awarded an aeronautical degree. Though the accomplishment is cited in several texts, we have been unable to verify.

2. In 1911, Barber was the first pilot in Great Britain to carry commercial cargo. He flew a consignment of Osram lamp bulbs from Shoreham to Hove. This was a publicity stunt staged by Barber and the Osram Company. He took the £100 purse that he earned from this flight and established the Britannia Trophy, an annual prize awarded to the most accomplished aviator.

3. He was the first person to fly an all British-made aeroplane.

4. He was the first person to use a patented electrolytic method to apply a protective copper coating to a propeller.

5. He was the first person to employ a professional test pilot, his chauffeur Mr. Bertie Woodrow.

6. In 1912, he was the first person to write an aviation insurance policy after Lloyds of London requested that he write his own.

7. He is reputed to be the first British aviator to see active service during a 1912 trip to Turkey.

8. He coined and was thus the first person to use the term "aerobatics"

9. He was possibly the first person to carry a lady passenger as an Air Service, Miss Treyhawke-Davies.

10. At a very early time in aviation history, Barber installed a rudimentary form of dual controls in his Valkyrie. He may have actually have been the first to do so, although this is difficult to state categorically.

11. Barber was most likely the first person to install a contra-rotating propeller in an aeroplane. By this is meant contra-rotating propellers on the crankshaft of an engine such as seen on aircraft today - not the system of an engine driving two propellers on different shafts by use of figure-of-eight chains such as those used by the Wright Brothers in the US. This system was patented by Frederick W. Lanchester (of Lanchester motorcar fame) in 1907. As early as 1909, Barber had built an aeroplane with such an arrangement. This aeroplane failed to fly but this was due to the weight of the steel frame and not the propeller system, although he never used the system afterward.

12. He was the first person to use a gasoline-powered boat on the gold mining area of Larder Lake, in Ontario, Canada.

Appendix 5: Barber's Signatures

From Barber's first marriage certificate, 1898

From Barber's second marriage certificate 1903

Letter from Barber to lawyer A.N. Morgan in 1906

From post card on the occasion of the first airmail flight September 9, 1911

George Hotel, Amesbury guest book 1914

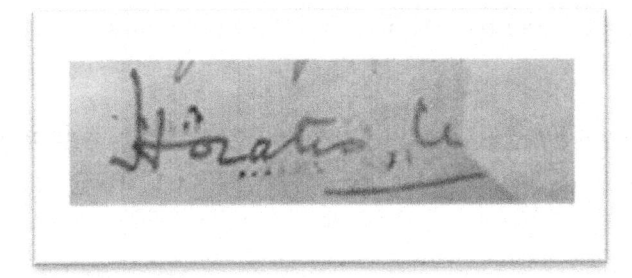

Registration with the Central Park Arsenal, New York, September 16, 1918

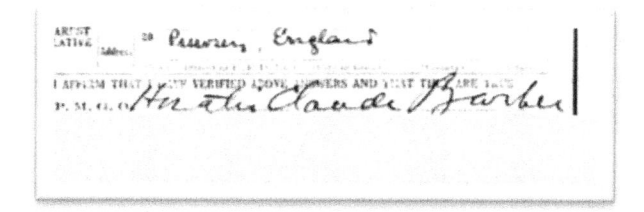

From an insurance document ca 1930s

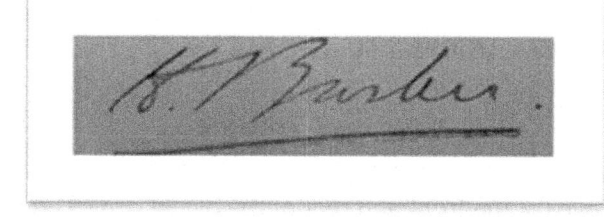

From his letter to his son John October 20, 1961

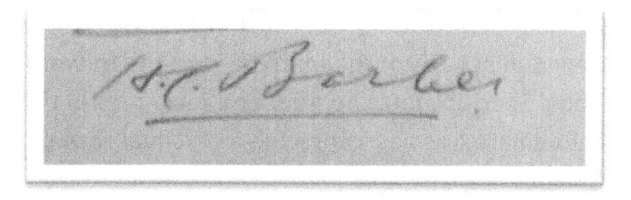

From Barber's will, 1963

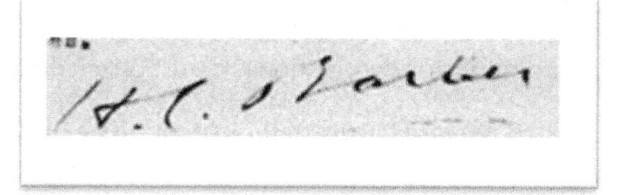

Appendix 6

Barber's Patents

Throughout his aviation period, Barber applied for and was granted several patents. Some of these are described here.[183]

His first patent No. 1999 seems to be what was later called his "automatic stability system" which was fitted to his first machine. It is simply titled "Improvements in Aeroplanes."

Barber applied for the patent January 27, 1909, and it was granted on November 25, later that year.

Improvements in Aeroplanes GB190901999A, UK

Abstract

Balancing automatically by pivoted supporting- planes connected together in pairs to move in opposite directions. The hinges at the front and rear of the planes are so arranged so that the rear part of the wing rises to a greater extent than the forward part. The plane b hinged at d to the chassis a, are connected by cords e passing over pulleys and by cords g attached to the pivot bar h. the rear spars c of the wing are crossed, and are hinged to toe chassis a on the side opposite to the wing; or, the forward part of the chassis is triangular, the hinges d Fig 4 [not shown] of the rear spars being placed nearer to the longitudinal axis of the machine than the forward spars. In the form described in the first Provisional Specification, the front and rear spars of the wing are hinged at an equal distance from the longitudinal axis so as to provide no inequality of movement of the front and rear parts on the plane.

The time period between application of this patent and the approval covers the time that Barber was experimenting with his first aeroplane, which included the elements described in this patent. It is understandable, then, why Barber was somewhat secretive about this aeroplane at the time and why so few photographs or descriptions of the aeroplane exist.

On March 23, 1910, he submitted an application to the patent office for "Improvements in Monoplane Flying Machines." Patent No. 7289 was granted on February 16, 1911. The opening sentence of the abstract is intriguing: "Aerial machines adapted to travel also on land…" as to why one would want to travel on land in a Valkyrie is not explained. In general, this seems to be the patent for the Valkyrie. The diagram suggests that the patent related to the prototype Valkyrie, with the addition of the forward elevator, but before the forward frame construction was changed from being pointed to the curved arrangement favoured in all the subsequent models. Some photographs showing the metamorphosis of the prototype into the Valkyrie No. 1 are shown in Chapter 12.

---

[183] patents.google.com

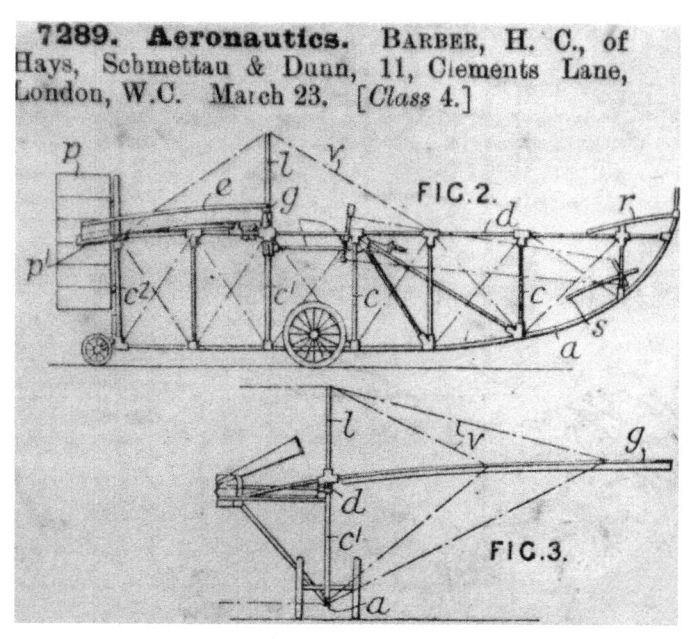

```
7289. Aeronautics. BARBER, H. C., of
Hays, Schmettau & Dunn, 11, Clements Lane,
London, W.C. March 23. [Class 4.]
```

From patents Journal July 19, 1911

Improvements in Monoplane Flying Machines GB191007289A UK and FR419436A France

Abstract

Aerial machines adapted to travel also on land, aerial machines without aerostats; shocks of landing, deadening; planes, arranged of- the front and rear ribs g of the main plane of a monoplane machine spring directly from uprights c1, c 2 respectively, which, with the further uprights c serve to connect the longitudinals d with the skids a. the uprights c1may be extended upwards at l for the connection of the plane stays v. A forward plane r is also provided. Steering- Simultaneously- operated rudders p, slotted as at p1 to accommodate the plane c, are pivoted to an extension of each rear upright c2, A forward elevator s is arranged below the plane r.

The term "aerostats" refers to airships or hot air balloons, which makes the title even less clear.

Barber's third patent was a method of electroplating wooden propellers with copper as a protection against the elements and, on the Valkyrie, exhaust emissions and engine oil.

The method involved soaking the propeller in plumbago (another term for graphite or for lead salts) in order to provide an electrically conducting base for the electroplating of copper onto the wood. Although new to aviation, this was a common method of taking prints from wooden engravings. It is not documented whether this method was employed by Barber on the Valkyrie or Viking aeroplanes. Barber applied for the patent "Wooden Propellers for Aeroplanes and the like with an Electrically Deposited Metal Coating" on December 10, 1910, and received approval on July 20, 1911. The brief abstract reads, "Screw propellers. - Wooden propellers for aeroplanes &c. are provided with an electrically deposited metal coating." Patent numbers GB191028783A in the UK and FR431719A in France.

Barber applied for his fourth patent October 7, 1912, and he received approval on June 26, 1913.

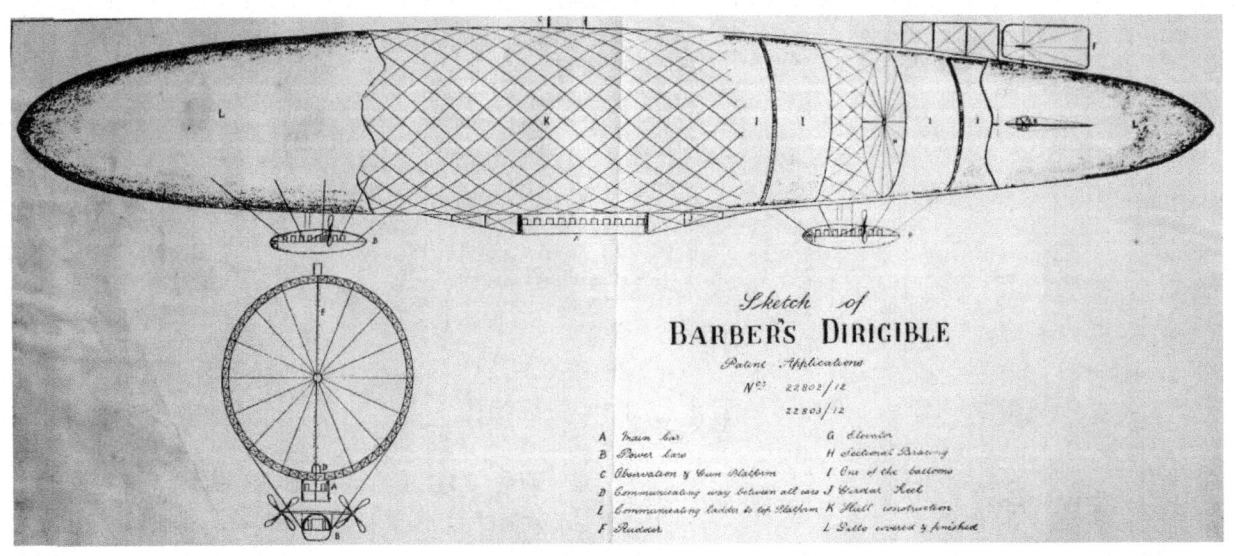

The sketch is not from the patent application, but serves to illustrate the novel construction. From Barber's personal scrapbook in the collection of the Hendon RAF Museum.

> **Improvements in or connected with Dirigible Balloons** GB191222802A UK
>
> Abstract
>
> Aerial machines with aerostats; cars; framework, A balloon is provided with a rigid frame made up of outer helical members 4, 5 connected by radial struts 3 with similar inner helical members 6,7. the various members may be partly solid and partly hollow, and are being braced together by wires 8, 9 10 the ends of which pass through screwed thimbles 20 carried by brackets 21, Fig 7. [not shown] To prevent distortion of the frame, staywires 23 may pass to a ring 22 from the frame, the wires serving to space apart the balloon sections, the envelope of the sections being fastened to the frame. The cars 13, 14 are slung from the frame by wires 16 with heads 17 pivoted to lugs fixed to plates 19 which are clamped to the members 4,5. At the ends of the balloon, certain of the wires may be replaced by wooden members. Preferably six or more balloon sections 25 are used, and they may be divided vertically into two parts. An observation car 15, controlling plane 11, and rudders 12 are provided. According to the Provisional Specification, vertical shafts containing ladders may be arranged in the balloon, allowing access to a gangway along the upper face of the vessel. The annular framework may be filled with gas admitted at the upper side of one end, the displaced air escaping at the lower side of the opposite end.

Although this airship was never built, similar construction was used by Barnes-Wallis in the construction of the R80 and R100 airships using metal alloy in place of wood and is referred to as geodetic. It was later used in the construction of Wellington bombers in WW2. However, we find that a very similar construction method was used in 1909-1911 by Professor Schütte.

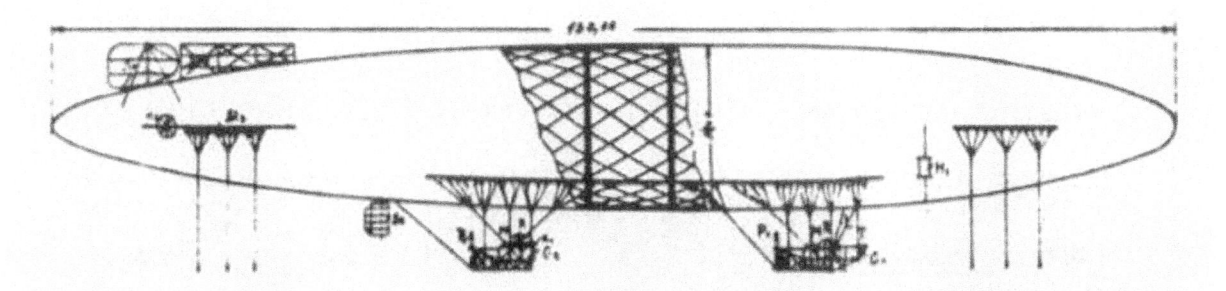

Oben: Nach Entwürfen von Professor Schütte entstand bei der Lanz-Werft in Rheinau 1909 – 1911 das starre Luftschiff SL 1. Darunter die Seitenansicht des Schütte-Lanz SL 1.

Translation: "Top: Based on designs by Professor Schütte, the rigid SL 1 airship was built at the Lanz shipyard in Rheinau between 1909 and 1911." The geodetic skeleton was of wood as in the Barber version. Note similarities of tail fin in both sketches! Hiveminer.com

Barber and William Cochrane submitted a fifth patent application on February 3, 1914. It was approved November 12, 1914.

> **Improvements in or connected with valve mechanism for Internal Combustion Engines**
>
> Abstract GB191402803A UK
>
> Cylinders, construction of castings, inlet and exhaust ports, both of which are spaced equidistantly around the walls of the combustion chamber, are controlled by an oscillating split ring valve 4, having equidistant ports, actuated by a grooved cam 22 in a grease box18 on the cylinder head. The inlet and exhaust ports are formed in a ring-shaped casting 2 which is secured between the cylinders 1 and the cylinder head. There may be a single row of ports in the valve and in the valve- chest as shown, leading to inlet and exhaust passages7,9, or there may be separate rows of ports for inlet and exhaust. The passage 7, 9 increase in width towards the pipe connection8,10.

According to the *Illustrated London News,* (see image, next page) Barber applied for a patent that involved hiding an airship above the clouds where it remained invisible to the enemy while an observer was suspended below the clouds on a long rope. The observer was connected to the airship via telephone. This seems to us now as a rather far-fetched idea but possibly not in its day. It does show that Barber's mind was never idle and that his ideas were certainly eclectic.[184]

We have not found a record of this patent.

---

[184] *Illustrated London News* September 6, 1913

MOISTURE AS A MASK: CLOUDS AS COVER FOR SCOUTING AIRMEN.

DRAWN BY OUR SPECIAL ARTIST, W. B. ROBINSON.

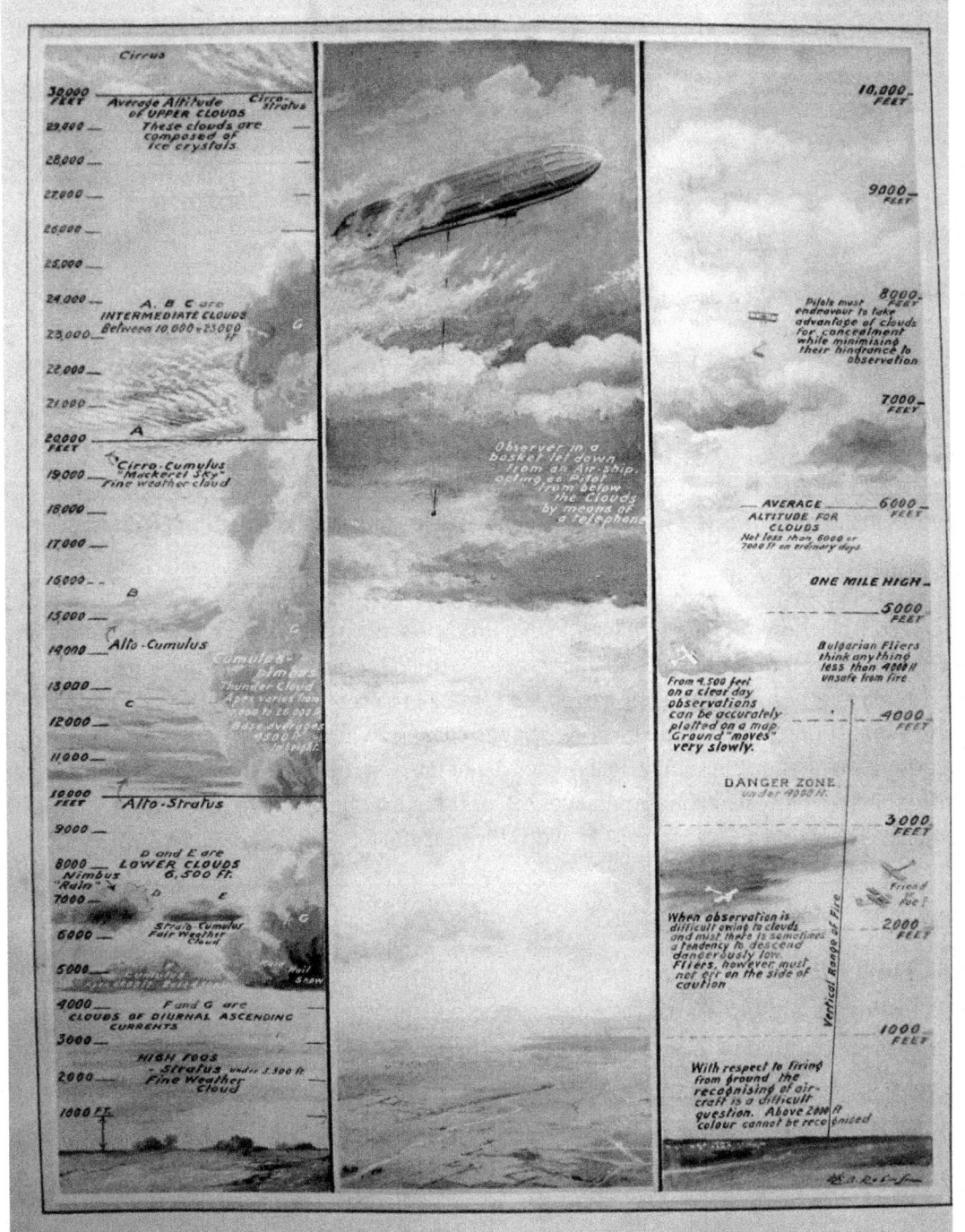

HIDING IN THE HEAVENS: CLOUDS USED AS PLACES OF CONCEALMENT BY THE FLYING CORPS; ALTITUDES AND DEPTHS OF CLOUDS; AND A SUGGESTION.

Amongst the announcements made in connection with the Army Manoeuvres is one to the effect that the War Office has had prepared a booklet which advises officers on the arts of using and fighting air-craft. A point is made in this of the value of clouds as cover for observers on duty aloft. Thus attention is once more called to a subject very well dealt with not long ago by Major Sykes. With regard to the very instructive drawings on this page, particular attention must be drawn to that in the centre, which illustrates a suggested method of making observations from a dirigible balloon hidden from the enemy by clouds. The observer is let down from the air-ship in a basket and communicates with those aboard the balloon by means of a telephone. In such a position—below the clouds, while the dirigible is above them and so hidden from those on the ground—the observer can see all that he wants with very little risk of being seen by the enemy and still less risk of being hit, and, in addition, can pilot the "invisible" air-craft. The idea is that of the well-known airman Mr. Barber, and a patent has been applied for.

Appendix 7

Dear John. A letter from Horatio to his son.

First page of a letter written by Horatio Barber to his son John October 20, 1961. Both a handwritten and typewritten copy of the letter are held in the Hendon RAF Museum Archives. The papers were donated to the museum by John Barber.

When he was 85 years old, Horatio wrote a letter to his son John Barber in response to a suggestion that the senior Barber should record his memoirs. The longhand version is written on Barber's personal stationery addressed Balmoral Terrace, Trinity Hill, Jersey, Channel Islands. Telephone Central 1427. We have transcribed the entire letter here and our comments follow. We have broken the text into paragraphs, for the sake of clarity.

216

20th October 1961

Dear John

I have received your letter suggesting that I set down my first thoughts about flying and how they developed up to my first successful flight. You seem to think that it could be done in a few words but it would take a volume to cover the subject and I do not feel that I could undertake that. I fear that what I have to say hereafter will be too scrappy for your liking but to go into further detail, including problems of design and my work as a pilot including episodes of cross-country flights etc., would be a laborious affair - and so I will scribble the following.

Early in 1908 I was at a loose end living in that apartment house in the Rue de Pressbourg overlooking the Arc de Triomphe in Paris, engaged in nothing useful and thinking vaguely of building and racing fast motor-boats or doing something in Kenya. One fine morning strolling down the Avenue des Champs-Élysées in Paris, France on the way to the British Club where English papers awaited me, I ran into a friend just arrived from England and who was leading an uncertain life like myself. He joined me on my way to the club. Passing near the Grand Palais he pointed to it remarking that it contained an exhibition of the mad contraptions of cranks who thought they could make flying machines and he suggested that we should see them. We did so and laughed at the weird vehicles which looked like hen-coops on wheels. Only one of them had made a short flight or hop. It was designed by a Brazilian named Santos-Dumont and was almost uncontrollable in the air. Santos-Dumont, a gallant and very likeable young man, did achieve some short but hair-raising flights.

I had no engineering knowledge but it was easy to see that the inclination of the plane surfaces when driven through the air with sufficient speed would induce an upward lifting reaction. It seemed to me that the wiring of the support struts was in many instances opposed to anything sensible. However, I was impressed by the general idea of gaining flight by using the lifting result of driving inclined planes against the air. That seemed to me, indeed, the only sound thing I got from the crazy looking objects exhibited.

Well, having nothing better to do, I thought about that, also the problem of balance and control. That long "think" ended with conclusion that in the event of flight becoming practical it would have a tremendous effect upon transportation and the whole economy of life including national defence. These thoughts took control of me and within a month I was in England, found a suitable workshop in some disused railway arches in Battersea, designed a machine and commenced building.

Having no engineering knowledge of any kind I gave a fairly free go ahead signal to a Consulting Engineer. That was a mistake that put me back some time. I transported the machine, powered with a 50 h.p. French Antoinette engine to Salisbury plain and during its first flight (greatest height about 30 ft) it crashed completely. I severed connection with the Consulting Engineer, hired a number of craftsmen, made scores of models driven by propellers actuated by twisted rubber and carried out hundreds of trial flights noting carefully the qualities of each model and such points as centre of gravity, lift and drift and directional and horizontal stabilities, etc., etc. One model showed exceptional stability also outstanding lift for weight, and assumed a correct gliding path to earth when the propeller stopped.

These experiments lasted about three months and I then started to build a full-size aircraft to the scale of the successful model, with a 30hp Green engine of all British materials and labour. Indeed, after my first successful flight I followed a rule of only using British materials and labour although later on I did break that rule for once by using for a time the French Gnome rotary engine. I felt from the defence point of view that it was essential to develop British materials and labour.

I made my first successful flight (after many hops) early in 1909 from where my hangar was situated on Durrington Down to Larkhill a distance of about two and a half miles, by far the longest flight then attained by any aeroplane in England. I flew at an altitude of only about forty feet, having a strong regard for the improved efficiency of the controls and thinking it advisable to avoid unnecessary risks, I flew in a direct and horizontal course and, the ground rising towards Larkhill I alighted there with little use of the elevator. I made turning flights before breakfast. I first alighted near some twenty horses from a racing stable which were being exercised under the direction of their trainer. I would not care to record his language which was not modified when I told him that before long hundreds of aeroplanes would be using Salisbury Plain.

I remember very vividly that midway in flight I saw before me a solitary bicyclist. Just before I flew over him, he dismounted and looking downwards between my knees, I saw his upturned face with wide open mouth and astonished expression. It was almost certainly the first aeroplane in flight he had seen. That evening some three thousand people arrived in my runway and rendered it impossible for me to carry out customary trial flights. Where they came from in that thinly populated area, I cannot imagine.

It was a wonderful ground for experimental flying and I would never have been able to proceed so quickly and so successfully but for the interest and kindness of Sir Edward Grey, The Secretary of State for War who gave me permission to use the Plain. It took me three months after many rebuffs by elegant frock-coated young men for me to gain admission to him at the War Office. I remember well going to the War Office once more and in desperation arriving with a package of food and drink declaring to the usual polite but negative young man that I was going to stay there until I saw his Chief. Twenty minutes after that I was ushered into Sir Edward's room. He received me most kindly and apologized for the difficulty I had met with and, more to the point, after some conversation said that if I would call at the War Office at 12 o'clock, I would receive a lease of a plot of land at Durrington Down upon which I might erect a hangar and with the right to fly over the Plain.

I was the first to design, build and fly an all British aeroplane. There have been bitter controversies over that record and I have kept aloof from them. I believe A. V. Roe was the first Britisher to design and fly an aeroplane in England but his engine was not British. He was an exceptionally modest and pleasant man and shunned publicity. A much-publicised early flight of a machine designed and built by a commercial firm for a Britisher was said to have made the first continuous circular flight of a mile. That flight was made in foggy weather and the machine could not be seen during the whole flight by an observer holding one position. It was said (but not published) that a mechanic at the distant part of the field saw the machine touch the ground several times during the flight thereby rendering the flight not continuous but a series of hops. That aspect of the flight was well known to the pioneers of flight but they have regarded it as of little importance to the value of such records not then being appreciated.

I am firmly of the opinion that A. V. Roe was the first Englishman to design, build and fly a British aeroplane and that opinion is based upon the very close watch I kept of developments in aviation. By "fly" or "flight" I mean flying above the ground for not less than about three hundred feet in distance and alighting without accident to the machine. That definition was accepted generally by the pioneers; Anything else was called a hop.

I gave up building aeroplanes in 1912 because the march of progress became too quick for my limited financial resources. I had spent in the game sufficient to decrease my investment income by about £1500 pound a year and to continue in that path seemed unsound. I could have continued commercially but I had no business experience and baulked at entering that unknown world. Just at that time, underwriters of Lloyd's asked me to advise them and I had no hesitation in proceeding along that line. That developed into my organising the British Aviation Insurance Group at Lloyd's and my Chairmanship of Lloyd's technical committee in Aviation. You know the rest.

I will conclude by mentioning the seven men whose interest and kindness helped me so much. Firstly, Sir Edward Grey.

Also Col. J. E. B. Seeley, Secretary of State for War (now Lord Mottistone). I was in close touch with him for some years. I found him very frank and far sighted and unlike so many others, he never dismissed anything just because it was new. We discussed many aspects of the British aviation situation. He acted very quickly in accepting my suggestion that a British Aviation Inspection Department be installed for which I thought there was a great need by reason of the sharply increasing number of personal accidents.

Bluff and hearty Sir Godfrey Payne was a great figure, much respected. I was, as a newly gazetted 2nd Lt., under his command at The Central Flying School soon after the start of the first World War. I was there to pass the necessary exams for my Wings. He did embarrass me somewhat when he ordered me to stand forward at a parade of the whole school and passed me without examination. I had occasion to meet him on various occasions during the War and he was invariably kind and helpful.

Another was Brigadier General McClean, another Commandant of the C. F. S. I served under him for nearly two years. A severe disciplinarian but always just. I learned much from him and he is one of my best memories.

Then Cuthbert E. Heath, known to many as The Father of Lloyd's. He sponsored me there in 1921 and subsequently in the United States where over a period of six years I established aviation insurance, needless to say I passed much reinsurance to his syndicate at Lloyd's. We first met in 1911 when I applied to Lloyd's for insurance to cover passengers in my aircraft. I believe that resulted in the first instance of an aviation policy being issued at Lloyd's. Mr Heath requested me to write the terms of the policy suggesting only that I try to be fair to both sides. That was my first lesson in underwriting and one I never forgot. His unfailing friendship and support over a long period of years was invaluable and helped me over many a high fence.

Again, there was Sir Henry Coulton, Chairman of Lloyd's. I met him frequently over a period of several years and developed a great admiration for him. During all that time we differed on only one point. When I told him in 1922 that I intended to go to America because I could see no prospect for many years of a sufficient volume of aviation risks in Europe, he said, "An Angel of Heaven could not succeed in such an enterprise." I certainly had a difficult time for the first few years but subsequently was very well compensated for my labours, also I started the ball rolling which is still producing annually millions of dollars for England.

Another was Charles Rose, Chairman of the Royal Aero Club, who died from heart failure directly after his first flight. Fortunately, not one of my aircraft. I lost a staunch friend there and missed him very much. His untimely end had the effect of shelving an enterprise we had jointly planned.

Alan Burgoyne, MP was a particularly good friend of mine and he did a lot of good work publicly and privately to advance the cause of British aviation. The following episode in which he was the driving force made aeronautical history. He dropped in to see me one day in 1911 and told me that Col. Seeley, at that time Secretary of State for War, was much concerned by the then slump in British aviation and the decrease in building aeroplanes, an increase in which was essential for the supply of aircraft to the recently formed Flying Corps. It looked as though the whole movement was fizzing out. Very small funds were being voted by the House of Commons to finance the Flying Corps so that they were unable to place orders for aircraft with commercial firms. Burgoyne asked me whether I could suggest some means to put life into the movement. I thought over the problem and made the suggestion that if a private individual could be found to donate a number of aircraft to the Government and that offer was accepted then the House of Commons might be shamed into voting sufficient funds to enable the Flying Corps to place orders for aircraft which might save the industry. He carried this suggestion to Seeley who approved of it and sent me a message asking me to think a bit harder and suggest the name of a possible donor. Well I could not think of anyone but, feeling very disturbed by the situation which I felt might jeopardise not only my flying hobby but also the future defence of the country, I offered to present four aircraft to the Government. That offer was accepted and produced a storm of protest in the house, members rising to say that greater financial support for the Flying Corps could more properly be given by the Government. Final result: considerably larger funds voted than in the past and the situation saved. Unfortunately, I got a lot of complimentary publicity which led it to being put about privately that I had an ulterior motive - that I was to get something for it - and I had no defence because of course I could not disclose the conversation between myself, Burgoyne and Seeley. Ancient history now but still unknown.

I have no objection to this screed or any part of it being made public after I have joined my old friends who have passed away. In the meantime, it may interest you and your brothers.

Love from Daddy,

H. C. Barber

*** *** ***

The Authors Comment

Whilst this letter is a valuable resource, we must take into account the number of years between the dates of the events he described and the date of writing. His words should not be taken as absolute. Barber was 85 years old when he wrote to John in 1961, at least seventeen years since he had been diagnosed with some form of dementia.

With this caveat in mind, we offer our comments on what he had to say to John.

I fear that what I have to say hereafter will be too scrappy for your liking but to go into further detail, including problems of design and my work as a pilot including episodes of cross-country flights etc., would be a laborious affair1 - and so I will scribble the following.

With his sometimes love of publicity and obvious skill and fondness for writing, one might wonder why Barber never produced an autobiography. To do so, of course, would have required a description of his life before aviation. It would seem that particular part of his life remained very much a secret to his friends, colleagues, and family during his lifetime. It is a great pity that he did not at least put down a more detailed account of his aviation days.

Early in 1908 I was at a loose end living in that apartment house in the Rue de Pressbourg overlooking the Arc de Triomphe in Paris, engaged in nothing useful and thinking vaguely of building and racing fast motor-boats or doing something in Kenya.

Consider the interesting use of the singular "I" in this sentence. We might infer that he was living there alone, without his family. Note also that he refers to the timing as "early" 1908.

We know that Elsie and their two children departed Canada in July 1907 for the UK. Barber was not with them according to the passenger lists. We have not been able to find his travel record for any destination in 1907 or 1908.

Based on his numerous interviews, the current understanding is that after his mining days in Canada, he either travelled to France directly, or eventually settled there after a stop at another European country. We know from Elsie's divorce decree that the family lived in Paris, but on the Rue Benjamin Goddard.

Horatio tells John that he was "engaged in nothing useful," without purpose or direction. We suggest that he was keeping a low profile after his premature and rapid exit from Canada.

In the same paragraph that starts "Early in 1908…" Barber writes:

Passing near the Grand Palais [his friend from England] pointed to it remarking that it contained an exhibition of the mad contraptions of cranks who thought they could make flying machines and he suggested that we should see them.

Barber has either confused the timing, or has conflated his memories of the events in Paris. He may have arrived "early in 1908" but the aeroplane exhibit at the Grand Palais was held at the end of December.

I had no engineering knowledge… and later, *I had no engineering knowledge of any kind.*

As was the case with many mine promoters during the Cobalt and Larder Lake booms, their advertisements were filled with exaggerations, if not outright lies. In regards to Barber's claims of being a mine engineer, he was simply writing ad copy to sell shares, and saying whatever needed to be said to sound like an authority.

Well, having nothing better to do, I thought about that, also the problem of balance and control.

These were his initial thoughts which gave rise to his patent application a few weeks later.

…I gave a fairly free go ahead signal to a Consulting Engineer. That was a mistake that put me back some time.

At the end of Appendix 3, we describe a letter in *Aero* magazine signed "An Aviator." We suspect that the writer was Barber. In the sentence in his letter to John, we feel that Barber is making a reference to the situation that prompted him to write to the press in 1910. The consulting engineer he refers to is possibly the designer W. O. Manning. Although Barber said, "That was a mistake," Manning was known to have been consulted on Barber's second aeroplane as well as on the Valkyrie in its early form.

I made my first successful flight (after many hops) early in 1909…

This claim is at odds with the known facts. During those early experiments, Barber's chauffeur Bertie Woodrow was doing most if not all of the flying. It was Woodrow who first described that first flight, including the details of the bicyclist. Here we must take into account Barber's age and dementia. He hasn't lost his ability, however, to write with style.

I was the first to design, build and fly an all British aeroplane.

Although Barber claims to be the first person to fly an all British aeroplane, which is fairly well documented, he then contradicts himself by suggesting it was A. V. Roe when he wrote, "I am firmly of the opinion that A. V. Roe was the first Englishman to design, build and fly a British aeroplane."

I could have continued commercially but I had no business experience and baulked at entering that unknown world.

Barber claims to have had no business experience by 1912. This we know to be completely untrue. It is interesting that even at this late stage in his life he was still unwilling to divulge even to his family, his less than illustrious businesses from his pre-aviation days.

We also find it amusing that he was unsure of venturing into the unknown. Ever since he left England in the early 1890s, his signature trademark was adventures in uncharted territory – literally and figuratively.

He did embarrass me somewhat when he ordered me to stand forward at a parade of the whole school and passed me without examination

Is this false modesty? Barber should not have been so embarrassed, as it seems that many experienced airmen were awarded their brevets in this way without examination. Harry Busteed also was awarded his brevet in a similar fashion.

Appendix 8

Herbert Campbell Barber

In Chapters 6 and 7, we tell the story of Horatio Claude Barber's brokerage business in Cobalt and Larder Lake. During that time, he wrote two pamphlets to spread the word about investment opportunities in the mines.

We also show that Horatio Barber lived in Toronto, Ontario from 1904 to 1907 with his wife and two children. We have a letter that connects H. C. Barber to the Open Call Mining Exchange, Canada Mines, and his home address at 76 Admiral where he and his wife Elsie Barber (nee Porter) were living.

We are satisfied beyond any doubt that Horatio Claude Barber was the man who wrote these two pamphlets.

A Misattribution

Very early in our research, we found both of these documents on archive.org, an online repository. In 2012, the University of Alberta Libraries scanned and uploaded both *Cobalt the Mining District* and *The Goldfields of Larder Lake*. However, the works were attributed to Herbert Campbell Barber.

The original microfilm is copyright 2000 and was produced by Canadian Institute for Historical Microreductions (CIHM). On their technical notes the CIHM indicated that the files were reprinted with the permission of the rights holder, David Campbell Barber. He was Herbert Campbell's son.

Since the University has made the pamphlets available for download, the misattribution has been perpetuated. Other versions of the same documents are available by online booksellers, who have reprinted the original using the incorrect author's name.

We suggest that the pamphlets were part of Herbert Campbell Barber's estate and his son David donated them to be microfilmed. Perhaps as a young man, Herbert took a passing interest in the silver rush in Cobalt. After all, few people escaped the excitement and headline news. He may have invested in a mining company or two. But we have no evidence of this.

We do not believe that Herbert Campbell worked as an engineer in mining. We are certain he did not work as a stock promoter.

Herbert Campbell Barber 1885 to 1962

Regarding the authorship of the promotional material for the Canada Mines brokerage: Horatio Claude wrote the pamphlets and not Herbert Campbell. But in anticipation of questions from readers who search for the documents themselves, we present here what we've learned about the "other" H.C. Barber.

We can account for Herbert Campbell Barber's education and employment history in Toronto from 1901 to 1911. To acquire his education in electrical engineering, Herbert attended the Model School of Upper Canada College (UCC) from 1901 to 1904. The School of Practical Science records show Herbert in attendance from 1905-1908.

According to the 1908 Toronto University yearbook, after graduating from UCC, he worked for Canada General Electric (CGE) for a year. He also spent his university holidays with CGE.

BARBER, HERBERT CAMPBELL

Bert was born in Toronto and spent his early years at the Model School and U.C.C. He spent a year with the C.G.E. before coming to the School and has since spent his holidays with them. He is an enthusiastic sailor and has held down a place on the crew of both the Temeraire and the Crusader, besides sailing innumerable smaller boats to victory. He was made a life member of the R.C.Y.C. in recognition of his bravery in saving a fellow yachtsman who had been carried overboard. He is well up in both his practical and school work and we all expect to see him take his place among the foremost engineers of the country.

Torontonensis, *1908 The yearbook for the University of Toronto – see Appendix 5 for signature comparison*

Herbert graduated with a BASc. in 1910 and worked as a representative for the Standard Underground Cable Co. of Hamilton. In the 1911 University of Toronto calendar, H. C. Barber, a graduate of 1908 was then associated with the electrical department of the City of Toronto.

158   UNIVERSITY OF TORONTO CALENDAR 1910—1911

1908—Continued.

Course.	Name and address.	Occupation.
1.*R. M. Anderson	Toronto, Ont.	Post-Graduate Course in Engineering, University of Toronto.
5. J. R. Arens	Orillia, Ont.	
3. H. C. Barber	Toronto, Ont.	Electrical Department, City of Toronto.

September 10, 1913, Herbert Campbell Barber married Ethel Mary Steinhoff. His occupation was electrical engineer. The couple had four children; David Campbell was the eldest.

> BARBER, Herbert Campbell; care Henry Barber, 88 St. Alban St., Toronto. " '01-'04; S. of Hy. Barber, Accountant, 18 Wellington St. E., Toronto; Model Sch., Toronto; Age 15-9"; Grad. S. P. S., '08; B.A.Sc., Univ. Tor., '10; Rep. Standard Underground Cable Co., Hamilton.

From the list of "Old Boys and Present Pupils" of Upper Canada College 1917

No Mining, No Cobalt

We have found no references to a Herbert Campbell Barber who was involved in mining or investments in newspapers or other mining journals or reports.

Herbert would have been 20 in 1905 when the Cobalt mining boom was in full swing. Judging from his academic career where "he was well up in both his practical and school work", he was occupied with his electrical engineering studies and therefore would not have been experienced in mining from around the world as is stated in the prefaces of the two pamphlets. We know, on the other hand, that by this time, Horatio Barber was a world traveller, having spent time in the gold mining areas of Australia and Western Canada and possibly Africa, Mexico, and the USA.

The *Goldfields* pamphlet includes group photographs in which H. C. Barber is named. These pictures show a rather long-faced individual, perhaps 30-something, with large protruding ears, consistent with the likeness to Horatio Barber in other photos. These images in the pamphlet are certainly not the 21-year-old, more handsome Herbert Campbell Barber.

Herbert Campbell served in WWI and returned from overseas in 1919. His obituary from the Toronto Star on January 22, 1962, sheds no further light on his life story.

> BARBER, HERBERT CAMPBELL; 11 Highview Crescent, Toronto, Rep. for Ontario of the Standard Underground Cable Co., Hamilton; E. September '01, from the Model Sch., Toronto; aged 15-9; L. April '04; son of Henry Barber, Toronto; Grad., S.P.S. '08; B. A.Sc., Univ. Tor., '10; Q.O.R., Pte. Enlisted, June 15, 1916; R.N.V.R., Sub-Lt.; O.S., June 15, 1916; Lt., June; Irish Coast Patrol, October; discharged, March 2 1919; ret'd from O.S., March 26, 1919.

The Roll of Service 1914-1919 / The War Book of Upper Canada College

> BARBER, Herbert Campbell—At his home, 100 Wychwood Park, on Sunday, Jan. 21, 1962. Herbert Campbell Barber, beloved husband of the late Ethel Mary Barber, dear father of David and Beverley (Mrs. Robin Ross Taylor). At the chapel of Morley B. Bedford, 159 Eglinton Ave. W. (at Lascelles Blvd.). Service on Tuesday at 3 p.m.

Toronto Star, January 22, 1962

Bibliography and Resources

Almond, Peter; *Aviation; the Early Years* (Konemann) 1998

Angus, Charlie; *Silver City, An Alternative History of a Frontier Town* (Unpublished)

Baldwin, Douglas; *Cobalt: Canada's Forgotten Silver Boom Town,* (Indigo Press) 2016

Barber, H.; *The Aeroplane Speaks* (Unknown publisher)

Barber, H. C.; *Cobalt - The Mining District Containing the richest deposits in the world of Silver and Cobalt* (Canada Mines Ltd.) 1906

Barber, H. C.; *The Gold Fields of Larder lake* (Canada Mines Ltd.) 1907

Barber, Horatio; *Aerobatics* (R. M. McBride & Co) 1928

Barber, Horatio; *Airy Nothings* (McBride, Nast Co) 1918

Barber, Captain H.; *How to Fly a Plane; The First World War Pilot's Manual* (Amberley) 2014

Blainey, Geoffrey; *The Rush that Never Ended*; (Melbourne University Press) 1963

Brett, R Dallas; *History of British Aviation 1908-1914* (Air Research Publications) 1988

Brown, Antony; *Cuthbert Heath; Maker of the Modern Lloyd's of London* (David & Charles) 1980

Brown, L. Carson; *Cobalt; The Town with the Silver Lining* (Canadian Geographic Journal) 1963

Brown, Peter C.; *Shoreham Airport an Illustrated History* (Amberly Publishing) 2014

Brown, Timothy C.; *Flying with the Larks; the Early Aviation Pioneers of Lark Hill* (The History Press) 2013

Bullock, William Starr; *Cobalt and its Silver Mines* (New York, by W. S. Starr) 1906

Burrough, Bryan; *The Big Rich: The Rise and Fall of the Greatest Texas Oil Fortunes*, (Penguin) 2009

Calvert, Albert F.; *My Fourth Tour in Western Australia* (The Library of UCLA) 1901

Canadian Mining Journal *The Davis Handbook* 1910

Chajkowsky, William E.; *Royal Flying Corps; Borden to Texas to Beamsville* (Boston Mill Press) 1979

Cooke, William; *Wings Over Meir; The Story of the Potteries Aerodrome* (Amberley Publishing) 2010

Crawford, T. S.; *Wiltshire and the Great War; Training the Empire's Soldiers* (The Crowood Press) 2012

Cruddas, Colin; *In Wiltshire's Skies* (Tempus Publishing) 2004

Daniels, Peter, and Sawyer, Rex; *Images of England: Salisbury Plain* (The History Press) 1996

Dowsett, Alan; *Handley Page; A History* (Tempus Publishing) 2004

Driver, Hugh; *The Birth of Military Aviation; Britain, 1903 - 1914* (The Royal Historical Society and Boydell Press) 1997

Dufresne, Vernon and Thompson, Clark; *The Goldfields of Larder Lake; Canada's forgotten gold Rush* (Township of Larder Lake) 1999

Fancy, Peter; *A Coleman Township Road Guide to Historic Cobalt* (Temiskaming Abitibi Heritage Association) 1994

Fancy, Peter; *A Guide to historic Cobalt* by Peter Fancy (Temiskaming Printing Co) 1994

Ferris, Neal; *Aspirational Heritage: The History & Archaeology of the Bath House-Hotel and Bath Stream-Spring Landscape, Nevis.* Report Prepared for the Nevis Historical & Conservation Society (NHCS) April 2019

Gibbs-Smith, Charles H.; *Aviation; An Historical Survey from its origins to the end of WWll* (Science Museum London) 1985

Gillespie, W.G.; *Souvenir of Cobalt; The Silver City* (published in Sudbury by W.G. Gillespie) 1906

Grahame-White, Claude, and Harper, Harry; *Heroes of the Air* (Hodder and Stoughton) 1912

Grahame-White, Claude and Harper, Harry; *With the Airmen* (Oxford University Press) 1918

Grayer, Jeffrey; *Rails across the Plain* by (Noodle Books) 2011

Hale, Don; *Those Magnificent Men in their Flying Machines* (Ads2life) 2016

Hales, H. K.; *The Autobiography of "The Card"* (Samson Low, Marston Co) 1937

Hales, H. K.; *The Chariots of the Air* (Wright & Brown) 1936

Hall, Malcolm; *From Balloon to Boxkite; The Royal Engineers and Early Aeronautics* (Amberley Publishing) 2010

Hubbard, T. O'Brien and Turner C. C.; *The Boys' Book of Aeroplanes* (Grant Richards) 1912

Hunt, C. W.; *Dancing in the Sky; The Royal Flying Corps in Canada* (Dundurn Press Toronto) 2009

James, Derek N.; *Bristol Aeroplane Company* (Chalford) 1996

Jane, Fred T.; *Jane's all the world's Airships; 1909* (David & Charles Reprints) 1969

Jarrett, Philip; *Pioneer Aircraft; Early Aviation before 1914* (Putnam) 2003

Lanchbery, Edward; *A. V. Roe; A Biography of Sir Alliott Verdon-Roe, Pioneer of British Aviation* (The Bodley Head) 1956

Land, William A.; *Australian Dictionary of Biography; Barber, George Walter (1868-1951)* 1979

Langham, Rob; *Bloody Paralyser. The Giant Handley Page Bombers of The First World War* (Fonthill) 2015

Larocque, Robert; *Selected Chapters of Temiskaming Heritage: Chapter 2. Historical Photo Analysis of the Landscape of Early Cobalt, Methods of Interpretation of Cobalt's Early Landscape Images* (White Mountain Publications, 2019)

Lee, Arthur Gould; *The Flying Cathedral* (Methuen & Co) 1965

Lefebvre, George; *The Darby Mine, Thomas Edison's Latchford Venture*; in *Selected Chapters of Temiskaming Heritage – Proceedings of the 2017 Speaker's Symposium* (2017)

Maclean's Magazine; *Have you forgotten your Bank Balance?* March 15, 1932

Manning, W. O.; *Airplanes and Engines (Airsense)* (Pitman) 1941

MacCarron, Donal; *Letters from an Early Bird; the Life and Letters of Denys Corbett Wilson 1882-1915* (Pen & Sword Aviation) 2006

Merriam, Frederick Warren; *First through the Clouds; the Autobiography of a Box-Kite Pioneer* (Air World Books) 2018

Middleton, Edgar, C.; *The way of the Air* (William Heinemann) 1917

Munson, Kenneth; *Pioneer Aircraft 1903-14* (MacMillan) 1969

Nesbit, Roy Conyers; *The RAF in Camera; 1903-1939* (Alan Sutton Publishing) 1995

North, Debra B.; A *Northern Hope; One Family's Life in Cobalt and Haileybury 1904-1928* (White Mountain Publications) 2018

Oliver, David; *Hendon Aerodrome; A History* (Airlife Publishing) 1994

Ormes, Ian; *Leading Edge; the Pioneering Years of Aviation Insurance* (Michael Rainbird Publishing) 1988

Parker, Norman; *Norman's View; History of Amesbury and Surrounding Area* (PPS Printers) 2018

Penrose, Harald; *British Aviation; the Pioneer Years* (Cassell) 1980

Pixton, Stella; *Howard Pixton; Test Pilot and Pioneer Aviator* (Pen and Sword Aviation) 2014

Priddle, Rod; *Wings over Wiltshire* (Ald Design & Print) 2003

Sergiades, A. O.: *Silver Cobalt Calcite Vein Deposits of Ontario* (Ontario Department of Mines) 1968

Smith, Clive R.; *Flying at Hendon; A Pictorial Record* (Routledge and Kegan Paul) 1974

Stemp, P. D.; *Kites, Birds and Stuff-Over 150 Years of British Aviation* (Lulu) 2013

Taylor, John W. R.; *Horatio Barber's Canards* (unknown publication)

Temiskaming-Abitibi Heritage Association; *From Cobalt to James Bay; Preserving our History. Proceedings of The History Workshop* (Roseanne Fisher Publishing) 2000

Torres, Ophelia A. and Victor M.; *Caribbean Folk tales and Short Stories*, (Iuniverse Inc.) 2005

Turner, Major C. C.; *The Old Flying Days* (Arno Press) 1971

Villard, Henry Serrano, Henry; *Contact! The Story of the Early Birds* (Bonanza Books) 1967

Walker, Percy B.; *Early Aviation at Farnborough: Balloons, Kites and Airships v. 1: History of the Royal Aircraft Establishment* (Macdonald) 1971

Wallace, Graham; *Claude Grahame-White; A Biography* (Putnam) 1960

Online Resources

Amesbury History Centre - amesburyhistorycentre.org.uk

Ancestry.com

Archive.org – links to the two promotional pamphlets written by Horatian Claude Barber. N.B. that these have been misattributed to Herbert Campbell Barber – see Appendix 8.

- *Cobalt - The Mining District Containing the richest deposits in the world of Silver and Cobalt* (Canada Mines Ltd.) 1906. archive.org/details/cihm_992263
- *The Gold Fields of Larder lake* (Canada Mines Ltd.) 1907. archive.org/details/cihm_992262

Cobalt Historical Society - heritagesilvertrail.ca

Facebook sites

- Cobalt Mining Museum
- Flying with the Larks

Findmypast.com

Flight Global - flightglobal.com/pdfarchive – digital archive of *Flight* magazine

Grace's Guide to British Industrial History - gracesguide.co.uk/Horatio_Claude_Barber

Mindat.org – database of mines and minerals around the world.

National Library of Australia - trove.nla.gov.au - including digital newspaper archives

Nevis Historical and Conservation Society - nevisheritage.org

Newspapers.com

Outback Family History - outbackfamilyhistory.com.au - dedicated to the history of goldfields of Western Australia including Kalgoorlie.

PaperofRecord.com – newspaper archive including the *New Liskeard Speaker*.

Patents.google.com

Royal Air Force Museum in Hendon - rafmuseum.org.uk

Smithsonian National Air and Space Museum - airandspace.si.edu/archives

The Cobalt Adventure - an interactive educational site dedicated to telling the story of Cobalt, Ontario. virtualmuseum.ca/sgc-cms/expositions-exhibitions/cobalt/en/index.php

Their Flying Machines - flyingmachines.ru

Tod, Chris; *A Magnificent Man: Legendary flying machine in Steyning* Tod is the former curator of the Steyning Museum. He wrote the story of Barber's unexpected landing in Steyning in 1911. steyningmuseum.org.uk/boxfiles/ttplane.html

Toronto Public Library - torontopubliclibrary.ca - including digital telephone and street directories as well as the Tyrell Blue Books of high society.

INDEX

A

Abercrombie, Capt. R. O., 124
Abitibi & Cobalt Mining Company, 44-48, 50-52, 85
Aero Engineering and Advisory Services Inc., 163-164
Aero Indemnity Co., 161-164
Aero Insurance Co., 161-164
Aero Underwriters Corporation, 159, 162, 164
Aerobatics, 130, 173
Aerobatics, 105, 130, 200
Aerograms, 160
Aeronautical Syndicate Limited (ASL), 58, 99 -100, 103-105, 108-109, 111, 114, 116-121-129, 132, 134-135, 138-140, 143, 146-148, 170-171
Aeronautics magazine "Pioneers of British Aviation", 127
Airy Nothings, 78, 153, 166, 169, 171-172, 198-200, 227
American Express, 160
Amesbury, town of, 1-2, 99, 104, 138, 209
Amesbury History Centre, 1, 100
Antoinette: **aeroplane**: 95, 100, 204-206; **engine:** 97, 133-134, 169, 172, 199, 204-206, 217
ASL monoplane, 99, 132, 134-135, 170-171
Atlantic Clipper, 175
Australia, 3, 9-18, 24, 26, 30, 42, 63, 70, 165, 189, 191-193, 226
Australian Army and Air Force Medical Service, 193
autogyro, 203
Aviation Insurance Association, 130, 156-158, 190
Avis monoplane, 94, 97, 169

B

Barber and Baldwin Inc., 159, 163-164, 190
Barber, Barbara Edith, 5
Barber, Charles Worthington, 2, 5-7, 191
Barber, Claude Percy, 27, 152, 187, 189
Barber, Conrad Hope, 28, 152, 175, 187, 189, 195-196
Barber, Edith Muriel, 191, 195
Barber, Frederick, 191, 194
Barber, George Walter, 9, 191-194
Barber, Herbert Campbell, 55, 224-226
Barber, Horatio Claude: **divorce**: 18, 78, 150-150-155, 190, 195; **education** 2, 7, 74, 85, 187, 189, 173; **family** 5-7, 9, 191-197; **illness**, 100, 124, 177, 187; **inventions,** 94, 97, 125; **legal problems,** 17, 22-26, 49-50, 72-77, 85, 150, 183; **marriage** 2, 15, 19-20, 153; **patents,** 99, 122, 211-215
Barber, Isabella, 2, 6-7, 136, 191
Barber, Lilian, 191
Barber, Maude, 7, 191, 194
Barber, Percy Charles, 7, 195
Barber, William, 5
Barber, Cecil Harry 191, 195
Basset Manor, 175
Battersby, Christopher Hayes, 58, 99
Battersby, Charles Worsley, 58, 99, 119
Battersea, England, 93-94, 98, 100, 102, 128, 132, 168-170, 189, 200, 217
Bean, Charles Edwin Woodrow, 192-193
Bedford Hospital, 191
Bedford Modern School, 7, 189
Bedford Grammar School, 106
Belmont, 174
Benson, Bernard, 108-109, 118
Bermuda, 174-175, 177-178, 190
Bernal, Capt., 123
Birdwood, General, 193
Bishop, Mr., 109
Bishop's Palace, Toronto, Ontario, 15-16
Black, Archibald, 159, 190
Blackburn, 203

232

Bleriot Company, 121
Blue Riband Trophy, 203
Bradshaw, Robert, 182-183
Branch, Mrs. Edmund, 178
Britannia Trophy, 130, 190, 203, 208
British Columbia, 13-16, 18, 31, 42
Brooklands, 107 - 113
Brown, Anthony, 157-158
Brown, Tim, 1
Browne, Robert H. C., 29, 56, 79
Buck, Francis P., 61
Burnley, town of, 198-203
Burnley Aero Club, 198, 203
Burnley Motor Omnibus Company, 94
Burnley Motor Pleasure Co., 198
Busteed, Harry, 124, 223

C

California, USA, 17-18, 20, 22, 24, 86, 100
Cambers, Mr., 129
Cammell, Reginald Archibald, 111-112, 114, 118
Canada General Electric, 225
Canada Mines Limited, 28, 35, 41-42, 50, 58-62, 67, 70-74, 77, 87-88, 165, 189, 224-225
Canadian Aeroplanes Limited, 16
Canadian Club, 16
Canadian Mining Journal (CMJ), 37-38, 70, 72-77, 87, 186
Capone, Federico, 94, 97
Central Flying School, 125, 14, 190, 219
Channel Islands – see Jersey
Civil Aviation Authority, 157
Clapham, England, 102
Cobalt Lake, 22, 28-29, 47-48, 57
Cobalt, Ontario, 2-3, 27, 29-32, 37-44, 47, 53-57, 76, 79-85, 165
Cody, Samuel, 106-107, 186
Coleridge, Samuel Taylor, 179
Constantinople, 3, 121-122
Cooke, W. E., 94, 98, 132, 198-203
Coolgardie, Western Australia, 10-11, 13
Corfu, 78, 153, 168

Crocker, W. R., 123
Croydon, town of, 94

D

Darragh, Ernest, 22
Davis Handbook, 44, 76
Dimmock, Lieut., 129
Dirigibles, 122-123, 172, 213-214
Downs, Lieutenant G.E., 193
Doyle, Simon, 7, 9, 191
Dublin Bay, 69-70
Dunne monoplane, 103
Dunne, J. W., 117

E

Eagle Star and British Dominions Insurance Co., 130, 157
East Lancashire Aeroplane Co., 198, 199, 201
Edison, Thomas A., 71
Elk Lake, town of, 58
Empyrean Policy for Aviators, 159
EVN monoplane, 169
Excess Insurance Co., 130, 157

F

Farman Brothers, 119, 128
Farman, Maurice, 122, 124, 128
Fenton, Robert, 5
Fergusson. Mr., 119
Ferris, Neal, 179
Finlan, Reeve, 31
Flight - a Rhapsody, 172
Forrest, Fred, 69
Fulton, Captain, 99, 112, 129

G

George Hotel, Amesbury, 1, 209
Gibson, Homer L., 49-50, 85-86
Globe Underwriters Exchange Inc., 163
Gnome engine, 110-111, 116, 119, 129, 144, 218
Gowganda, town of, 59
Grace, Terry, 1, 36

Graces Guide, 2
Graham, Captain G. C., 193
Grahame-White Type V1, 120, 123, 149
Grahame-White, Claude, 106-108, 120-123, 148
Grand Palais des Champs-Élysées, Paris, France, 78, 128, 217, 222
Greece, 2, 78, 153, 168
Green Engine, 99, 103-104, 110-111, 135, 138-139, 218
Guggenheim, Daniel and Murray, 51

H
Handley-Page, Frederick, 117, 119
Harrods Limited, 119
Harrow School, 7
Hartford Insurance Company, 159
Hawaii, 3, 18, 24, 26
Heath, Cuthbert Eden, 157-158, 220
Hendon, 2, 101, 103-108, 110-111, 113, 115-116, 119, 121, 128-129, 139-141, 144, 156, 167, 189, 229
Highland Mary Mine, 75-76, 87
Honolulu, 8, 18
Hounslow Heath, 124
How to Fly a Plane, 130, 165
Hudson Bay Extended Mine, 33, 44
Hudson, Frank, 201-205
Huggins, Mr. John, 179
Hunter, Cromwell Orrick, 81
Hunter J.H., 29, 34, 41, 79-82, 88
Hunter, Joseph Hendricks, *see Hunter, J.H.*

I
Imperial Bank, 31-32, 53-56, 85
Incorporation and Securities Co. of Canada, 27, 35, 189
Inwood, John, 24-25

J
Jersey, Channel Islands, 164, 174, 177 190
Jersey City, New Jersey, 2, 20, 189

K
Kalgoorlie, 9, 13-15, 165, 189, 192, 231
Kalgoorlie Hospital 9, 15, 165, 189, 192
Kipling. R., 166
Knighton Down, 2, 169

L
Labour Union, 91,182
Lanchester, F. W., 93, 132, 203, 208
Larder Lake, 1, 3, 11, 28, 38, 49-51, 58-77, 79, 84, 87-88, 90, 99, 167, 180, 185, 208, 222, 224
Larder Lake Proprietary Goldfields Mine, 11, 59-61, 66, 72-74, 76, 77, 87
Lark Hill, 1, 30, 92, 94, 95, 96, 97, 98, 99, 100, 101, 128, 132, 138, 140, 144, 169, 170, 189, 200
Larose Mine, 22,
Law & Co., 74, 75
Law, Frank, 74-76, 87, 187
Lee, Arthur, 106, 108
Lennox and Lennox 72, 76-77, 87, 88
Lennox, T. Herbert, 61, 76, 87
Leno, Dan 102
Leno, Herbert 102
Lewis, Lt. R. E., 124
Lindbergh, Charles, 158
Lloyd's of London, 122-123, 126, 129-130, 152, 156-159, 190, 208, 219-220
Londonderry Mine, 10-11, 70
Long Lake *see Cobalt Lake*
Long Lake, Charlton, 34-37, 82-83, 87
Loughborough, Isabella, 6

M
Manchester, 5, 199
Manning, W. O., 97, 99, 135, 137, 170, 200,
Manning Chambers Building, 27-28
Manningford Abbotts, 124, 126
Marsh. Capt. W. A., 29, 31, 34, 41, 82
Marskey, John. F., 60-61, 65, 72-73
McKinley, James, 22
Meeze Miss, 129

Merchant Navy, 164, 191
Metzgar and Leno, 102-103
Metzgar, Ted and Bert, 102
Mexico, 3, 26, 42, 70, 90, 179, 226
Miller, W. G. Dr., 27, 34, 43, 165
Miller, T. M., 17
Mills, John, 11
Moore-Brabazon, J.C., 93
Moore, C.H., 29, 53, 79, 80, 81, 88
Moore, Clifton Henry, *see C.H. Moore*
Morgan, Albert Norton, 35 -37, 87-88, 209
Murray, Bertha and Mildred, 16
Murray, W. Parkyn, 16
Mustard, Ted, 1

N
Napier, Mike, 124
Nelson, Horatio, 179
Nevis,174, 177-184, 187, 190
Nevis Historical & Conservation Society, 179, 184
New Westminster, B. C., 15, 16
Nipissing Mine, 45, 51, 80
North American Accident Co., 16
North, J.D., 120, 148
Northern Automobile Co., 203
Northern Ontario Navigation Co., 70

O
O'Connor, Mike, 124
Olympia Aero Exhibition, 106, 149, 198, 201
Ontario Bureau of Mines, 44, 77, 79
Ormes, Ian., 158, 159
Osborne, John, 179
Oxford University, 7, 173

P
Page & Miles Ltd., 130
Palmer Mrs., 129
P. & O. Steam Navigation Company, 15
Parker, J. Brooks, 159, 190
Parker, Norman, 1, 78, 98, 174
Pearson, Rev. William Dewhurst, 7

Perez, George Neaves, 24-25
Pewsey, village of, 124, 126, 154
Phillips, Horatio, 93
Piper, Dr. David H., 61, 72-73, 78
Pippe, Edle Annita Margarete, 15-18, 189, 195
Pixton, Howard, 106, 107
Pixton, Stella, 106
Porter, Elsie Mabelle, 2, 19, 20, 28, 152, 189, 195, 224
Poulainville, 192
Premier Mine, 7

Q
Queen's Hospital, Honolulu, 8

R
Reddick, Dr., 50, 59 -60, 69
Reserve Aeroplane Park, 125
Reserve Aeroplane Squadron, 125
RFC School Shoreham, 124
Rheims Aero Show, 203
Richthofen, Baron Manfred von., 192- 194
Ridley- Prentice, 115, 119, 129
RMS Titanic, 25
Roe, A.V., 93, 106-107, 186, 219, 223
Rolls, C.S., 93
Rossia Insurance Company, 163
Rossland, B. C., 13, 61
Royal Aero Club, 94, 95, 130, 168, 190, 220
Royal Aeronautical Society, 2
Royal Air Force, (RAF), 16, 96, 113, 125 -126, 130, 132- 134, 137, 139, 156, 187, 190, 195, 200, 213, 216
Royal Flying Corps, (RFC), 16, 124-127, 130, 158, 161, 190, 195
Ryerson, Col. G. Sterling, 61, 72-73

S
S. S. Canada, 24-25
Salisbury Plain, 92, 94, 103-104, 128, 166 - 169, 171-172, 217-218
Samson, Lieutenant, 111, 118

San Francisco, 17, 18, 22- 24, 26, 157, 189
Santa Clara, 22, 24, 25
Santos-Dumont, 92, 100, 135, 217
Schmettua, Herman, 99
School of Practical Sciences at Toronto University, 225
Shakespeare, W., 166
Short Brothers, 93, 168
Silver, 2, 3, 4, 22, 27, 29, 32-34, 37-38, 41-42, 44-46, 51, 53, 57-58, 65, 70, 76, 79, 84, 87-88, 185, 224
Silver Bird Mine, 76
Silver Centre, 59
Sinclair, Colonel T., 193 -194
Smith, Archie "Coolgardie", 13-14
Society of British Aircraft Constructors, 157
South Africa, 6-7
Speculator(s), 3, 11, 15-18, 21, 31, 65, 185, 186
Spirit of St. Louis, 158
St. Kitts and Nevis, 174, 178-180, 183
Standard Underground Cable Co., 225
Stemp, P. D., 98, 199
Steyning, 112-113
Strathy, G. B., 70, 77
Sullivan, Alan, 16

T
Tegusiewabi, 62
Temiskaming, 22, 29, 34, 62, 71
Temiskaming and Northern Ontario Railway (T&NOR), 22, 29
The Bath House, 178-179, 182, 184, 187, 190,
The Cobalt Open Call Mining Exchange (COCME), 2, 29- 32, 36, 39, 42, 48, 58, 79, 81, 189
The *Geisha*, 69-70
The Goldfields of Larder Lake, 11, 38, 50, 59, 61, 74, 90, 185, 224
The Packway, 95, 169
The Red Baron, *see Richthofen, Baron Manfred von*
The Royal Mail Steam Packet Co., 179
Thomas, Mr. George Holt 119, 129

Tomstown, 62
Toronto, 15, 26-29, 36, 41-42, 49, 60, 61, 126, 189, 224
Torquay, 166, 168
Torren's Law Title Act, 46
Treyhawke-Davies, Eleanor, 112, 130, 208
Turkey, 3, 121-122, 208
Turner, C. C., 136

U
Ulrey, Senator Lewis Valentine, 51, 60, 64-66, 70, 72-73, 78, 87-91
Upavon, 124, 154, 190

V
Valkyrie 1, 101-103, 105, 137, 139-140
Valkyrie II, 141
Valkyrie C type, 140-141
Valkyrie Type B Racer, 116, 140-142, 144
Valkyrie Prototype, 102, 135-137, 144, 170, 211
Valkyrie School, 108
Vedrines, Jules, 110
Verne, Jules, 104
Vernon Hotel, 17, 38
Victoria. B.C., 17, 18
Viking Biplane, 116-117, 130, 146-148, 212

W
Walker, Eleanor, 5
Walker, Maria, 5
Walker, Thomas Kenyon, 5
Wandsworth Gas Company, 93
Waterous, Chas. H. Jr., 61
Watson-Salmond, Janet (Jessie), 9, 192
White, Col. Solomon, 24, 31, 37, 82-84,
Who's who of American Authors, 173
Wildcat [Mines], 9-10, 28, 31, 33, 43-44, 46-47, 49, 51, 60-61, 64, 70, 74-76, 84, 87-88, 165, 185
Willows, Ernest Thompson, 123
Willis Abbott and Co., 41
Wilson, Maggie, 1-4, 36, 179

236

Woodrow, Bertie, 98-101, 103-104, 134-135, 166, 167, 206, 208, 222
World War l (WWl), 126, 161, 192, 219
World War ll. (WWll), 91
Worthington, Col. A. N., 61
Wright Brothers, Wilbur and Orville, 92, 128, 135, 146, 208

Wright, Howard T., 93-100, 102-103, 128, 132-133, 135, 169-172, 189, 198- 204, 206,
Wright Warwick, 93

Y

York, Ontario, 15, 27-28, 189 *see also Toronto*

Made in the USA
Middletown, DE
01 December 2019